Programming the ESP32 in MicroPython
Second Edition

Harry Fairhead & Mike James

I/O Press
I Programmer Library

Harry Fairhead & Mike James,
Programming the ESP32 in MicroPython
Second Edition
ISBN Paperback: 9781871962932
ISBN Hardback: 9781871962284
First Printing, 2025
Revision 1

Published by IO Press   www.iopress.info
In association with I Programmer   www.i-programmer.info
and with I o T Programmer   www.iot-programmer.com

The publisher recognizes and respects all marks used by companies and manufacturers as a means to distinguish their products. All brand names and product names mentioned in this book are trade marks or service marks of their respective companies and our omission of trade marks is not an attempt to infringe on the property of others.

For updates, errata, links to resources and the source code for the programs in this book, visit its dedicated page on the IO Press website: iopress.info.

Preface

The ESP32 is a remarkable device. It is low cost but with many different subsystems that make it more powerful than you might at first think. You can use it for simple applications because it is cheap but you can also use it for more sophisticated applications because it is capable. For this book the language of choice for programming the ESP32 is to use MicroPython. While it is a slower language than C, most of the time this doesn't matter and it is so much easier to use.

As a high-level language, MicroPython is based on Python 3 and is fully object-oriented. This means that you can create classes to encapsulate hardware and make your code easier to use and understand. It also allows you to implement complex algorithms and so make your data processing easier. In general, you can take an existing Python 3 program and simply run it under MicroPython, usually with no changes. If there are any changes then they are generally minor.

Another good thing about MicroPython on the ESP32 is that it is very easy to get started. After a simple installation procedure you have a working MicroPython machine which you can program almost at once using the Thonny IDE.

The purpose of the book is to reveal what you can do with the ESP32's GPIO lines together with widely used sensors, servos and motors and ADCs. After covering the GPIO, outputs and inputs, events and interrupts, it gives you hands-on experience of PWM (Pulse Width Modulation), the SPI bus, the I2C bus and the 1-Wire bus. We also cover direct access to the hardware, adding an SD Card reader, sleep states to save power, the RTC, RMT and touch sensors not to mention how to use WiFi.

New in this edition is coverage of the ESP32 S3 which is rapidly becoming the device of choice. The standard ESP32 S3 DevKitC from Espressif is covered and so is the Arduino Nano ESP32, and the programs should work seamlessly with other ESP32 devices.

This book doesn't teach you Python or MicroPython in the sense of basic programming, but a knowledge of how to program in almost any language is all you really need. All examples are written in a very simple style that avoids the use of some features of Python that are very "neat" but tend to obscure the meaning of the code. You can easily refactor any of the examples into classes that suit your particular purpose and programming style.

This is not a projects book, although there isn't much left for you to do to round out the embryonic projects that are used as examples. Instead it is about understanding concepts and the acquisition of skills. The hope is that by the end of the book you will know how to tackle your own projects and get them safely to completion without wasting time in trial and error.

Thanks to our tireless editors Sue Gee and Kay Ewbank. Programming is the art of great precision, but English doesn't come with a built-in linter. Errors that remain, and we hope they are few, are ours.

For the source code for the programs in this book, together with any updates or errata, links to resources including recommendations for obtaining electronic components, visit its dedicated page on the IO Press website: iopress.info.

You can also contact us at harry.fairhead@i-programmer.info or mike.james@i-programmer.info

Harry Fairhead
Mike James
January, 2025

Table of Contents

Chapter 5
Some Electronics   **63**

Chapter 6
Simple Input   **85**

Chapter 7
Advanced Input – Interrupts   **101**

Chapter 8

Pulse Width Modulation   **113**

Chapter 9

Controlling Motors And Servos   **129**

Chapter 10
Getting Started With The SPI Bus   **157**

Chapter 11
Using Analog Sensors   **177**

Chapter 12
Using The I2C Bus   **191**

Chapter 13
One-Wire Protocols **213**

Chapter 14
The Serial Port **239**

Chapter 15

Using WiFi   **259**

Chapter 16

Sockets   **275**

Chapter 17
Asyncio And Servers 295

Chapter 18
Direct To The Hardware 317

Chapter 1

The ESP32 - Before We Begin

The ESP32 is a remarkable device. It is cheap enough to be used for tasks that were marginal for a microcontroller yet powerful enough to tackle tasks that until recently were too much for such a low cost device. It has two cores, WiFi, Bluetooth and low-power consumption modes. It has a fast processor with enough memory to get most jobs done. It also has a great many built-in peripherals and can talk to devices such as the PWM, I2C, SPI, and UART without much trouble. It also has some novel peripherals such as a motor controller PWM device, a remote control subsystem, touch input and an ultra low power processor that can run while the main processors are in sleep mode.

All of this makes the ESP32 suitable for very simple tasks such as a door or window open sensor or something much more sophisticated like a motor controller.

The ESP32 Family

The ESP32 is designed by Espressif Systems, a Chinese company that gained reputation by its first processor, the ESP8266, which incorporated a WiFi subsystem in a very small, low-cost, package. The ESP8266 gained a loyal following from enthusiasts but in the early days it was difficult to find out about the device because of the lack of English documentation. With the release of the ESP32 family much of these difficulties are behind us – there is a lot of good documentation, a stable SDK and MicroPython support.

The ESP does suffer from the fact that there is no single reference implementation. With devices like those in the Arduino family and from Raspberry Pi there is a single source of product and information and this makes things simpler. However, most of the variation in the ESP32 devices we can buy are minor and in practice there are only one or two variations you need to be concerned with and they are very compatible with one another.

The first thing to be clear about is that the ESP32 family is not based on the very common ARM processors. Currently ESP32 devices either use an Xtensa LX6 or LX7 processor or, less commonly, an open source RISC-V processor. As there is SDK and MicroPython support for both of these processors, there is no difficulty in using either. However, most ESP32 development devices use the LX6.

At the time of writing there are five commonly encountered ESP32 devices; the S series based on the LX6/7 processor and the C series using the RISC-V processor:

The S Series:

- ESP32 – (2014) LX6 using single or dual core WiFi 4 and Bluetooth
- ESP32-S2 (2019) LX7 dual core WiFi 4 only
- ESP32-S3 (2020) LX7 dual core WiFi 4 and Bluetooth

The C series:

- ESP32-C3 (2020) RISC-V Wifi 4
- ESP32-C6 (2021) RISC-V Wifi 6

The devices also differ in terms of memory configuration, GPIO lines and other features. Newer devices seem to be using the RISC processor in preference to the LX6/7. At the time of writing the ESP32 is the cheapest and most commonly encountered. However, the upgraded ES32 S3, which is considerably faster, is also readily available. The ESP32 and the ESP32 S3 are both used as examples in this book.

Development Boards

In most cases the development boards that you are likely to use are constructed using surface mount modules that contain the basic device. These take the form of the small silver box mounted on the development board.

It is this "silver box" which determines the characteristics of a development system. Manufacturers select a module and add some components to create a development board. It is also worth pointing out that you can buy the modules not mounted on a PCB and design them into your own electronics for a 100% custom ESP32.

The main task of the development board is to convert the TTL serial port to a USB connector that provides power and a serial connection to the development machine. You can see a typical circuit diagram below:

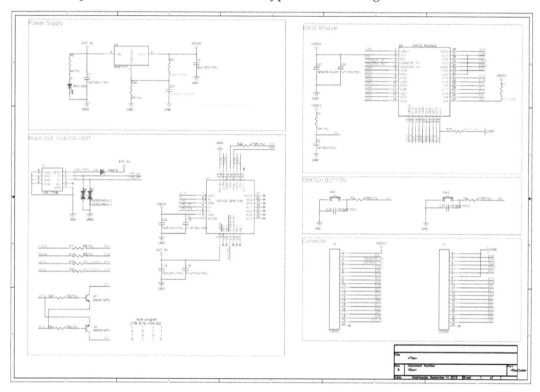

This is for the ESP32 dev kit produced by Espressif and it is taken as the starting point for every other development board.

The key thing is that the development board generally adds very little to the ESP32 module used. That is, the main characteristics of the board are determined by the ESP32 module in use, but they can still differ in what GPIO lines are brought out to external pins and what additional hardware is provided – some provide an LED connected to GPIO 2.

At the time of writing there are two main module families – WROOM and WROVER are what you will mostly encounter. The main difference between the two families is that the WROVER family has a serial RAM device that is needed to support video devices. Other than this the two are identical. Nearly all development boards feature a WROOM or a WROOM S3 module and these come in a range with mostly minor differences. The most commonly encountered are:

Name	Flash Memory
ESP-WROOM-32	4 MB
ESP32-S3-WROOM-1	8 MB
ESP-WROOM-32-8M	8 MB
ESP-WROOM-32-16M	16 MB

While the ESP32 uses an LX6 dual-core processor, the S3 uses an LX7. There are other configurations that offer features for specific use cases. The 32U series, ESP-WROOM-32U etc, has an external U.FL (IPEX) connector for an external antenna rather than the internal PCB antenna and the HT series can withstand higher temperatures. Some very small development boards also make use of the ESP-Pico module which comes in a range of flash memory sizes.

Development boards also differ in which GPIO lines are brought out to external connectors.

A typical ESP32 is shown below:

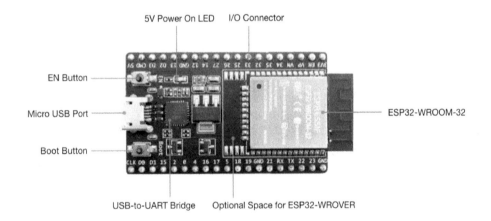

The S3 usually has two connectors, a UART and a USB, and usually has an addressable RGB LED connected to GPIO38:

The Arduino Nano ESP32 is another popular development board as it offers integration with the wider Arduino ecosystem:

Typical of the smaller development boards, the Nano ESP32 brings out slightly fewer GPIO lines and this can be a problem. It also uses a different way of numbering the GPIO lines that it does make available. This is supposed to be a simplification, but it is often the source of confusion. Also at the time of writing, it isn't as well supported as other Arduino hardware and its support for MicroPython is still "experimental". In many ways the Espressif development boards work better with Arduino software than the Nano ESP32.

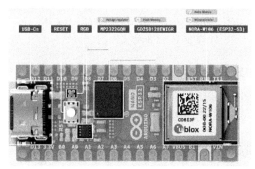

There are usually one or two switches, a boot loader and a reset, and a power LED that can be a nuisance as you can't turn it off without a soldering iron. A serial UART to USB chip is also often included and this is often a CP2120 or a CH340. Some users claim that one is better than the other, but in practice they both work well. Most development boards use the same pinout as the Espressif designed boards, but you will encounter minor variations and smaller form factors which expose fewer GPIO lines to the outside world. The USB connection is used to power the board and to program it.

As already mentioned, you can also find development boards that don't have a USB connector. These are generally powered directly via the power pins and they are programmed using the UART serial interface without the help of the USB conversion. Working with this sort of board is slightly more difficult as you have to find a way to connect to the UART, but it works in exactly the same way once you have sorted out supplying power and making the serial connection.

What all this means is that despite there being a confusing number of ESP32 development boards they are all highly compatible and programmable in the same way. Apart from potential problems of differing amounts of memory and speed, a program written for one should run on another. The only exception to this rule is if the development board doesn't make the GPIO line available for external use, but all of the standard size boards have the same set of external connections.

The key points about the ESP32/S3 hardware that you are most likely to encounter in a development board:

- Dual-core LX6/LX7 processor, flexible clock running up to 240 MHz
- 520KB of SRAM, and 4/8MB of on-board Flash memory
- USB 1.1 with device and host support
- Low-power sleep and dormant modes
- 34/48 × multi-function GPIO pins 10/14 touch (capacitive) sensors
- 4 × SPI, 2 × I2C, 3 × UART, 2 x I2S, CAN bus, 1/2 × 12-bit ADC, 2 x 8-bit DAC (ESP32 only) and 16 PWM outputs
- Accelerated cryptographic hardware on-chip
- Separate low-power processor

Reset and Boot

It is worth knowing what the two buttons that are part of almost every development board actually do and why you generally don't need to make use of them.

As its name suggests, the reset/enable button resets the system and reboots it. If you press the boot button nothing happens until you press the reset/enable button when the system will enter "firmware download mode" and run the loader to allow new code to be downloaded via the serial port.

Once in download mode you have to use a utility such as esptool to download the code, see the next chapter. The actual protocol used is documented, but usually you can ignore the details.

The reset enable button is connected to the EN line on the module and reset/enable button is connected to GPIO0. This means that you cannot use GPIO0 for other purposes:

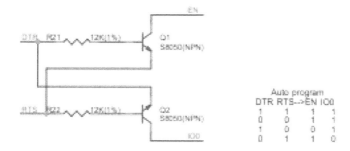

In practice you rarely need to use the boot button to download code because most development boards use the standard configuration and connect the serial port's DTR and RTS control lines to EN and GPIO0:

You can see that by toggling the serial control lines you can reset the system or set it into firmware upload mode. What this means is that you usually don't have to press the buttons because the software you are using to upload or run code does the job for you. It is important to know this because if you use the serial port for other purposes you need to be careful about how the RTS and DTR lines are used, see Chapter 14 on the serial port for more.

What To Expect

There are no complete projects in this book – although some examples come very close and it is clear that some of them could be used together to create finished projects. The reason for this is that the focus is on learning how things work so that you can move on and do things that are non-standard.

What matters is that you can reason about what the processor is doing and how it interacts with the real world in real time. This is the big difference between desktop and embedded programming. In the desktop world you don't really care much about when something happens, but when you are programming a physical system you care very much.

This is a book about understanding general principles and making things work at the lowest possible level. This knowledge isn't always necessary when you are working on a relatively slow system in MicroPython, but it is always helpful for understanding what is going on when things go wrong. When you are working directly with the hardware knowing what is happening matters.

All of the examples are as basic as possible and the code is designed to be as easy to understand as possible. In most cases this means avoiding the use of constants that appear to come from nowhere and functions that make it difficult to see the basic steps. Also error handling is reduced to a bare minimum – simple programs look complicated if you add error handling code. Of course, there is no reason not to refactor these examples into something that looks more like production code and the effort in doing this is much less than getting the basic programs working in the first place.

Rather than going through multiple possible configurations for a development environment, this book uses Thonny. If you want to work in a different way then there are a number of alternatives such as PyCharm, VSCode and even an Arduino-based editor but they are all less developed than Thonny.

What Do You Need?

Well – an ESP32 or an ESP32 S3 at least! In fact you probably are well advised to buy more than one just in case something goes wrong. The price that you have to pay for an ESP32 board varies according to the quantities you require. If buying single boards, the cheapest source is China with a single ESP32 board costing around $3 and an ESP32 S3 around $5, plus postage, of course. An Arduino Nano ESP32, by contrast, will cost around $20.

You also need a machine to run the software to create programs which can be downloaded into the ESP32 – the development machine. The good news is that you can use almost any desktop machine – PC, Mac or Linux system.

As to additional hardware over and above the ESP32, you will need a solderless prototype board and some hookup wires, also known as Dupont wires. You will also need some LEDs, a selection of resistors, some 2N2222 or other general purpose transistors and any of the sensors used in later chapters. See the Resources page for this book on the I/O Press website for links.

A solderless prototype board and some Dupont wires

The typical ESP32 development board presents a particular problem for prototyping as it is too wide to fit on a standard board. There are some "slim" development boards that make a virtue out of being able to fit on a standard prototype board but a simple solution is to use two prototyping boards and plug one side into one board and the other into the other:

There is also an art to inserting and removing a large device such as the ESP32 from a prototype board. The trick is to use a plastic lever to slowly move each end of the device up from the board working evenly and slowly.

While you don't need to know how to solder, you will need to be able to hook up a circuit on a prototyping board. A multimeter (less than $10) is useful, but if you are serious about electronic projects, investing in a logic analyzer (less than $100) will repay itself in no time at all.

You can get small analyzers that plug in via a USB port and use an application to show you what is happening. It is only with a multichannel logic analyzer that you have any hope of understanding what is happening. Without one and the slight skill involved in using it, you are essentially flying blind and left to just guess what might be wrong.

A Low Cost Logic Analyzer

Finally, if you are even more serious, then a pocket oscilloscope is also worth investing in to check out the analog nature of the supposedly digital signals that microcontrollers put out. However, if you have to choose between these two instruments, the logic analyzer should be your first acquisition.

It is worth noting that the ESP32 can generate signals that are too fast to be reliably detected by low-cost oscilloscopes and logic analyzers, which work at between 1MHz and 25MHz. This can mean that working with pulses much faster than $1\mu s$ can be difficult as you cannot rely on your instruments. There are reasonably priced 200MHz and 500MHz logic analyzers and one of these is certainly worthwhile if you are serious about hardware. It is worth knowing that both instruments can mislead you if you try to work with signals outside of the range that they can work with.

It is also assumed that you are able to program in Python. While there are some differences between it and MicroPython, the programs are easy enough to follow and any out-of-the-ordinary coding is explained.

Community

Because so many companies produce ESP32 boards there isn't a single ESP32 community as there is for the Arduino or the Raspberry Pi. Espressif runs a lively forum at:

`https://www.esp32.com/index.php`

and this is a good place to ask questions and to see if there are already answers. There is an ESP32 forum hosted by MicroPython:

`https://forum.micropython.org/viewforum.php?f=18`

which is useful for specific MicroPython questions.

The Arduino forum has a section for Nano ESP32 questions:

`https://forum.arduino.cc/c/official-hardware/nano-family/nano-esp32`

There is also Stack Overflow of course.

On any forum, the quality of answers varies from misleading to excellent. Always make sure you evaluate what you are being advised in the light of what you know. Be kind and supportive of anyone offering an answer that indicates that they misunderstand your question.

You also need to keep in mind that the advice is also usually offered from a biased point of view. Experts in other language will often give you a solution that abandons MicroPython. Electronics beginners will offer you solutions that are based on "off-the-shelf" modules, when a simple alternative solution is available, based on a few cheap components. Even when the advice you get is 100% correct, it still isn't necessarily the right advice for you. As a rule never follow any advice that you don't understand.

Summary

- The ESP32 from Chinese manufacturer Espressif is a remarkably powerful device given its low cost and is ideal for building prototypes, one-offs and production devices.

- There appear to be so many different ESP32 development boards that it can be difficult to know where to start. However, there are only a small number of ESP32 modules which are used to create development boards and these differ only in small ways.

- The original ESP32 is still available at a lower cost than its replacement ESP32 S3.

- Start with a WROOM-32 EPS32 or ESP32 S3 development board with a full set of pins exposed.

- The Arduino Nano ESP32 offers an ESP32 S3 integrated with the rest of the Arduino family, but it is more expensive.

- You will need a pair of prototyping boards and some prototyping wires. You also need a multimeter and preferably a logic analyzer. After these basic instruments you can add what you can afford.

- There is an active ESP32 community forum hosted by Espressif and if you get stuck it's the place to ask for advice. If you have a specific MicroPython question then use the ESP32 forum at the MicroPython website. However, always evaluate any advice proffered and, in general, don't accept it unless you understand it.

- Thonny provides an easy-to-use and efficient development environment, irrespective of the type of development machine you choose.

Chapter 2

Getting Started

The easiest language to use to program the ESP32 is MicroPython. This is a reasonably full implementation of Python 3 plus special modules to work with the ESP32's hardware. If you know the Python language you will have no problem working in MicroPython. However, getting used to the ideas involved in working with hardware is another matter – you have to think a little differently. To put it simply, time matters. What this means will become clear in the rest of the book, but exactly when and in what order things happen are fundamental concerns to this sort of hardware programming, and this usually means needing the most efficient programming language possible. Sometimes, however, you don't need speed, even in an IoT application. For example, if you just want to flash a few LEDs or read a temperature sensor in a human timescale, then you can write in almost any language and MicroPython is ideal. You can also often avoid having to react at the highest possible speed by using the range of peripheral devices that the ESP32 has. In other words, you can offload time critical operations to specialized hardware.

Speed, or rather lack of speed, can be a problem with coding in Python, but it is worth explaining that while Python may not be fast, it is sophisticated. There are ways of writing code in MicroPython that would require a lot of work to implement in lower-level languages. You may not have raw speed, but you do have mature sophistication.

So MicroPython is worth learning and the ESP32 provides low-cost hardware to experiment with. How do we get started?

Installing MicroPython
The key to understanding how everything works is to realize that what we are about to do is convert an ESP32 into a MicroPython machine. That is, we are going to download the MicroPython system onto an ESP32 and from this moment on the device behaves quite differently because every time you switch it on it is running the MicroPython system.

We get the MicroPython program onto the ESP32 using the basic way of getting any program onto the ESP32. The difference is that we are only going to do this once. If nothing goes wrong after we have installed MicroPython we can use it to download and run any MicroPython programs we write in future. You only have to repeat the installation if something damages the MicroPython system or you load some other program onto the ESP32.

The most basic way of getting any program installed on the ESP32 is to use the Python esptool which communicates with the ESP32 using the USB connection as a serial port. It has lots of options, but if all you want to do is install MicroPython there are only a small number of commands you need to know.

The recommended and the simplest way to install MicroPython and run programs, however, is to bypass esptool and use Thonny as an intermediate. It makes use of the commands introduced in this section, but is much simpler to use. Unless you want to do things the slightly harder way skip to the next section.

To install esptool use:

```
pip install esptool
```

This will install esptool and usually your only problem is working out where it has been installed. You can use esptool to do a great many things with the connected ESP32 but the two actions that you need to get started with MicroPython are:

```
esptool.py --port /dev/ttyUSB0 erase_flash
```

and:

```
esptool.py --chip esp32 --port /dev/ttyUSB0 write_flash
                          -z 0x1000 micropythonfile.bin
```

The first erases the flash memory on your ESP32 so that you can install new software without interference from existing code. The second installs new software – in this case MicroPython. The only difficulty in using either of these commands is discovering the serial port to use. Under Linux it will generally be dev/ttyUSB0 if you only have one USB port connected. You also don't need to install a driver under Linux, but the chances are you will under Windows.

If you are using a board with a CP210x serial to USB connection then you will most likely need to install the CP210x Universal Windows Driver, available from Silicon Labs:

```
https://www.silabs.com/developers/usb-to-uart-bridge-vcp-drivers
```

If you are using a board with a CH340 serial to USB then the driver should be already installed, but you can find drivers by searching the web if you need them. Under Windows the serial ports are called COMn and you need to use the device manager to find which one the USB to serial chip is connected to.

If esptool reports that it cannot find the ESP32, or that it isn't responding, then the problem is almost certainly that you are using the wrong serial port or haven't installed a necessary driver. The only other common problem is using a USB cable that is power only and doesn't allow a data connection.

There is also the question of which bin file to install on the ESP32. If you go to the MicroPython download page and select the ESP32 filter you will see that there are many different versions for specific development boards.

If you can see one that matches exactly the board you have then use it. If not then use the generic ESP32 or ESP32 S3 file, At the time of writing the current version is v1.24.1, but this will change as MicroPython is updated.

Once you have installed MicroPython it will start running whenever you connect the ESP32 to power or when you reset the machine. You don't have to install MicroPython again unless you need to upgrade or repair it.

When MicroPython starts running it makes a REPL, (Read Evaluate Print Loop) a simple interactive code editor available via the serial port.

To run a program you can do it the hard way and connect to the ESP32 running MicroPython via a serial terminal and use the interactive REPL to type in or copy and paste in MicroPython commands. However, it is much better to move away from the command line and use an IDE such as Thonny which sets the REPL into paste mode and uploads and runs your program automatically.

It is worth knowing that the REPL controls the running of the Python program and adds a "soft reset" which doesn't reboot the ESP32 but simply restarts the MicroPython interpreter.

The control commands are:

- ◆ Ctrl-A on a blank line enters raw REPL mode. This is like a permanent paste mode, except that characters are not echoed back.
- ◆ Ctrl-B on a blank line goes to normal REPL mode.
- ◆ Ctrl-C cancels any input or interrupts the currently running code.
- ◆ Ctrl-D on a blank line does a soft reset.
- ◆ Ctrl-E starts paste mode.

When you perform a soft reset the interpreter will automatically start to run the code stored in the file `main.py`.

When you perform a real hardware reset, using the reset/enable button or using the software equivalent, then the interpreter will automatically start to run the code stored in the file boot.py:

Action	
hardware reset	Runs `boot.py` followed by `main.py`
soft reset Ctrl-D	Runs `main.py`
Ctrl-C	Stops the running program

If you find you cannot interrupt a running program using Ctrl-C for any reason the solution is to reflash MicroPython using esptool.

Arduino Nano ESP32

In principle, the procedures outlined above should just work on the Nano ESP32 with a little configuration. At the time of writing, MicroPython support for the Nano ESP32 isn't complete and there are problems in using it with Thonny, for example. Most of the problems are caused by the way that it downloads programs. The Nano ESP32 uses a DFU (Device Firmware Upgrade) bootloader which neither esptool nor Thonny can use to upload programs. The problem is that the USB port is used in three different configurations - DFU, Bootloader and Serial port. The default configuration of the Nano ESP32 is DFU mode and this is what the Arduino IDE expects when it uploads programs.

The MicroPython site suggests using the dfu-util program to download MicroPython. This is involved and difficult to get working, especially under Windows, but it does work as long as the ESP32 is in DFU mode. Download it from https://dfu-util.sourceforge.net/ and unzip it. Download the latest MicroPython in app-bin format and save it somewhere accessible. Connect the Nano ESP32 and use the command:

```
dfu-util.exe dfu-util -d 0x2341:0x0070 -R
    -D path to\ARDUINO_NANO_ESP32-20241129-v1.24.1.app-bin
```

replacing *path to* with the correct path to the file.

A better, but little-documented, way to install MicroPython on the Nano ESP32 is to make use of the, currently experimental, installer from Arduino Labs at https://github.com/arduino/lab-micropython-installer. You simply download the binary for your system and unzip it. Then run the setup program. The installer is easy to use, as long as it detects the connected board:

It will detect the board even if it is in DFU or bootloader mode. It will then install the latest MicroPython to the board and convert the USB port to a standard serial port. This means you cannot use it to install MicroPython twice in a row without restoring the USB port to DFU mode.

🐍 **MicroPython Installer**

Install MicroPython on your Arduino board

Detected Boards

Arduino Nano ESP32

Reload

INSTALL MICROPYTHON

☐ Use Preview Builds 🚩

OR

Drag & drop custom firmware here or choose file

Once MicroPython has been installed you can start Thonny or connect to the serial port and start programming in MicroPython using the command line.

It can be difficult to know what upload mode the board is in and you can use the Windows device manager to work it out.

If you see a single COM port allocated to the Nano ESP32 then it could be in bootloader mode or serial port mode. If you see:

then the board is in DFU mode and you should be able to use it with the MicroPython Installer or the Arduino IDE.

The installer works under Linux and Mac, but there isn't a release that works under non-x64 intel Linux. So, for example, it doesn't work on a Raspberry Pi. In this case you have to install MicroPython using another machine. Once MicroPython is installed it works perfectly under Thonny on all systems.

There is also a lab project to create an Arduino MicroPython IDE but, at the moment, Thonny is much better.

To set DFU mode press the reset button once, wait for the LED to come on and then press it again before the LED turns off. If this has worked, the LED should slowly flash green. If you press reset again, the device DFU configuration is lost. To make it permanent you have to power cycle it or use the Arduino IDE to download a program.

Hello World Using Thonny

The Thonny IDE is preinstalled on many Linux systems and you can install it on Linux, Mac or Windows from the Thonny website. You can use it to install MicroPython onto a connected ESP32 and to develop programs.

If you already have it installed you need to check that it is up to date. Visit the Thonny website:

`https://thonny.org/`

and download the latest version. If you are working with Debian Linux you can use:

`sudo apt install thonny`

Once installed, start it running and make sure that the ESP32 is connected via a USB cable as Thonny and the other IDEs communicate with it via the serial port provided by the USB cable.

A newly installed Thonny runs in simple mode to make it easier to use for beginners. You need to use Thonny in "regular" or "expert" mode which presents the full range of menu options. Select the regular or expert mode link from the top right-hand corner and restart Thonny. After this you should see all of the menus. You can change the mode using the Options menu item and select the General tab and set the mode:

Once you are in regular mode you can set the Python interpreter to use, but if you are going to use Thonny to install MicroPython on the ESP32 then it is a good idea to install esptool.py. To do this select Tools, Manage Packages

In the dialog box that opens type in esptool and search for this in PyPI:

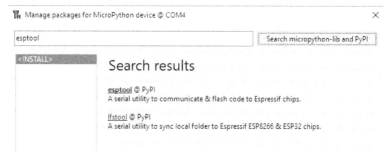

Select esptool from the list of possible targets and wait while Thonny installs it for you. One advantage of this method of installation is that Thonny ensures that it is installed in a location that is on the execution path.

After you have installed esptool you can move on to installing MicroPython. First make sure you have an ESP32 device connected via USB. Thonny installs its own full copy of Python for you to use, but it can also make use of other Python interpreters including MicroPython for a range of different devices including the ESP32. Use the Interpreter tab in the Options dialog and select MicroPython(ESP32) as the interpreter.

Next, click on the Install or Upgrade MicroPython link in the bottom right-hand corner:

As discussed earlier, this works on ESP32 and ESP32 S3 but not on the Arduino Nano ESP32. In the case of the Nano ESP32 you have to install MicroPython before using it with Thonny

You don't need to have downloaded the MicroPython you want to use if it is one of the versions that Thonny offers you. If you want something different you have to download a .bin file from the MicroPython site. You also need to know which serial port the ESP32 is connected to:

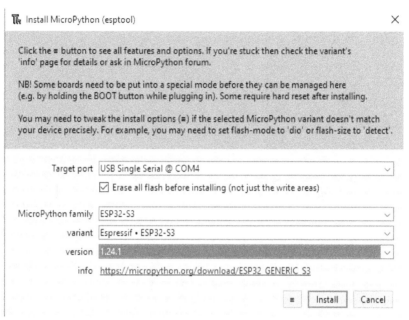

As long as you have these two entries specified correctly you can click the Install button and wait while MicroPython is installed – it takes a few minutes and you can follow the progress in the status bar at the bottom left which displays Done when the process is complete.

After you have installed MicroPython you can move back to the Interpreter tab and specify the port to use. As long as the ESP32 is connected, and no other program is making use of its serial connection, Thonny should be able to find it automatically. If it fails try setting the port that you know the ESP32 is connected to.

As long as this works you will see an editing window and a Shell that you can type immediate MicroPython instructions into and see the commands that Thonny issues to the ESP32.

Enter the following program:

```
print("Hello ESP32 World")
```

This will print the message to the console at the bottom of the Thonny window.

Once the program is entered you can click the Run icon and you will see the result in the shell window at the bottom of the screen:

You can save your program either on the local development machine or on the ESP32. In most cases you will want to store the program on the development machine so that you can open it and continue editing it. Saving the program on the ESP32 allows you to run the program without downloading it and to set it as the default program when the ESP32 is first started.

You can see all of the files stored on the local machine or the ESP32 by selecting View, Files:

You can manage the files in the usual way and load files from either source into the editor. The file in the editor is always copied down to the ESP32 when it is run. If a program that you are trying to run makes use of other programs, via an import statement say, then you have to ensure that the appropriate files are stored on the ESP32.

MicroPython creates a small filing system on the ESP32 and you can save and open files stored there using Thonny.

Thonny is a good way to get started as it is simple and quick, but it lacks many of the facilities you may be used to in other IDEs. In particular it lacks any debug options and it has no intelligent prompting (intellisense) or syntax checking for MicroPython.

MicroPython Remote Control

The `mpremote` program is a standard Python program that can communicate with the REPL on any MicroPython device. It has commands to manipulate files and the machine's state. Most of the time you won't need it, but occasionally it can be an essential component.

To install it use:

```
pip install mpremote
```

There are now several commands you can use, but you probably won't need any of them:

- `mpremote connect` *`device`* where *`device`* is any of:
    `list, auto, id:usb` serial number, `port:port`
- `mpremote disconnect`
- `mpremote resume`
- `mpremote soft-reset`
- `mpremote repl` *`options`* where *`options`* are:

    `--capture` *`file`*, to capture output of the REPL session to *`file`*

    `--inject-code` *`code`*, to specify characters to inject at the REPL when Ctrl-J is pressed

    `--inject-file` *`file`*, to specify a file to inject at the REPL when Ctrl-K is pressed
- `mpremote eval python code`
- `mpremote exec code`
- `mpremote run` *`file`* where *`file`* is a MicroPython file on the local machine
- `mpremote fs` *`command`* where *`command`* may be:

    `cat` *`file`*... to show the contents of a file or files on the device

    `ls` *`dir`*... to list the given directories

    `cp -r src...` `dest`   to copy files; use ":" as a prefix to specify a file on the device

    `rm` `src`... to remove files on the device

    `mkdir dirs`... to create directories on the device

    `rmdir dirs`... to remove directories on the device

    `touch file`... to create the files (if they don't already exist)
- `mpremote edit` *`file`*... copies each file from the device to a local temporary directory and then launches your editor for each file (defined by the environment variable `$EDITOR`). If the editor exits successfully, the updated file will be copied back to the device
- `mpremote mip install` packages... install packages from `micropython-lib` (or GitHub) using the mip tool

- ◆ `mpremote mount` *options* *local-dir* where *options* are `-l` which allows unsafe file access outside of the local directory. If the device is soft restarted then the directory is remounted unless `main.py` is running. To mount the directory you can use Ctrl-B to start the REPL when the directory is remounted.

- ◆ `mpremote unmount`

The trick in using `mpremote` is to realize that you can chain the commands to form a small procedure. If any command leaves you in the REPL you can exit it using Ctrl-]

For example:

```
mpremote connect com6 fs cp main.py :main2.py
```

connects to the device using COM6 and then copies `main.py` from the local machine to the ESP32 and renames it `main2.py`. To check that the files are there you can use:

```
mpremote connect com6 fs ls
```

Notice that you can use the `cp` command to upload files from the ESP32 to the local machine. For example:

```
mpremote connect com6 fs cp :main.py main2.py
```

uploads `main.py` from the ESP32 to the local machine under the name `main2.py`.

If you mount a directory then it replaces the devices filing system. For example if you create a directory called `myDir` containing `myProgram.py` then:

```
connect com6 mount myDir
```

will start the REPL and when you use `os.listdir()` you will see `myProgram.py`.

To leave the REPL use Ctrl-] and then use `unmount` to remove the mount or `resume` to return to the REPL with the directory still mounted.

If you want to download and run a program use:

```
mpremote connect com6 run main.py
```

The file `main.py` is downloaded, run and then deleted from the ESP32.

Summary

- MicroPython is a powerful and sophisticated language and, with the ESP32's speed, you can achieve a great deal.

- Before you can start using MicroPython, you have to download it and install it on any ESP32 you want to use.

- Installing it onto an ESP32 is a matter of using `esptool`. Use the generic ESP32 binary file unless you know better.

- Once MicroPython is installed on an ESP32 it is a MicroPython machine every time you switch it on.

- To program a MicroPython machine you can use the command prompt, but it is much easier to use an IDE.

- The standard IDE for MicroPython is Thonny and this works with the ESP32 without any additional configuration.

- You may also need to use `mpremote` to work with the file system of the ESP32.

Chapter 3

Getting Started With The GPIO

In this chapter we take a look at the basic operations involved in using the ESP32's General Purpose Input/Output (GPIO) lines with an emphasis on output. We'll consider questions such as how fast can you change a GPIO line, how do you generate pulses of a given duration and how can you change multiple lines in sync with each other?

ESP Pins

The first thing to make ourselves familiar with is the layout and range of GPIO pins available on a typical development board – some development boards have fewer or differently arranged pins. Most development boards are based on the ESP32-DevKitC or the ESP32-S3-DevKitC but they sometimes have additional onboard LEDs or reduced GPIO pins. The pins are usually described on the PCB and you can use this to confirm that the development board you are using has a particular pin configuration.

All of the pins have multiple uses, most of which we will explore in later chapters, but here we concentrate on their simplest use as GPIO lines. A GPIO line can be configured as an input or an output, but what is important even at this early stage is that you know that the ESP32 is a 3.3V device. This means that a GPIO line works with two voltages, 0V and 3.3V. If you try to use a GPIO line at a higher voltage then you risk damaging the ESP32.

You can power the ESP32 via the USB port, which is the easiest way while you are developing software. You can also supply 5V via the 5V pin and it will be regulated down to 3.3V or you can connect a 3.3V supply to the 3.3V pin. You can only use a single method of powering the ESP32.

The ESP32 usually has 34 physically accessible GPIO lines in four groups:

GPIO0 to GPIO19, GPIO21 to GPIO23, GPIO25 to GPIO27
and GPIO32 to GPIO39.

Pins GPIO34 to GPIO39 are input only.

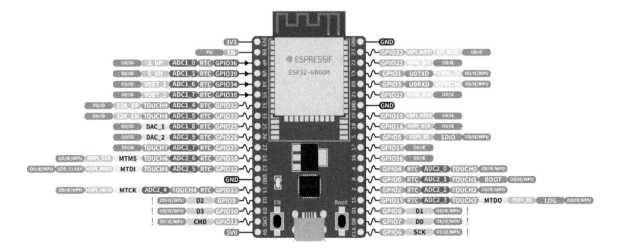

Notice that GPIO37 and GPIO38 are not available on most development boards. The following GPIO lines are used for other purposes and should be avoided:

GPIO0	Used at boot to signal Firmware upload
GPIO1	Used for USB serial Tx
GPIO2	Sometimes used to drive onboard LED
GPIO3	Used for USB serial Rx
GPIO6-11	Shared with Flash memory
GPIO16-17	Not available on WROVER modules

The ESP 32 S3 has 45 GPIO lines but also has 34 only physically accessible GPIO lines in two groups:

GPIO0 to GPIO 21 and GPIO35 to GPIO48

All GPIO lines are input/output.

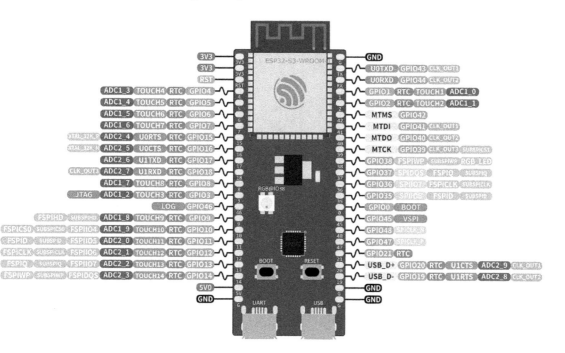

You can see that while there is a lot of overlap, GPIO assignments and use in the ESP32 and ESP32 S3 are not the same. The following GPIO lines are used for other purposes and should be avoided:

GPIO0	Used at boot to signal Firmware upload
GPIO19-20	Used for USB connection
GPIO38-42	Not available on WROVER modules SPI

The Arduino Nano ESP32 has 21 GPIO lines, which is fewer than the ESP32 or ESP32 S3:

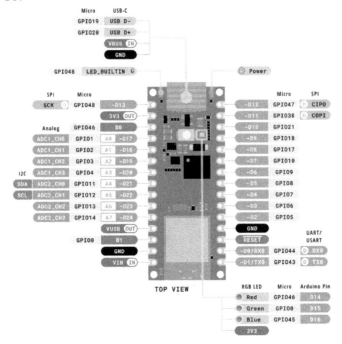

Notice that the Arduino diagram uses two different ways to indicate GPIO pins, GPIO numbers and Arduino Pin names. For example, GPIO02 is also labeled A1, standing for Analog 1. This is because the Arduino family of devices has an Analog 1 input and this has been mapped to GPIO02, which can be used as an analog input in the case of the ESP32. In practice, it is less ambiguous to use GPIO numbers and this is what MicroPython does.

Despite the pins being labeled as digital or analog, they are all standard ESP32 pins and can be used in any GPIO mode.

In the rest of the book, all pin numbers used in programs and diagrams will be GPIO numbers. If you want to use Arduino numbering then you can always make use of variables like D1=43 or A1=2.

The mapping between the two sets of names can be seen below:

ESP32	Nano	ESP32	Nano
GPIO0	BOOT1	GPIO12	A5
GPIO1	A0	GPIO13	A6
GPIO2	A1	GPIO14	A7
GPIO3	A2	GPIO17	D8
GPIO4	A3	GPIO18	D9
GPIO5	D2	GPIO21	D10
GPIO6	D3	GPIO38	D11
GPIO7	D4	GPIO43	D1
GPIO8	D5	GPIO44	D0
GPIO9	D6	GPIO46	BOOT0
GPIO10	D7	GPIO47	D12
GPIO11	A4	GPIO48	D13

As is the case with most microprocessors, each GPIO line has multiple uses as you can see in the pin layout diagrams. You can select what mode a pin is used in and in this chapter we concentrate on using pins in the simplest GPIO mode. Even so, which pins you select for general-purpose use should take into account what other uses you might put pins to.

Another complication is that some pins are used when the ESP32 boots to set its state. Pins GPIO0, 2, 5, 12, 15 on the ESP32 and pins GPIO0, 3, 45, 46 on the ESP32 S3 are "strapping pins" and if you use pull-up or pull-down resistors to set their initial state, you will change the behavior at boot time. Each of the strapping pins has an internal resistor that will pull it either high or low and hence supplies the default behavior. If the strapping pins are connected to anything then these weak resistors are overcome and you can set the pins to any initial state. Strapping pins are useful in that you can use them to set up the ESP32 but they are often a nuisance when you forget that they exist and accidentally set them. Notice that the state of the pins is sampled and saved when the system boots – after this you can use them as general GPIO lines without worry.

Pins GPIO1, 3, 5, 14-15 are also used by the system at start up to send boot status data. This means that on booting up these pins change state rapidly and could trigger any devices connected to them, leading to difficult-to-find bugs.

Another consideration is that if you plan to use JTAG debugging you need to avoid pins GPIO12-15 in the ESP32 which implement the JTAG protocol. Notice that JTAG is generally only useful if you are working in C and it is not used for debugging a Python program. You can disable the JTAG protocol by programming an eFuse, but this isn't generally a good idea. The EPS32 S3 uses GPIO39-42 for JTAG, but this is normally disabled and you have to program an eFuse to turn it on. In most cases, you are better using the built-in JTAG adapter via the USB connector.

In general, with the ESP32 you can use pins GPIO4, 5 and 12-33 for general I/O without restrictions and pins GPIO34-39 for input only. GPIO2 can also be used for general I/O if it isn't connected to an onboard LED.

For an ESP32 S3, you can usually use pins GPIO1, 2, 4-21, 38-44, 47 and 48 without worrying about strapping or other uses. Notice that the two ranges only overlap in GPIO13-33 range.

The Arduino Nano ESP32 has pins GPIO1-14, 17-18, 21, 38, 43-44 and47-48.

All three overlap in only a small number of usable GPIO lines:

GPIO 2, 4, 5, 12, 13, 14, 17, 18 and 21.

It is also worth knowing at this early stage that there is a second set of GPIO lines referred to as RTC GPIO which use the same pins as the standard GPIO lines, but are only active in deep-sleep or ultra low power mode. Their purpose is to allow the processor to control things while in low-power mode. You can ignore these additional lines for the moment and concentrate on using the standard GPIO lines.

Notice that, unlike when programming directly to the hardware, MicroPython doesn't use the idea of setting the GPIO pin into a particular mode. Instead it provides classes that make use of GPIO pins in particular ways. For example, if you were programming directly to the hardware you would first set the pins you wanted to use to the mode you wanted to use, e.g. PWM (Pulse Width Modulation) and then you would start working with PWM operations. In MicroPython you would simply create a PWM object using the pin in question and expect it to take care of setting the pin to the correct mode. Notice, however, that you are still restricted to using pins that support the mode you are using.

There is no standard notation for which physical pin to connect to, but if the development board is based on the or similar the two connectors on either side are called J2 and J3 or J1 and J3 and the pins are numbered sequentially:

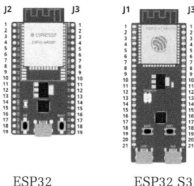

ESP32   ESP32 S3

Basic GPIO Functions

The MicroPython `Pin` class allows you to create an object which controls the way a single GPIO line works. The simplest form of the constructor is:

`Pin(id, mode = mode)`

where id is the number of the GPIO line you want to use and mode is `Pin.IN` or `Pin.OUT`. There are other possibilities and these are discussed later.

Notice that *id* is the GPIO number and not the hardware pin number. For example, 5 means GPIO5 and not "connector pin 5" but connector J3 pin 10.

There is also an `init` method which can be used to change the configuration of the pin. For example, `pin.init(mode = Pin.IN)` might be used to change a pin from output to input.

A number of methods are provided to work with the state of a `Pin` object:

Method	Description
`value(x)`	Sets the line to x, usually 0 or 1, but x can be anything that evaluates to true or false
`on()`	Sets the line to high
`off()`	Sets the line to low

There are a number of other methods and properties, but these are the most basic. You can discover the current state of a GPIO line using `state = pin.value()` and you can set the initial state of a GPIO output using `value =` in the constructor or in the `init` method.

45

Blinky

By tradition, the first IoT program you write is Blinky which flashes an LED. A program to flash an LED uses a general I/O line and an external LED. Some development boards have an LED already connected to GPIO2. With this in mind, let's flash an LED connected to GPIO2 which will either use the onboard LED or an external LED you have connected.

The ESP32 S3 including the Nano ESP32 has an addressable RGB LED connected to GPIO48. This is more complicated than a simple LED and differs on each machine – a simple external LED works on everything.

Enter the program:

```
from machine import Pin
import time

pin = Pin(2, Pin.OUT)
while True:
    pin.value(1)
    time.sleep(1)
    pin.value(0)
    time.sleep(1)
```

The program doesn't use any constants in order to make what is happening clearer. It first initializes GPIO2 to be an output and sets it repeatedly high and low with a pause of one second in between. If the board you are using has an LED connected to GPIO2, pin A1 on a Nano ESP32, you will see it flashing. If not and you want to connect an LED to see the "blinking" for real then this is easy enough, but you do need a current-limiting resistor to avoid the LED drawing more current than the GPIO line can supply and possibly damaging the chip. A 200Ω resistor is a good choice, see Chapter 5, where a better way to drive an LED is also discussed.

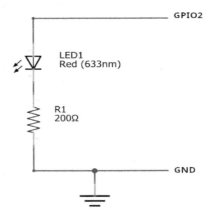

How you build the circuit is up to you. You can use a prototyping board or just a pair of jumper wires. The short pin and/or the flat on the side of the case marks the negative connection on the LED – the one that goes to ground.

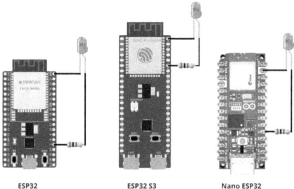

| ESP32 | ESP32 S3 | Nano ESP32 |

If you can't be bothered to go through the ritual of testing "Blinky" with a real LED, then just connect a logic analyzer to J3 Pin 15 and you will see pulses at 1-second intervals.

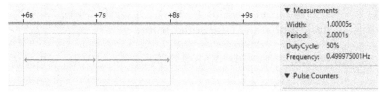

Adding A Function Toggle

The ESP32 doesn't support a toggle function, but it is easy to add one:

```
def toggle(pin):
    temp = pin.value()
    temp = not temp
    pin.value(temp)
```

This sets a line high it if it is low and low if it is high. This form of the function shows how it works, but in practice you would probably write it in a more compact form:

```
def toggle(pin):
    pin.value(not pin.value())
```

With toggle it is even easier to implement Blinky:

```
from machine import Pin
import time
pin = Pin(2,Pin.OUT)
while True:
    toggle(pin)
    time.sleep(1)
```

Summary

- The ESP32 and ESP32 S3 have 34 GPIO lines in total, but some are already used by the development board and the Nano ESP32 has 21 GPIO lines.

- The pin numbering used isn't standardized between the two Espressif devices, but using the GPIO numbers that the ESP32 module uses is a safe option. While the Nano ESP32 tends to use its own numbering, it is still better to use ESP32 GPIO numbers.

- The ESP32 GPIO lines are organized in four groups, GPIO0 to GPIO19, GPIO21 to GPIO23, GPIO25 to GPIO27 and GPIO32 to GPIO39. Pins GPIO34 to GPIO39 are input only.

- The ESP32 S3 GPIO lines organized in two groups, GPIO0 to GPIO21 and GPIO35 to GPIO48.

- The Nano ESP32 has one major group of GPIO lines, GPIO1 to GPIO14 and then a few additional lines.

- The only GPIO lines that all three have in common are: GPIO 2, 4, 5, 12, 13, 14, 17, 18 and 21.

- All these ESP32s are 3.3V devices and the GPIO lines should not be used at a higher voltage.

- MicroPython provides the Pin class to control a single GPIO line and its basic methods let you set the line high or low and to discover what it is currently set to.

- A Blinky program is usually the first IoT program you write on a new machine. For all these ESP32s you can easily arrange to make an externally connected LED blink on and off.

- An externally connected LED needs a current limiting resistor.

Chapter 4

Simple Output

A GPIO line is either configured to be an input or an output. The electronics of working with inputs and outputs are discussed in the next chapter, but first we focus on the software side of the task of using GPIO lines in output mode. While it isn't possible to ignore electronics entirely, keep in mind that more details are provided in Chapter 5.

It is worth noting at this stage that output is easy. Your program chooses the time to change a line's state and you can use the system timer to work out exactly when things should happen. The real problems only start to become apparent when you are trying to change the state of lines very fast or when they need to be changed synchronously. This raises the question of how fast the ESP32 can change a GPIO line and this is something we consider at this early stage because it puts constraints on what we can easily do.

Basic GPIO Functions

We have already met the basic methods of the Pin object that let you work with a single GPIO line:

Method	Description
init(mode)	Sets mode to input or output
value(x)	Sets the line to x, usually 1 or 0, but can be anything that evaluates to True or False
on()	Sets the line to high
off()	Sets the line to low

Using these methods is very straightforward, but notice that there is no way to set multiple lines in one operation. This can be a problem, something we'll come to later.

Signal

There is a fundamental problem with controlling devices via a GPIO line – does the concept of "on" correspond to a high or a low level on the output line? Some things switch on with a high voltage, others switch off. My personal preference is to always work with line states – on is high and off is low – but you might not agree.

You can take a Pin object and wrap it in a Signal object which can be configured to make on correspond to a high or a low voltage. For example:

```
signal = machine.Signal(pin,invert=False)
```

gives you a signal object with signal.on() corresponding to a high voltage on the GPIO line, whereas:

```
signal = machine.Signal(pin,invert=True)
```

gives you a signal object with signal.on() corresponding to a low voltage on the GPIO line. Of course, signal.off() works in the same way.

Slightly more confusing is signal.value(x) where x can be anything that converts to True or False. In this case True corresponds to "on" and False to "off" and what this means in terms of GPIO line voltage depends on how he Signal was defined. So signal.value(1) could mean high or it could mean low depending on the constructor used.

How Fast?

A fundamental question that you have to answer for any processor intended for use in embedded or IoT projects is, how fast can the GPIO lines work?

Sometimes the answer isn't of too much concern because what you want to do only works relatively slowly. Any application that is happy with response times in the tens of millisecond region will generally work with almost any processor. However, if you want to implement custom protocols or anything that needs microsecond, or even nanosecond, responses, the question is much more important.

It is fairly easy to find out how fast a single GPIO line can be used if you have a logic analyzer or oscilloscope. All you have to do is run the program:

```
from machine import  Pin
pin = Pin(2, Pin.OUT)
while True:
    pin.value(1)
    pin.value(0)
```

If you run this program on an ESP32 you will discover that the pulses are about 5.7μs and not even, the up time is 5.7μs but the down time is 6.1μs (S3 timings are 2.9μs and 3.4μs):

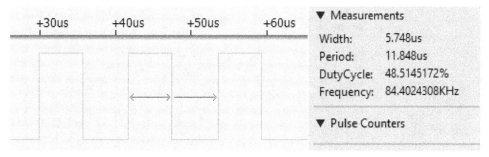

The unevenness is due to the internal workings of MicroPython. If you change the way that the code is specified, you are likely to see changes in timing. For example, if you try the equivalent code:

```
from machine import Pin
def flash():
    pin = Pin(2, Pin.OUT)
    while True:
        pin.value(1)
        pin.value(0)
flash()
```

you will discover that the pulse width has dropped to around 3.8μs (S3 1.9μs). This is not what you might expect given that a function call is an additional step!

There is a facility to compile functions to native code and this gives the largest speed increase without going to exceptional lengths. If you want a function to be compiled all you have to do is add the @micropython.native decorator:

```
from machine import Pin

@micropython.native
def flash():
    pin = Pin(2, Pin.OUT)
    while True:
        pin.value(1)
        pin.value(0)
flash()
```

Notice that the decorator can only be applied to a function.

If you run this program you will find that not only does the pulse time drop to 2.7μs (S3 1.5μs), but the pulses are nearly symmetrical - high time is 2.72μs and low time is 2.76μs (S3 1.46μs and 1.47μs):

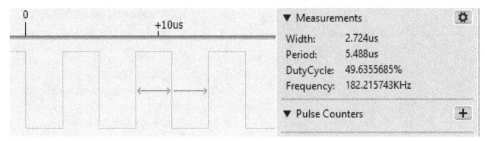

The reason that the pulses are almost symmetrical is that now Python is not involved in running the while loop and the machine code is much faster.

One problem with tight loops with native code is that it is very easy to write a program that cannot be interrupted. The solution is to reinstall MicroPython using esptool.

Including Pauses

To generate pulses of a known duration we need to pause the program between state changes. In the Blinky programs we used sleep to slow things down, but without properly introducing it.

Using sleep(*seconds*) gives a pause or "wait" for the specified number of seconds. As *seconds* is a floating-point number you can specify fractions of a second. So for half-second pulses you could use:

```
from machine import Pin
import time
pin = Pin(2, Pin.OUT)
while True:
    pin.value(1)
    time.sleep(0.5)
    pin.value(0)
    time.sleep(0.5)
```

As well as sleep there are also sleep_ms and sleep_us which pause the program for the specified number of milliseconds and microseconds respectively. You can use utime or time to import the functions.

Of course, when creating pulses of a given time the waits add to the basic pulse time.

So for example:

```
from machine import Pin
import time
pin = Pin(2, Pin.OUT)
while True:
    pin.value(1)
    time.sleep_us(10)
    pin.value(0)
    time.sleep_us(10)
```

creates pulses that are 16μs wide (S3 11.7μs) not 10μs. In general, you have to add about 5μs (S3 2μs) to the wait time to get the pulse length.

The traditional way of introducing a busy wait (also known as a spin wait) is to simply use a time-wasting for loop which produces short wait times:

```
from machine import Pin
import time
pin = Pin(2, Pin.OUT)
n = 10
while True:
    for i in range(n):
        pass
    pin.value(1)
    for i in range(n):
        pass
    pin.value(0)
```

which generates pulses according to the setting of n:

n	ESP32 Time in μs	ESP32 S3 Time in μs
1	13-17	8
2	17-21	10
3	21-25	12
4	25-28	14
5	28-32	16
6	32-35	19
7	35-39	21
8	39-43	23
9	43-46	25
10	46-50	27

These figures are subject to change as MicroPython versions are optimized and the time for operations varies.

Fixed Time Delay

A common problem is making sure that something happens after a fixed time delay when you have a variable amount of work to do during that time interval. Consider the program snippet:

```
pin.value(1)
for i in range(n):
    pass
time.sleep_ms(1)
pin.value(1)
```

where the for loop is intended to stand in for doing some other work. The intention is that the GPIO line should be set high for 1ms, but clearly how long the line is set high depends on how long the loop takes, which is given by n plus 1ms of sleep time.

What is needed is a pause that takes into account the time that the loop uses up and simply delays the program for the remaining amount of time to make it up to 1ms. This is where the functions ticks_ms() and ticks_us() come in useful. They give the time since the machine was switched on in milliseconds or microseconds respectively. These both wrap around at some unspecified point and to take account of the wrap you need to use:

```
ticks_add(ticks,number)
ticks_diff(ticks1,ticks2)
```

to do arithmetic that takes account of the wrap.

We can now write the program snippet given earlier as:

```
from machine import Pin
import time
pin = Pin(2, Pin.OUT)
n = 5
while True:
    t = time.ticks_add(time.ticks_us(), 1000)
    pin.value(1)
    for i in range(n):
        pass

    while time.ticks_us() < t:
        pass
    pin.value(0)
```

Now we obtain the ticks before setting the line high and add 1000 to it. No matter how long the for loop takes, the while loop will provide a delay of 1ms, as long as the loop takes less than this time. You can try the program out by modifying the value of n. No matter what it is set to you should get 1ms pulses.

This is a very general technique and one that can often make difficult timing problems very simple.

Output with bitstream

The MicroPython `bitstream` function can be a great simplification when trying to generate a set of pulses of set lengths:

```
machine.bitstream(pin, encoding, timing, data)
```

The pin specifies the pin to use for the output – it is up to you to configure it as output and set its initial level. At the moment encoding is always `0` and this forces timing to be a four-element tuple:

```
(high_time_0, low_time_0, high_time_1, low_time_1)
```

This specifies the high and low times for the pulses corresponding to a zero and a one in the data. The data is usually specified as a bytes object or byte array. The idea is that you can code up a zero or a one using a "bit cell" – a high followed by a low for fixed times:

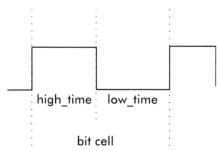

If the high_time and low_time values are different for a zero and a one this can be used to decode the bitstream into data. There are two different ways to encode the data – you can set different high_time and low_times for zero and one but ensure that they add up to the same value. This keeps the bit cell time the same and the decoding is a matter of measuring the times between the rising and falling edges on each pulse. If you allow the cell time to vary then decoding can be done just by measuring the width of the cell which is usually easier.

On most machines, `bitstream` is implemented in software and the speed of the CPU limits the width and accuracy of the pulses. The ESP32 has a special hardware feature, RMT, which was designed to provide signal processing for infrared remote controllers. This can generate pulse streams that are fast and accurate – plus or minus 5ns at the highest speeds. The smallest pulse that you can generate using the default setup for RMT is 80ns. The latest version of MicroPython uses the RMT to implement bitstream and this makes it faster and more accurate.

For example:

```
import time
from time import sleep
import esp32
from machine import Pin
import machine
pin = Pin(2,Pin.OUT,value=0)
buf = bytearray(b"\x55\x55")
print(buf)
machine.bitstream(pin,0,(80,90,100,110),buf)
```

The data consists of a stream of alternating zeros and ones and the timings produce the following pulse stream:

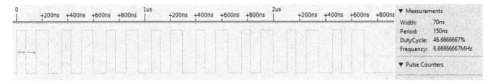

The actual pulse widths produced are (70,80,95,105) which is close, but might not be good enough to be decoded correctly by a receiver. The accuracy gets much better as soon as you are working above 100ns.

There are eight channels of RMT, 0 to 7, and you can select which is used with the function:

```
esp32.RMT.bitstream_channel(n)
```

If you set n to None the original software implementation is used and the performance is severely reduced. Even at 800ns there is still an error of 20ns and there are occasional glitches.

The bitstream command seems to be the ideal way of creating a pulse train, but there are problems. If you are trying to implement a data transfer protocol there are usually start and stop bits to implement and these are usually outside of the specification for zero and one bits. That is, there are generally additional bits that you have to implement outside of the bitstream command and this can be difficult.

It is also a problem that sending repeated bitstreams puts a 400µs gap between the signals. That is it takes about that long to set up the RMT hardware. As long as the signaling protocol allows data to be grouped into bitstreams with gaps between, the RMT approach is a good one. Unfortunately the 400µs gap also occurs between start and stop bits and the bitstream and this is usually much more of a problem.

Using RMT (advanced)

MicroPython provides direct access to the RMT, but this facility is still in beta and doesn't provide all of the available features. In particular, it only allows you to send data and not receive data.

The RMT was designed to allow the ESP32 to implement an infrared controller and, with its eight channels and ability to work with 12.5ns pulses, it is capable of encoding and decoding many different protocols.

You can create a RMT object using:

```
esp32.RMT(channel, pin=None, clock_div=8,
                      idle_level=False, tx_carrier=None)
```

You can select any of the eight channels, 0 to 7, and connect it to the specified pin. An eight-bit value, clock_div, sets the resolution of the signal, e.g. setting it to 256 provides 256 time increments reported in microseconds. The channel resolution is 1/(source_freq/clock_div) which, as the source_freq is fixed at 80MHz, is a maximum of 1/(80/256) = 3.2µs.

The idle_level sets the resting value of the pin when no data is being transmitted. The carrier parameter allows you to set a waveform to be sent when the signal is high specified as a tuple (frequency, duty, level) which transmits a signal with the specified frequency and duty cycle during either the high or low period of the bitstream.

For example, if you are using RMT as an infrared signal the carrier frequency is set to 38 or 36KHz, duty to 50 and level to True for high. This make the infrared led pulse at the frequency for each high level in the bit stream.

The MicroPython driver is currently set to use an 80MHz clock and this cannot be changed. The most important method is the one that sends a bitstream using the initialized RMT:

```
RMT.write_pulses(duration, data=True)
```

This looks simple but there are three ways to specify the duration and data:

- ◆ Mode 1: duration is a list or tuple of durations. The optional data argument specifies the initial output level. The output level will toggle after each duration.

- ◆ Mode 2: duration is a single positive integer and data is a list or tuple of output levels. Each high or low state has the same duration.

- ◆ Mode 3: duration and data are lists or tuples of equal length, specifying individual durations and the output level for each.

Notice that Mode 2 and 3 allow you to specify the duration of each bit precisely which makes it possible to encode start and stop bits as well as the more regular data bits.

For example:

```
import esp32
from machine import Pin
import machine
pin=Pin(2,Pin.OUT,value=0)
rmt=esp32.RMT(0,pin=pin)
rmt.write_pulses((1000,400,200,300,200,300),1)
```

outputs:

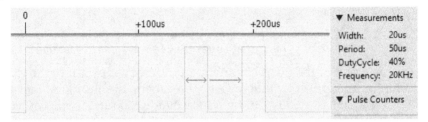

The pulse widths are very accurate at these timings and resolution. Notice that the times specified are for both high and low periods and you can send as many or as few bits as you need. If you send multiple bitstreams using individual calls to write_pulses the gap between each set is around 20µs.

There are some other useful RMT functions:

◆ rmt.source_freq()
Returns the source clock frequency. Currently the source clock is not configurable so this will always return 80MHz.

◆ rmt.clock_div()
Returns the clock divider.

◆ rmt.wait_done(timeout = 0)
Returns True if the channel is idle or False if pulses are being transmitted. The timeout, if specified, makes the function block until the channel is idle or the timeout is up.

◆ rmt.loop(enable_loop)
Repeats sending the data. If set to True the next pulse stream will repeat until loop is called with False.

RMT provides a powerful way of generating bitstreams without the need for the main processor to be involved while the data is sent. If the receive side of the RMT was available it would be ideal for decoding bitstreams, but it isn't and as the RMT is in beta you have to think carefully before using it.

Phased Pulses

As a simple example of using the output functions, let's try to write a short program that pulses two lines, high and then low, out of phase.

The simplest program to do this job is (Nano ESP32 GPIO4 is A3):

```
from machine import Pin

pin1 = Pin(2, Pin.OUT)
pin2 = Pin(4, Pin.OUT)
while True:
    pin1.value(1)
    pin2.value(0)
    pin1.value(0)
    pin2.value(1)
```

There is no delay in the loop so the pulses are produced at the fastest possible speed and `pin2` goes low when `pin1` goes high and vice versa. Using a logic analyzer reveals that the result isn't what you might expect:

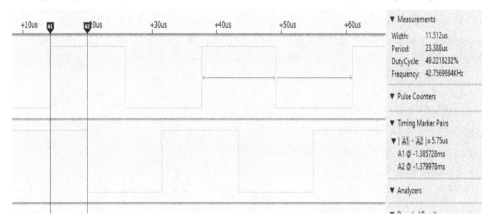

Although the intent is for both actions to occur at the same time, the top train switches on and the bottom train takes about half a pulse before it switches off.

The point is that it does take quite a long time to access and change the state of an output line. If we include a delay to increase the pulse width then the delay caused by accessing the GPIO lines in two separate actions isn't so obvious, but it is still there. There are applications where the switching speed is so low that the delay between switching doesn't matter – flashing LEDs for instance. With a delay of around 5μs you could flash a line of around 2000 LEDs before the lag between the first and the last became apparent. On the other hand, if you use out-of-phase pulses to control a motor, then the overlap when both GPIO lines were on would burn out the drivers quite quickly. Of course, any sensible, cautious, engineer wouldn't feed a motor control bridge from two independently generated pulse trains unless they were guaranteed not to switch both sides of the bridge on at the same time.

Setting Multiple GPIO Lines

There is no way of using MicroPython methods to change multiple GPIO lines at the same time, even though the hardware makes it possible. To do the job you need to write some code that accesses the hardware directly, see Chapter 19 for more details. In this chapter we simply present and make use of the function explained there:

```
def gpio_set(value, mask):
    machine.mem32[0x3FF44004] =
 machine.mem32[0x3FF44004] & ~mask | value & mask
```

The address used in machine.mem32 is for the ESP32 for the ESP32 S3 and Nano ESP32 change this to 0x60004004.

This works by directly accessing the GPIO registers. The function gpio_set uses a mask to determine which lines will be set and a value that gives the states to set them to. Any bits not set in the mask leave the corresponding GPIO line unchanged.

It is easy to create a mask for any GPIO lines. For example, if you want to modify only lines GPIOn and GPIOm then mask is:

```
mask = 1<<n | 1<<m
```

and so on if you have more lines to modify.

The value can be constructed in the same way. If you want to set the lines to a and b then value is:

```
value = a<<n | b<<m
```

Notice that if the corresponding bit isn't set in mask then the bit in value has no effect. That is, mask determines which bits you are going to modify and value determines what those bits are set to.

Making use of this we can write the previous program without lags as when value and mask are used to update the GPIO register all of the lines change at once:

```
from machine import Pin
import machine

def gpio_set(value, mask):
    machine.mem32[0x3FF44004] =
            machine.mem32[0x3FF44004] & ~mask | value & mask

pin = Pin(2, Pin.OUT)
pin = Pin(4, Pin.OUT)
value1 = 1 << 2 | 0 << 4
value2 = 0 << 2 | 1 << 4
mask = 1 << 2 | 1 << 4
while True:
    gpio_set(value1, mask)
    gpio_set(value2, mask)
```

The address used in machine.mem32 is for the ESP32 for the ESP32 S3 and Nano ESP32 change this to 0x60004004.

As we are changing the same pins each time, we only need a single mask. The value, however, changes each time. If you run this program you will see an almost perfect pair of out-of-phase $27\mu s$ pulses:

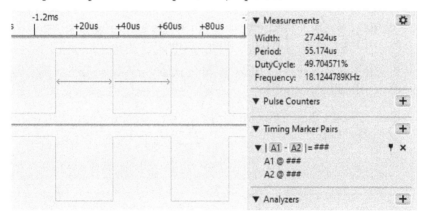

If you add the annotation @micropython.native to the start of the gpio_set function then the pulses are faster, around $18\mu s$.

61

Summary

- Output is easy because the program decides when to change the state of a line. Input is hard because you never know when an input line will change state.

- GPIO lines can be set to act as inputs or outputs when you create a Pin object.

- If a line is set to output it can be set high or low using a number of Pin Methods functions.

- You can generate pulses as short as 5.7μs or 3.4μs using the S3.

- If you compile a function that changes the GPIO lines you can generate reliable 2.7μs or using the ESP32 S3 1.5μs pulses.

- A delay can be introduced into a program using the `sleep`, `sleep_ms` or `sleep_us` functions.

- An alternative is to use a busy wait loop which is simply a loop that keeps the CPU busy for an amount of time. It is easy to obtain an equation that gives the delay per loop repetition.

- By using the tick methods you can set an action to have an exact repeat time, even if what it does varies in time.

- Producing pulses which are in accurately in phase is not possible using the Pin methods.

- If you access the hardware directly you can change multiple lines in one operation.

Now that we have looked at some simple I/O, it is worth spending a little time on the electronics of output and input. We cover the electronics of input before looking at how the software handles input because we need to understand some of the problems that the software has to deal with.

First some basic electronics – how transistors can be used as switches. The approach is very simple, but it is enough for the simple circuits that digital electronics makes use of. It isn't enough to design a high-quality audio amplifier or similar analog device, but it might be all you need.

How to Think About Circuits

For a beginner electronics can seem very abstract, but that's not how old hands think about it. Most understand what is going on in terms of a hydraulic model, even if they don't admit it. The basic idea is that an electric current running in a wire is very much like a flow of water in a pipe. The source of the electricity plays the role of a pump and the wires, the pipe. The flow of electricity is measured in Amps and this is just the amount of electricity that flows per second. The flow is governed by how hard the pump is pumping, which is measured by voltage and how restrictive the pipe is, the resistance which is measured in Ohms.

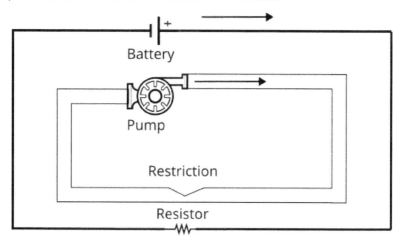

It is true that when you are doing electronics you are basically doing plumbing with a fluid that you generally can't see that flows in pipes called wires.

The only difficult one of these three ideas is the idea of pumping force. We tend to think of a pump providing a flow at the location of the pump but there is something, "a pumping force" that keeps the water flowing around every part of the circuit. In your imagination you have to think of the water being forced ever onward at every point in the pipe. In particular when there is constriction in the pipe then you might need more pumping force to get the water through. In a sense the pump provides the total pressure available and this distributes itself around the circuit as needed to push the flow through each restriction.

In electric circuits the pumping force is called EMF or ElectroMotive Force or just voltage. We also assume that the force needed to push electricity through wires is negligible and resistors are the only place that a voltage is needed to make the current flow.

The relationship between these quantities is characterized by Ohm's law:

V=IR or I=V/R or R=V/I

where V is the voltage in Volts, I is the current in Amps and R is the resistance in Ohms.

It is worth pointing out that we generally work in Volts (V) and milliamps (mA), one thousandth of an amp, in Ohm's law and this automatically gives resistance in kilo-ohms (kΩ).

You can see that if you increase the voltage, the flow, then the current increases. If you increase the resistance then the current decreases. Slightly more difficult is the idea that for a given resistance you need particular pumping force to achieve a given flow. If you know the actual flow and the resistance then you can work out the pumping force needed to get that flow.

The following points should be obvious. The flow through a pipe has to be the same at each point in the pipe – otherwise water would backup or need to be introduced. The total pressure that the pump provides has to be distributed across each of the resistances in the pipe to ensure the same flow. These pressures have to add up to the total pressure that the pump provides.

Slightly less obvious, but you can still understand them in terms of water flow, pressures add, currents add and resistances to flow in the same pipe add.

One of the main reasons for understanding electrical flow is that you can use Ohm's law to avoid damaging things. As a current flows through a resistor it gets hot. The rule here is that the energy produced is proportional to VI. If you double the current, you double the heating effect. Most electronic devices have current limits beyond which they are liable to fail. One of the basic tasks in designing any electronic circuit is to work out what the current is and, if it is too high, add a resistor or lower the voltage to reduce it. To do this you need a good understanding of the hydraulic model and be able to use Ohm's law. There are examples later in this chapter.

It is also worth pointing out that there are devices which do not obey Ohm's law – so-called non-Ohmic devices. These are the interesting elements in a circuit – LEDs, diodes, transistors and so on, but even these devices can be understood in terms of the flow of a fluid.

This is a lightning introduction to electronics, pun intended, and there is much to learn and many mistakes to make, most of which result in blue smoke.

Electrical Drive Characteristics

If you are not familiar with electronics, the important thing to understand is the relationship between voltage, current and resistance. Voltage is like pressure and it makes the electrons flow. The current is the size of the flow and the resistance is what it sounds like – a resistance to the flow. For a fixed resistor the current flowing increases in proportion to the voltage. The relationship between voltage current and resistance is summarized by Ohm's law, $V = IR$ where V is the voltage in volts, I is the current in amps and R is the resistance in ohms.

So we need to know what voltages are being worked with and how much current can flow. The most important thing to know about the ESP32 is that it works with two voltage levels – 0V and 3.3V. Even though you can power most development boards from 5V there is a DC to DC chip that converts whatever you supply it with to 3.3V. It is theoretically possible to run the ESP32 digital portion at 1.8V and use 3.3V to run the analog portion of the chip, but the majority of development boards don't make this available.

If you have worked with other logic devices you might be more familiar with 0V and 5V as being the low and high levels. The ESP32 uses a lower output voltage to reduce its power consumption, which is good, but you need to keep in mind that you may have to use some electronics to change the 3.3V to other values. The same is true of inputs, which must not exceed 3.3V or you risk damaging the ESP32.

An important question is how much current the GPIO lines can handle without damaging the chip. This isn't an easy question and at the time of writing the documentation isn't clear on the matter. According to the documentation, each GPIO line can be set to "drive" up to 40mA. However, this doesn't quite mean what you might think. This is not an upper limit on the supplied current, but a configuration that is needed to ensure that the output voltages of the GPIO line are within specification, even if you connect something that requires a lot of current – see later.

According to the datasheet for the ESP32, while GPIO16 and GPIO17 are limited to 20mA the other GPIO lines can provide up to 40mA. This doesn't mean, however, that you can use every GPIO line to supply the maximum current at the same time. The datasheet is very vague on what the actual maximum is, but it refers to reducing the current to half the maximum as the number of GPIO lines using that current increases. You also need to be aware of the fact the development board's power supply is limited to 1200mA and the WiFi components can draw 200mA while transmitting. Clearly, if all 34 GPIO lines were drawing the maximum 40mA the total would be 1360mA which is well beyond what the power supply can source. This is an extreme and unlikely example, but it indicates that it is the total current draw subject to each line being less than 40mA is the important consideration.

In practice, you need to work out the total current draw from all of the GPIO lines in a worst case and then consider if this is reasonable in terms of total power consumption. For reliable operation you need to stay away from the maximums.

Driving An LED

One of the first things you need to know how to do is compute the value of a current-limiting resistor. For example, if you just connect an LED between a GPIO line and ground then no current will flow when the line is low and the LED is off, but when the line is high, at 3.3V, it is highly likely that the current will exceed the safe limit. In most cases nothing terrible will happen as the ESP32's GPIO lines are rated very conservatively, but if you keep doing it eventually something will fail. The correct thing to do is to use a current-limiting resistor. Although this is an essential part of using an LED, it is also something you need to keep in mind when connecting any output device. You need to discover the voltage that the device needs and the current it uses and calculate a current-limiting resistor to make sure that is indeed the current it draws from the GPIO line.

An LED is a non-linear electronic component – the voltage across it stays more or less the same irrespective of the current passing through the device. Compare this to a more normal linear, or "ohmic", device where the current and voltage vary together according to Ohm's law, V =IR, which means that if the current doubles, so does the voltage and vice versa.

This is not how an LED behaves. It has a fairly constant voltage drop, irrespective of the current. (If you are curious about it, the relationship between current and voltage for an LED is exponential, meaning that big changes in the current hardly change the voltage across the LED.) When you use an LED you need to look up its forward voltage drop, about 1.7V to 2V for a red LED and about 3V for a blue LED, and the maximum current, usually 20mA for small LEDs. You don't have to use the current specified, this is the maximum current and maximum brightness. To work out the current-limiting resistor you simply calculate the voltage across the resistor and then use Ohm's law to give you the resistor you need for the current required. The LED determines the voltage and the resistor sets the current.

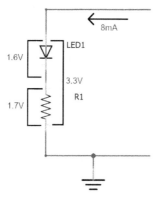

A GPIO line supplies 3.3V and if you assume 1.6V as the forward voltage across the LED, that leaves 1.7V across the current-limiting resistor since voltage distributes itself across components connected in series. If we restrict the current to 8mA, which is very conservative, then the resistor we need is given by:

R = V/I = 1.7/8 = 0.212

The result is in kiloohms, kΩ, because the current is in milliamps, mA. So we need at least a 212Ω resistor. In practice, you can use a range of values as long as the resistor is around 200 ohms – the bigger the resistor the smaller the current, but the dimmer the LED. If you were using multiple GPIO lines then keeping the GPIO current down to 1 or 2mA would be better, but that would need a transistor.

You need to do this sort of calculation when driving other types of output device. The steps are always the same. The 3.3V distributes itself across the output device and the resistor in some proportion and we know the maximum current – from these values we can compute the resistor needed to keep the actual current below this value.

LED BJT Drive

Often you need to reduce the current drawn from a GPIO line. The Bipolar Junction Transistor (BJT) may be relatively old technology, but it is a current amplifier, low in cost and easy to use. A BJT is a three-terminal device - base, emitter and collector - in which the current that flows through the emitter/collector is controlled by the current in the base:

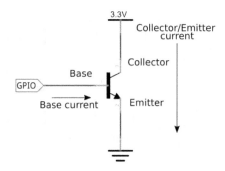

The diagram shows an NPN transistor, which is the most common. This diagram is a simplification in that, in reality, the current in the emitter is slightly larger than that in the collector because you have to add the current flowing in the base. In most cases you need just two additional facts. Firstly, the voltage on the base is approximately 0.6V, no matter how much current flows since the base is a diode, a non-linear device just like the LED in the previous section. Secondly, you need to multiply the current in the collector/emitter by the current gain of the transistor, specified as hFE or ß (beta) a value you can look up for any transistor you want to use. While you are consulting the datasheets, you also need to check the maximum currents and voltages the device will tolerate. In most cases, the beta is between 100 and 200 and hence you can use a transistor to amplify the GPIO current by at least a factor of 100.

Notice that, for the emitter/collector current to be non-zero, the base has to have a current flowing into it. If the base is connected to ground then the transistor is "cut off", i.e. no current flows. What this means is that when the GPIO line is high the transistor is "on" and current is flowing and when the GPIO line is low the transistor is "off" and no current flows. This high-on/low-off behavior is typical of an NPN transistor.

A PNP transistor works the other way round:

The 0.6V is between the base and the collector and the current flows out of

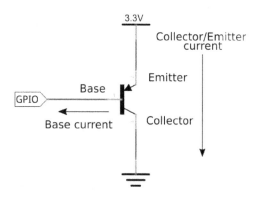

the base. In this case to switch the transistor on you have to connect the base to ground. What this means is that the transistor is off when the GPIO line is high and on when it is low.

This complementary behavior of NPN and PNP BJTs is very useful and means that we can use such transistors in pairs. It is also worth knowing that the diagram given above is usually drawn with 0V at the top of the diagram, i.e. flipped vertically, to make it look the same as the NPN diagram. You always need to make sure you know where the +V line is.

A BJT Example

For a simple example we need to connect a standard LED to a GPIO line with a full 20mA drive. Given that all of the GPIO lines work at 3.3V and ideally only supply a few milliamps, we need a transistor to drive the LED which typically draws 20mA.

You could use a Field Effect Transistor (FET) of some sort, but for this sort of application an old-fashioned BJT (Bipolar Junction Transistor) works very well and is cheap and available in a thru-hole mount, i.e. it comes with wires. Almost any general purpose NPN transistor will work, but the 2N2222 is very common. From its datasheet you can discover that the max collector current is 800mA and its hFE is at least 50, which makes it suitable for driving a 20mA LED with a GPIO current of at most 20mA/50 = 0.4mA.

The circuit is simple but we need two current-limiting resistors:

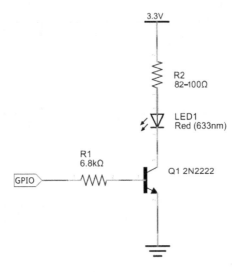

If you connected the base to the GPIO line directly then the current flowing in the base would be unrestricted – it would be similar to connecting the GPIO line to ground. R1 restricts the current to 0.39mA, which is very low and, assuming that the transistor has a minimum hFE of 50, this provides just short of 20mA to power it.

The calculation is that the GPIO supplies 3.3V and the base has 0.6V across it so the voltage across R1 is 3.3 - 0.6V = 2.7V. To limit the current to 0.4mA would need a resistor of 2.7V/0.4mA = 6.7kΩ. The closest preferred value is 6.8kΩ, which gives a slightly smaller current.

Without R2 the LED would draw a very large current and burn out. R2 limits the current to 20mA. Assuming a forward voltage drop of 1.6V and a current of 20mA the resistor is given by (3.3-1.6)V/20mA = 85Ω. In practice, we could use anything in the range 82Ω to 100Ω.

The calculation just given assumes that the voltage between the collector and emitter is zero, but of course in practice it isn't. Ignoring this results in a current less than 20mA, which is erring on the safe side. The datasheet indicates that the collector emitter voltage is less than 200mV.

The point is that you rarely make exact calculations for circuits such as this, you simply arrive at acceptable and safe operating conditions. Also notice that the transistor could be connected to a higher supply voltage than the 3.3V shown. Transistors are not just amplifiers, they are level shifters. You can also use the same design to drive something that needs a higher voltage.

For example, to drive a 5V dip relay, which needs 10mA to activate it, you would use something like:

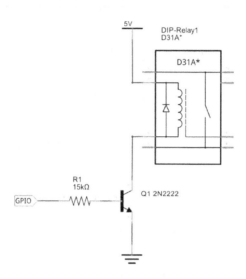

Notice that in this case the transistor isn't needed to increase the drive current – the GPIO line could provide the 10mA directly. Its purpose is to change the voltage from 3.3V to 5V. The same idea works with any larger voltage.

If you are using the 2N2222 then the pinouts are:

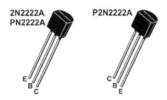

As always, the positive terminal on the LED is the long pin.

MOSFET Driver

There are many who think that the FET (Field Effect Transistor) or more precisely the MOSFET (Metal Oxide Semiconductor FET) is the perfect amplification device and we should ignore BJTs. They are simpler to understand and use, but it can be more difficult to find one with the characteristics you require.

Like the BJT, a MOSFET has three terminals called the gate, drain and source. The current that you want to control flows between the source and drain and it is controlled by the gate. This is analogous to the BJT's base, collector and emitter, but the difference is that it is the voltage on the gate that controls the current between the source and drain.

The gate is essentially a high resistance input and very little current flows in it. This makes it an ideal way to connect a GPIO line to a device that needs more current or a different voltage. When the gate voltage is low the source drain current is very small. When the gate voltage reaches the threshold voltage $V_{GS(th)}$, which is different for different MOSFETs, the source drain current starts to increase exponentially. Basically, when the gate is connected to 0V or below $V_{GS(th)}$ the MOSFET is off and when it is above $V_{GS(th)}$ the MOSFET starts to turn on. Don't think of $V_{GS(th)}$ as the gate voltage that the MOSFET turns on, but as the voltage below which it is turned off.

The problem is that the gate voltage to turn a typical MOSFET fully on is in the region of 10V. Special "logic" MOSFETs need a gate voltage around 5V to fully turn on and this makes the 3.3V at which the ESP32's GPIO lines work a problem. The datasheets usually give the fully on resistance and the minimum gate voltage that produces it, usually listed as Drain-Source On-State Resistance. For digital work this is a more important parameter than the gate threshold voltage.

You can deal with this problem in one of two ways – ignore it or find a MOSFET with a very small $V_{GS(th)}$. In practice MOSFETs with thresholds low enough to work at 3.3V are hard to find and when you do find them they are generally only available as surface-mount. Ignoring the problem sometimes works if you can tolerate the MOSFET not being fully on. If the current is kept low then, even though the MOSFET might have a resistance of a few ohms, the power loss and voltage drop may be acceptable.

What MOSFETs are useful for is in connecting higher voltages to a GPIO line used as an input – see later.

Also notice that this discussion has been in terms of an N-channel MOSFET. A P-channel works in the same way, but with all polarities reversed. It is cut off when the gate is at the positive voltage and on when the gate is grounded. This is exactly the same as the NPN versus PNP behavior for the BJT.

MOSFET LED

A BJT is the easiest way to drive an LED, but as an example of using a common MOSFET we can arrange to drive one using a 2N7000, a low-cost, N-channel device available in a standard TO92 form factor suitable for experimentation:

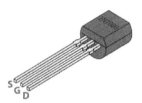

Its datasheet states that it has a $V_{GS(th)}$ typically 2V, but it could be as low as 0.8V or as high as 3V. Given we are trying to work with a gate voltage of 3.3V you can see that in the worst case this is hardly going to work – the device will only just turn on. The best you can do is to buy a batch of 2N7000 and measure their $V_{GS(th)}$ to weed out any that are too high. This said, in practice the circuit given below does generally work.

Assuming a $V_{GS(th)}$ of 2V and a current of 20mA for the LED the datasheet gives a rough value of 6Ω for the on resistance with a gate voltage of 3V. The calculation for the current-limiting resistor is the same as in the BJT case and the final circuit is:

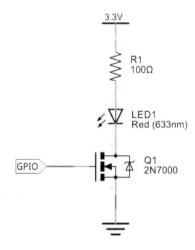

Notice that we don't need a current-limiting resistor for the GPIO line as the gate connection is high impedance and doesn't draw much current. In practice, it is usually a good idea to include a current-limiting resistor in the GPIO line if you plan to switch it on and off rapidly. The problem is that the gate looks like a capacitor and fast changes in voltage can produce high currents. Notice that there are likely to be devices labeled 2N7000 that will not work in this circuit due to the threshold gate voltage being too high, but encountering one is rare.

A logic-level MOSFET like the IRLZ44 has a resistance of 0.028Ω at 5V compared to the 2N2222's of 6Ω. It also has a $V_{GS(th)}$ guaranteed to be between 1V and 2V. It would therefore be a better candidate for this circuit.

Setting Drive Type

The GPIO output can be configured into one of a number of modes, but the most important is pull-up/down. Before we get to the code to do the job it is worth spending a moment explaining the three basic output modes, push-pull, pull-up and pull-down.

Push-Pull Mode

In push-pull mode two transistors of opposite polarity, one PNP and one NPN, are used:

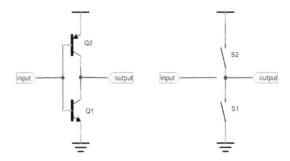

The circuit behaves like the two-switch equivalent shown on the right. Only one of the transistors, or switches, is "closed" at any time. If the input is high then Q1 is saturated and the output is connected to ground - exactly as if S1 was closed. If the input is low then Q2 is saturated and it is as if S2 was closed and the output is connected to 3.3V. You can see that this pushes the output line high with the same "force" as it pulls it low. This is the standard configuration for a GPIO output.

Pull-Up Mode

In pull-up mode one of the transistors is replaced by a resistor:

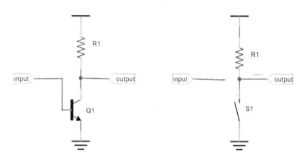

In this case the circuit is equivalent to having a single switch. When the switch is closed, the output line is connected to ground and hence driven low. When the switch is open, the output line is pulled high by the resistor. You can see that in this case the degree of pull-down is greater than the pull-up, where the current is limited by the resistor. The advantage of this mode is that it can be used in an AND configuration. If multiple GPIO or other lines are connected to the output, then any one of them being low will pull the output line low. Only when all of them are off does the resistor succeed in pulling the line high. This is used, for example, in a serial bus configuration like the I2C bus.

Pull-Down Mode

Finally the pull-down mode, which is the best mode for driving general loads, motors, LEDs, etc, is exactly the same as the pull-up, only now the resistor is used to pull the output line low.

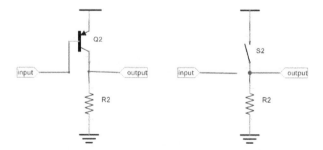

The line is held high by the transistor and pulled low by the resistor only when all the switches are open. Putting this the other way round, the line is high if any one switch is closed. This is the OR version of the shared bus idea.

Open Collector

There is one final output configuration – open collector or, when referring to a MOSFET, open drain. The idea is simple, you don't connect the collector or the drain to anything at all – you simply use it as the output:

There is no pull-up resistor, but you can supply one as an external pull-up if needed. You can also drive a device that needs a current flow through it rather than just a voltage – a coil is the standard example. However, a GPIO line usually cannot supply enough current for such devices.

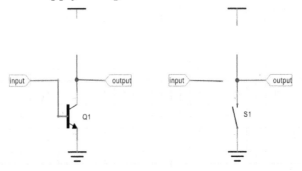

The real use of the open collector arrangement is to implement a shared data line:

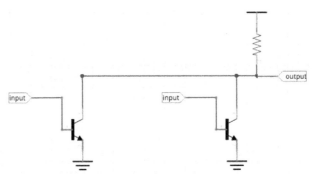

In this case two inputs control one output. If the first transistor is on then the output is low, irrespective of the state of the second transistor. The same is true if the second transistor is on. If you work through the possible combinations we have:

Input 1	Input 2	Output
Off	Off	High
Off	On	Low
On	Off	Low
On	On	Low

You might recognize this as the truth table for an OR gate. This is exactly what an open collector output used in this way implements. Early integrated circuits referred to as Resistor Transistor Logic or RTL implemented logic in this way. This was soon replaced by Transistor Transistor Logic or TTL because transistors are easier to implement in an integrated circuit.

In IoT applications, open collector connections are used to allow any number of devices to share a line. If all of the devices are configured to be open collectors then any one of them can pull the line low. In most cases only one device will be active and sending data at any one time.

Setting Output Mode

MicroPython's `Pin` class has some additional parameters in the constructor to set the mode for a GPIO line:

`machine.Pin(id, mode, pull, value)`

We have already met `id` and `mode` and the `pull` parameter can be any of:

- None   No pull-up
- Pin.PULL_UP = 1   Pull-up resistor enabled
- Pin.PULL_DOWN = 2   Pull-down resistor enabled

In addition to these you can also set `mode` to `Pin.OPEN_DRAIN = 2`, which gives you an active low and a high impedance for the 1 state.

The pull-up/down resistor is 45kΩ.

If you set the line to output, i.e. `OUT` or `OPEN_DRAIN` then you can set an initial state using `value`.

After you have created a `Pin` object you can change its configuration using the `init` method which takes the same parameters:

`Pin.init(mode, pull,  value)`

Only the parameters specified are changed.

The `init` method is particularly useful for changing a line from input to output and vice versa.

Not all of the ESP32's GPIO lines can be used in output mode. GPIO34 to GPIO39 are input only and they do not have pull-up/pull-down resistors.

Drive

The output drive strength isn't to do with how much current the GPIO line can source, it is about the voltage output at different currents. It is the effective output resistance. This is a sophisticated idea but it is easy to understand if you think of it as being similar to the current limiting resistor in an LED circuit.

All outputs have a limited ability to supply current at a given voltage. If an output is at 3.3V with no current, i.e. no connection, then as the current it supplies increases the voltage will drop. Think of this as being similar to the pressure in a pipe which is at a maximum when the tap is off and falls as the tap is opened.

To model this you have to add a resistor to the circuit which corresponds to the internal resistance of the current source:

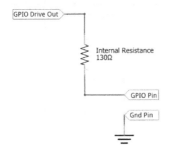

The GPIO Drive Out is internal to the device and any load you are trying to drive is connected between GPIO Pin and Gnd Pin. Now consider what the voltage is if the load draws 10mA. Using Ohm's law we have the voltage drop across the internal resistor as 130 x 10 = 1300 mV = 1.3V. This means that the 3.3V theoretically output by the GPIO line is reduced to 3.3-1.3=2V. Does this matter? It all depends on what the load is and what effect the reduction to 2V has on its operation. Notice, however, that it makes our calculation of current limiting resistors for loads such as LED more complicated.

If the internal resistance of a GPIO line is a problem you can change it by setting the drive keyword parameter in the constructor or the init method.

```
Pin.DRIVE_0: 5mA / 130Ω
Pin.DRIVE_1: 10mA / 60Ω
Pin.DRIVE_2: 20mA / 30Ω (default strength if not configured)
Pin.DRIVE_3: 40mA / 15Ω
```

Notice that the default is for an internal resistance of 30Ω and hence the voltage drop when drawing a current of 10mA is 30 x 10 =300mV=0.3V which makes the output voltage on the load 3V – which isn't as bad as our initial calculation with Drive_0 set.

The currents listed aren't maximum allowable current draw. Instead they are approximately the maximum safe current to draw if you want the output voltage to be high enough for another 3.3V device to recognize the output as a one – about 2.7V. That is, if the load draws more than the specified current the voltage falls below 2.7V and isn't guaranteed to be recognized as logic one by another 3.3V device.

Basic Input Circuit - The Switch

It is time to turn our attention to the electrical characteristics of GPIO lines as inputs. One of the most common input circuits is the switch or button. Many beginners make the mistake of wiring a GPIO line to a switch something like:

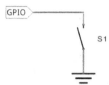

The problem with this is that, if the switch is pressed, the GPIO line is connected to ground and will read as zero. The question is, what does it read when the switch is open? A GPIO line configured as an input without pull-up or pull-down enabled has a very high resistance. The maximum current and input line will draw is 50nA. As it isn't connected to any particular voltage, the voltage on it varies due to the static it picks up. The jargon is that the unconnected line is "floating". When the switch is open the line is floating and if you read it the result, zero or one, depends on whatever noise it has picked up.

The correct way to do the job is to tie the input line either high or low when the switch is open using a resistor. A pull-up arrangement would be something like:

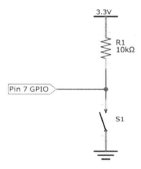

The value of the resistor used isn't critical. It simply pulls the GPIO line high when the switch isn't pressed. When it is pressed a current of a little more than 0.3mA flows in the resistor. If this is too much, increase the resistance to 100kΩ or even more - but notice that the higher the resistor value the noisier the input to the GPIO and the more it is susceptible to RF interference. This gives a zero when the switch is pressed.

If you want a switch that pulls the line high instead of low, reverse the logic by swapping the positions of the resistor and the switch in the diagram to create a pull-down:

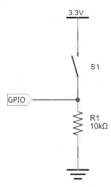

This gives a one when the switch is pressed.

The good news is that the ESP32 defaults to an input configuration with a pull-down resistor of around 45kΩ which means you can connect a switch directly to a default GPIO line of 3.3V and it will give a one when the switch is pressed.

Debounce

Although the switch is the simplest input device, it is very difficult to get right. When a user clicks a switch of any sort, the action isn't clean - the switch bounces. What this means is that the logic level on the GPIO line goes high then low and high again and bounces between the two until it settles down. There are electronic ways of debouncing switches, but software does the job much better. All you have to do is insert a delay of a millisecond or so after detecting a switch press and read the line again - if it is still low then record a switch press. Similarly, when the switch is released, read the state twice with a delay. You can vary the delay to modify the perceived characteristics of the switch.

A more sophisticated algorithm is based on the idea of integration to debounce a switch. All you have to do is read the state multiple times, every few milliseconds say, and keep a running sum of values. If you sum say ten values each time then a total of between 6 and 10 can be taken as an indication that the switch is high. A total less than this indicates that the switch is low. You can think of this as a majority vote in the time period for the switch being high or low.

The Potential Divider

If you have an input that is outside of the range of 0V to 3.3V then you can reduce it using a simple potential divider. In the diagram, V is the input from the external logic and Vout is the connection to the GPIO input line:

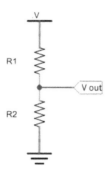

```
Vout = V*R2/(R1+R2)
```

You can spend a lot of time working out good values of R1 and R2. For loads that take a lot of current you need R1+R2 to be small and divided in the same ratio as the voltages. For example, for a 5V device R1=18KΩ or 20KΩ and R2=33KΩ work well to drop the voltage to 3.3V.

A simpler approach that works for a 5V signal is to notice that the ratio R1:R2 has to be the same as (5-3.3):3.3, i.e. the voltage divides itself across the resistors in proportion to their value, which is roughly 1:2. What this means is that you can take any resistor and use it for R1 and use two of the same value in series for R2 and the Vout will be 3.3V.

The problem with a resistive divider is that it can round off fast pulses due to the small capacitive effects. This usually isn't a problem, but if it is then the solution is to use a FET or a BJT as an active buffer:

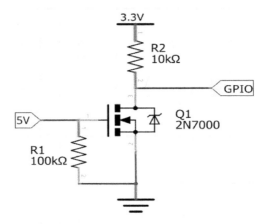

Notice that this is an inverting buffer, the output is low when the input is high, but you can usually ignore this and simply correct it in software, i.e. read a 1 as a low state and a 0 as a high state. The role of R1 is to make sure the FET is off when the 5V signal is absent and R2 limits the current in the FET to about 0.3mA. In most cases you should try the simple voltage divider and only move to an active buffer if it doesn't work.

This very basic look at electronics isn't all that you need to know, but it is enough for you to see some of the problems and find some answers. In general, this sort of electronics is all about making sure that voltages and currents are within limits. As switching speeds increase you have additional problems, which are mainly concerned with making sure that your circuits aren't slowing things down. This is where things get more subtle.

Summary

- You can get a long way with only a small understanding of electronics, but you do need to know enough to protect the ESP32 and things you connect to it.

- The maximum current from any GPIO line should be less than 40mA.

- All of the GPIO lines work at 3.3V and you should avoid directly connecting any other voltage.

- You can drive an LED directly from a GPIO line.

- Calculating a current-limiting resistor always follows the same steps: find the current in the device, find the voltage across the device and work out the resistor that supplies that current when the remainder of the voltage is applied to it.

- For any load you connect to a GPIO output, you generally need a current-limiting resistor.

- In many cases you need a transistor, a BJT, to increase the current supplied by the GPIO line.

- To use a BJT you need a current-limiting resistor in the base and generally one in the collector.

- MOSFETs are popular alternatives to BJTs, but it is difficult to find a MOSFET that works reliably at 3.3V.

- GPIO output lines can be set to active push-pull mode, where a transistor is used to pull the line high or low, or passive pull-up or pull-down mode, where one transistor is used and a resistor pulls the line high or low when the transistor is inactive.

- GPIO lines have built-in pull-up and pull-down resistors which can be selected or disabled under software control.

- When used as inputs, GPIO lines have a very high resistance and in most cases you need pull-up or pull-down resistors to stop the line floating. The built-in pull-up or pull-down resistors can be used in input mode.

- Mechanical input devices have to be debounced to stop spurious input.

- If you need to connect an input to something bigger than 3.3V then you need a potential divider to reduce the voltage back to 3.3V. You can also use a transistor.

Chapter 6
Simple Input

There is no doubt that input is more difficult than output. When you need to drive a line high or low you are in command of when it happens, but input is in the hands of the outside world. If your program isn't ready to read the input, or if it reads it at the wrong time, then things just don't work. What is worse, you have no idea what your program is doing relative to the event you are trying to capture. Welcome to the world of input.

In this chapter we look at the simplest approach to input – the polling loop. This may be simple, but it is a good way to approach many tasks. In Chapter 7 we'll look at a sophisticated alternative – interrupts.

GPIO Input

GPIO input is a much more difficult problem than output from the point of view of measurement and verification. For output at least you can see the change in the signal on a logic analyzer and know the exact time that it occurred. This makes it possible to track down timing problems and fine tune things with good accuracy.

Input on the other hand is "silent" and unobservable. When did you read in the status of the line? Usually the timing of the read is with respect to some other action that the device has taken. For example, you read the input line $20\mu s$ after setting the output line high. But how do you know when the input line changed state during that 20 microseconds? The simple answer is in most cases you don't.

In some applications the times are long and/or unimportant but in some they are critical and so we need some strategies for monitoring and controlling read events. The usual rule of thumb is to assume that it takes as long to read a GPIO line as it does to set it. This means we can use the delay mechanisms that we looked at with regard to output for input as well.

One common and very useful trick when you are trying to get the timing of input correct is to substitute an output command to a spare GPIO line and monitor it with a logic analyzer. Place the output instruction just before the input instruction and where you see the line change on the logic analyzer should be close to the time that the input would be read in the unmodified program. You can use this to debug and fine tune and then remove the output statement.

Basic Input Functions

The `Pin` object can be set to input mode using the constructor:

```
pin = Pin(4, Pin.IN)
```

You can also set the direction to input using the `init` method:

```
pin.init(mode=Pin.IN)
```

Once set to input, the GPIO line is high impedance so it won't take very much current, no matter what you connect it to. However, notice that the ESP32 uses 3.3V logic and you should not exceed this value on an input line. For a full discussion of how to work with input see the previous chapter.

You can read the line's input state using the `value` method:

```
result=pin.value()
```

Notice that this is an "overloaded" method. If you supply a value as a parameter then it attempts to set the value as output. If you don't specify a value then it gets the GPIO level as a zero or a one.

This is all there is to using a GPIO line as an input, apart from the details of the electronics and the small matter of interrupts.

As introduced in the previous chapter you can also set the internal pull-up or pull-down resistors using one of:

- ◆ `None`   No pull-up
- ◆ `Pin.PULL_UP = 1`   Pull-up resistor enabled
- ◆ `Pin.PULL_DOWN = 2`   Pull-down resistor enabled

in the constructor or the `init` method.

The pull-up/down resistors are 45kΩ.

The Simple Button

One of the most common input circuits is the switch or button. If you want another external button you can use any GPIO line and the circuit explained in the previous chapter. That is, the switch has to have either a pull-up or pull-down resistor either provided by you or a built-in one enabled using software.

The simplest switch input program using an internal pull-up is:

```
from machine import Pin
import time
pinIn = Pin(4, Pin.IN,Pin.PULL_UP)
pinLED = Pin(2, Pin.OUT)

while True:
    if pinIn.value():
        pinLED.on()
    else:
        pinLED.off()
    time.sleep(0.5)
```

As the internal pull-up resistor is used, the switch can be connected to the line and ground without any external resistors:

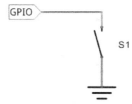

The program simply tests for the line to be pulled high by the switch not being closed and then sets GPIO2 high. If GPIO2 is connected, the on-board LED will light up while it is not pressed. Notice GPIO4 goes low when the switch is pressed.

If you change PULL_UP to PULL_DOWN, the way the switch has to be connected becomes:

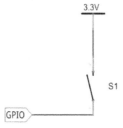

The program still works, but now GPIO4 is high when the switch is pressed and hence the LED is on when the switch is pressed.

Should you use an internal or external resistor? The answer is that it mostly doesn't matter as long as there is a resistor included in your circuit. So if you use None make sure there is an external resistor. The only problem with using an internal resistor is the possibility that the software fails to set the pull-up/down mode and leaves the input floating.

Also notice that this switch input is not debounced. The simplest way to do this is include a time delay in the loop before the line is sampled again.

If you want to respond to a button press, that is a press and a release event, then you have to test for a double transition:

```
from machine import Pin
import time

pinIn = Pin(4, Pin.IN,Pin.PULL_DOWN)
pinLED = Pin(2, Pin.OUT)

while True:
    while pinIn.value()==0:
        pass
    while pinIn.value()==1:
        pass
    pinLED.on()
    time.sleep_ms(1)
    pinLED.off()
```

In this case you really do need the debounce delays if you want to avoid responding twice to what the user perceives as a single press.

A 1-millisecond delay is probably the smallest delay that produces a button that feels as if it works. In practice, you would have to tune the delay to suit the button mechanism in use and the number of times you can allow the button to be pressed in one second.

Press or Hold

You can carry on elaborating on how to respond to a button. For example, most users have grown accustomed to the idea that holding a button down for a longer time than a press makes something different happen.

To distinguish between a press and a hold all you need to do is time the difference between line down and line up:

```
from machine import Pin
import time
pinIn = Pin(4, Pin.IN,Pin.PULL_DOWN)
pinLED = Pin(2, Pin.OUT)

while True:
    while pinIn.value() == 0:
        pass
    t = time.ticks_ms()
    time.sleep_ms(1)
    while pinIn.value() == 1:
        pass
    t = time.ticks_diff(time.ticks_ms(),t)
    if t<2000:
        pinLED.on()
        time.sleep(1)
        pinLED.off()
    else:
        for i in range(10):
            pinLED.on()
            time.sleep_ms(100)
            pinLED.off()
            time.sleep_ms(100)
```

In this case holding the button for 2 seconds registers a "hold" – the LED flashes 10 times and anything less is a "push" – the LED flashes just once. Notice the 1ms debounce pause between the test for no-press and press.

One of the problems with all of these sample programs is that they wait for the button to be pressed or held and this makes it difficult for them to do anything else. You have to include whatever else your program needs to do within the loop that waits for the button – the polling loop. You can do this in an ad hoc way, but the best approach is to implement a finite state machine, see later.

How Fast Can We Measure?

Buttons are one form of input, but often we want to read data from a GPIO line driven by an electronic device and decode the data. This usually means measuring the width of the pulses and this raises the question of how fast can we accept input?

89

The simplest way to find out how quickly we can take a measurement is to perform a pulse width measurement. Applying a square wave to GPIO4 we can measure the time that the pulse is high using:

```
from machine import Pin
import time
pinIn = Pin(4, Pin.IN)

while True:
    while pinIn.value()==1:
        pass
    while pinIn.value()==0:
        pass

    t=time.ticks_us()
    while pinIn.value()==1:
        pass
    t=time.ticks_diff(time.ticks_us(),t)
    print(t)
    time.sleep(1)
```

This might look a little strange at first. The inner while loops are responsible for getting us to the right point in the waveform. First we loop until the line goes low, then we loop until it goes high again and finally measure how long before it goes low. You might think that we simply have to wait for it to go high and then measure how long till it goes low, but this misses the possibility that the signal might be part way through a high period when we first measure it.

If you run this program and apply a square wave of a known frequency to GPIO4 you will see values printed that correspond to the pulse width in μs. If you increase the frequency you should see the value change in step until the program cannot keep up with the input when the time suddenly jumps to values that are too large as pulses are missed.

This can be measured down to around $12\mu s$ with a very poor accuracy at this limit and an accuracy of 5 to $10\mu s$ for longer times. It misses pulses at $10\mu s$ which makes the upper limit of operation as less than 50KHz.

Notice that in either case if you try measuring pulse widths much shorter than the lower limit that works, you will get results that look like longer pulses are being applied. The reason is simply that the ESP32 will miss the first transition to zero but will detect a second or third or later transition. This is the digital equivalent of the aliasing effect found in the Fourier Transform of general signal processing.

MicroPython also provides a special method that implements the algorithm used in the above program. The method:

```
machine.time_pulse_us(pin, level, timeout)
```

will block until the pin specified changes to the level specified or the timeout occurs. Once the pin attains the level specified it times how long it takes for it to change and returns the result in microseconds. The only problem is that, if the pin is already at the specified level, the timing begins at once.

Using this method the program above can be written more simply as:

```
import time
import machine

pinIn = machine.Pin(4, machine.Pin.IN)

while True:
    t = machine.time_pulse_us(pinIn, 1)
    print(t)
    time.sleep(1)
```

Notice that you will get some fractional measurements using this method. To get accurate results you would have to be sure that the line was at zero just before the method is used.

For example:

```
import time
import machine

pinIn = machine.Pin(4, machine.Pin.IN)

while True:
    while pinIn.value() == 1:
        pass
    t = machine.time_pulse_us(pinIn, 1)
    print(t)
    time.sleep(1)
```

The time_pulse_us method is not a big improvement on the more basic way of doing the job, but it is more accurate for lengthier intervals. It is also very useful when implementing protocols that use different length pulses to represent a zero or a one, see Chapter 13.

The Finite State Machine

If your project requires a complex set of input and output lines then you need an organizing principle to save you from the complexity. When you first start writing IoT programs that respond to the outside world you quickly discover that all of your programs take a similar form:

```
while(True):
    wait for some input lines
    process the input data
    write some output lines
    wait for some input lines
    read some more input lines
    write some output lines
```

For most programmers this is a slightly disturbing discovery because programs are not supposed to consist of infinite loops, but IoT programs nearly always, in principle if not in practice, take the form of an apparently infinite polling loop. A second, and more important, aspect is that the way in which reading and writing GPIO lines is related can be so complex that it can be difficult to see exactly when any particular line is read and when it is written.

It is natural to try to find implementations that make this simpler. In most cases programmers discover or invent the idea of the event or, better, the interrupt. In this case when something happens in the outside world a function is automatically called to deal with it and the relation between the external state and the system's response is seemingly well defined. Of course, in practice it isn't, as you have to deal with what happens when multiple events or interrupts occur at the same, or very nearly the same, time.

Often more sophisticated approaches are used to try and handle more external changes of state in a given time. Somehow the infinite polling loop is seen as wasteful. What is the CPU doing if it spends all its time looping round waiting for something to happen? Of course, if it has nothing better to do then it isn't a waste. In fact IoT devices are often dedicated to just getting one job done so the "polling is wasteful" meme, so prevalent in the rest of computing, is completely unjustified.

What is more, the polling loop is usually the way to get the greatest throughput. If a processor can handle X external state changes per second and respond to these with Y external state changes per second, then moving to an event- or interrupt-based implementation reduces both X and Y. In short, if a processor cannot do the job using a polling loop then it cannot do the job. This is not to say that there aren't advantages to events and interrupts – there are, but they don't increase throughput.

So how should you organize a polling loop so that what it does is self-evident by looking at the code? There are many answers to this according to the system being implemented and there are no "pure" theoretical answers that solve all problems, but the finite state machine, or FSM, is a model that every IoT programmer should know.

A finite state machine is a very simple program. At any given time the machine/program has a record of the current state, S. At a regular interval the external world provides an input I which changes the state from S to S' and produces an output O. That's all there is to a finite state machine. There are variations on the definition of the FSM but this one, called a Mealy machine because its outputs depend on both its state and the input, is the most suitable for IoT programming.

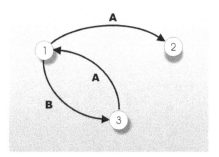

You can design an FSM with the help of a diagram. In the FSM shown there are three states 1, 2 and 3 and if you are in state 1 an input of A moves the system to state 2 and an input of B moves it into state 3.

Your program simply needs to take the form of a polling loop that implements a finite state machine. It reads the input lines as I and uses this and the current state S to determine the new state S' and the output O. There is some overhead in using this organization, but it is usually worth it. Notice that this organization implies that you read input once, make changes once and set outputs once in the loop. If you fix the time that the polling loop takes then you know the characteristic time for any changes to the system.

FSM Button

As an example, let's implement the simple button given earlier in the chapter. The first version used multiple loops to wait for changes in the state of the input line. The finite state version uses only a single polling loop:

```
from machine import Pin
import time

pinIn = Pin(4, Pin.IN)

s = 0
count = 0
while True:
    I = pinIn.value()
    t = time.ticks_add(time.ticks_us(),1000*100)
    if s == 0:    #button not pushed
        if i:
            s = 1
            count=count+1
            print("Button Push ",count)
    elif s == 1: #button pushed
        if not i:
            s = 0
    else:
        s = 0
    while time.ticks_us()<t:
        pass
```

This looks more complicated than the original, and there are more lines of code, but it is much easier to extend to more complex situations. In this case we have only two states – s = 0 for button not pushed and s = 1 for button pushed. Ideally the states that we use shouldn't refer to inputs or outputs, but to the overall state of the system. For example, if you were using a ESP32 to control a nuclear reactor you might use a state "CoreMeltdown" in preference to "TempSensorOverLimit". States should be about the consequence of the inputs and the outputs should be the consequence of the current state. In the example above the inputs and output are too simple to give rise to an abstract concept of "state". Even if you were to change the state labels to "LEDOn" or "LEDOff" they are directly related to the state of a single output line.

The key idea, however, is that the states indicate the state of the system at the time of the input. That is, s = 0 (button not pushed) is the state when the system reads in a low on the GPIO line (recall the line is pulled low so pushing the button makes it go high). You can see at the start of the polling loop we read the input line and store its value in the variable i. Next, a case statement is used to process the input depending on the current state. You

94

can see that if s = 0, i.e. button not pushed, then the state moves to s = 1, i.e. button pushed, and a message is printed giving the number of times the button has been pressed as a simple action. In general, the action could be setting a GPIO line high or doing anything that is appropriate for the new state. Notice that actions occur on state changes.

If the state is in s = 1, i.e. button pushed, then the input has to be 0 for anything to happen. In this case the state changes to s = 0 and any actions that are needed to take the system from state 1 to state 0 are performed – none in this case. Finally, if the state is anything other than 0 or 1, we set it to 0 as something is wrong.

Notice that the polling loop is set up so that the whole thing repeats every 100ms. The time is taken at the start of the loop and after everything has been processed we wait for 100ms to be up. What this means is that, no matter how long the processing in the loop takes, as long as it takes less than 100ms the loop will repeat every 100ms.

This is a very simple finite state machine polling loop. In practice, there is usually a set of ifs that deals with each current state, but there is often another set of if statements within each state case to deal with what happens according to different inputs. An alternative way of designing a finite state machine loop is to use a lookup table, indexed by state and input, which gives you the new state and the actions.

FSM Hold Button

As a slightly more complicated example of using the FSM approach, let's implement the button with hold. You might think that a button with hold has three states – button not pushed, button pushed and button held. You can implement it in this way, but there is an argument that there are still only two states – not pushed and pushed. The held state is better implemented as extra input data to the state, i.e. the time the button has been in the pressed state.

Remember, the output of a FSM depends on the state and the input and in this case the input is the line level and the time pressed:

```
from machine import Pin
import time
pinIn = Pin(4, Pin.IN)

s = 0
while True:
    i = pinIn.value()
    t = time.ticks_add(time.ticks_us(),1000*100)
    if s == 0:          #button not pushed
        if i:
            s = 1
        tpush = t
    elif s == 1:        #button pushed
        if not i:
            s = 0
            if time.ticks_diff(t, tpush) > 2000000:
                print("Button held \n\r")
            else:
                print("Button pushed \n\r")
    else:
        s = 0
    while time.ticks_us()<t:
        pass
```

It is clear that you can't know the time the button has been pressed until it is released so the actions are now all in the button-pushed state. While the button is in the pushed state it can be released and we can compute the time it has been pressed and modify the action accordingly.

FSM Ring Counter

Another very common input configuration is the ring counter. A ring counter moves on to a new output each time it receives an input and repeats when it reaches the last output of the set. For example, if you have three output lines connected to three LEDs then initially LED 0 is on, when the user presses the button LED 1 is on and the rest off, the next user press moves on to LED 2 on and another press turns LED 0 on. You can see that as the user keeps pressing the button the LEDs go on and off in a repeating sequence.

A common implementation of a ring counter has a state for each button press and release for each LED being on. For three LEDs this means six states and this has a number of disadvantages. A better idea is to have just two states, button pressed and button released and use a press counter as an additional input value. This means that what happens when you enter the button pressed state depends on the value in the counter.

We also change from using the measurement of the button as pressed or released and move to considering an "edge" signal. Generally we need inputs that indicate an event localized in time. Button "pressed" and button "released" are events that are extended in time but "press" and "release" are localized to small time intervals that can be thought of as single time measurements. In general we prefer "edge" signals because these indicate when something has changed.

Implementing this is fairly easy:

```
from machine import Pin
import time
pinIn = Pin(4, Pin.IN)
pinLED1 = Pin(1, Pin.OUT)
pinLED2 = Pin(2, Pin.OUT)
pinLED3 = Pin(3, Pin.OUT)
pinLED1.on()
pinLED2.off()
pinLED3.off()
s = 0
buttonState = pinIn.value()
while True:
    buttonNow = pinIn.value()
    edge = buttonState-buttonNow
    buttonState = buttonNow
    t = time.ticks_add(time.ticks_us(), 1000*100)
    if s == 0:
        if edge == 1:
            s = 1
            pinLED1.off()
            pinLED2.on()
            pinLED3.off()

    elif s == 1:
        if edge == 1:
            s = 2
            pinLED1.off()
            pinLED2.off()
            pinLED3.on()
    elif s == 2:
        if edge == 1:
            s = 0
            pinLED1.on()
            pinLED2.off()
            pinLED3.off()
    else:
        s = 0
    while time.ticks_us() < t:
        pass
```

First we set up the GPIO lines for input and output and set the outputs so that LED 0 is on, i.e. s = 0. Next we start the polling loop. Inside the loop there is a `switch` statement that manages three states. At the start of the loop the difference between the current button value and its previous value are used to calculate `edge` which is 1 only when the button has changed from pressed, 1, to released, 0. That is, `edge=1` only on a down-going edge. If the button has just been pressed then the state is moved on to the next state, 0→1, 1→2 and 2→0, and the LEDs are set to the appropriate values.

You might wonder why all three LEDs are set and not just the two that are changing? There are a number of reasons including it's easier to see what is happening from the code and it makes sure that all of the LEDs are in the state you intend. Notice that the polling loop is set up to repeat every 100ms so providing debouncing and a predictable service time. If you try this out you will find that the LEDs light up sequentially on each button press.

Like many more advanced methods the FSM approach can make things seem more complicated in simple examples, but it repays the effort as soon as things get more complicated. A polling loop with tens of states and lots of input and outline lines to manage becomes impossible to maintain without some organizing principle.

Summary

- Input is hard because things happen at any time, irrespective of what your program might be doing.

- You can call the `value` method at any time to discover the state of a GPIO line – the problem is when and how often to call it.

- You can choose between external or internal pull-up/down resistors.

- Mechanical input devices such as buttons have to be debounced.

- The power of software is that it can enhance a simple device. A simple button is either pushed or released, but you can use this to generate a third "held" state.

- Using a polling loop you can handle inputs as short as a few tens of microseconds.

- Most IoT programs are best written as a polling loop.

- The Finite State Machine (FSM) is one way of organizing a complex polling loop so that inputs are tested and outputs are set once for each time through the loop.

- Ideally the states of a FSM should not be simple statements of the inputs or outputs that determine the state, but for simple systems this can be difficult to achieve.

- It can be difficult to work out what constitutes the events of a FSM. Ideally they should be localized in time so that they indicate the moment that something happens.

Chapter 7

Advanced Input - Interrupts

When you start to work with multiple inputs that mean a range of different things, input really becomes a challenge. You can control much of the complexity using finite state machines and similar organizational principles, but sooner or later you are going to have to deal with the problem of input when your program isn't ready for it. Sudden urgent unexpected input is the most difficult to deal with and when in this situation it is natural to think of the interrupt because this is the essence of urgent! However, things are much more complicated than they seem at first and so we need to consider when and where it is appropriate to give up polling for an event and change to responding to an interrupt.

Interrupts Considered Harmful?

An interrupt is a hardware mechanism that stops the computer doing whatever it is currently doing and makes it transfer its attention to running an interrupt handler. You can think of an interrupt as an event flag that, when set, interrupts the current program to run the assigned interrupt handler.

Using interrupts means the outside world decides when the computer should pay attention to input and there is no need for a polling loop. Most hardware people think that interrupts are the solution to everything and polling is inelegant and only to be used when you can't use an interrupt. This is far from the reality. There is a general feeling that real-time programming and interrupts go together and if you are not using an interrupt you are probably doing something wrong. In fact, the truth is that if you are using an interrupt you are probably doing something wrong. So much so that some organizations are convinced that interrupts are so dangerous that they are banned from being used at all.

Interrupts are only really useful when you have a low-frequency condition that needs to be dealt with on a high-priority basis. The reason is that polling for an event that rarely occurs is a time waster and treating the rare event using an interrupt makes reasonable sense. Interrupts can simplify the logic of your program, but rarely does using an interrupt speed things up because the overhead involved in interrupt handling is usually quite high.

If you have a polling loop that takes 100ms to poll all inputs and there is an input that demands attention in under 60ms then clearly the polling loop is not going to be good enough. Using an interrupt allows the high-priority event to interrupt the polling loop and be processed in less than 100ms. However, if this happens very often the polling loop will cease to work as intended. An alternative is to simply make the polling loop check the input twice per loop.

For a more real-world example, suppose you want to react to a doorbell push button. You could write a polling loop that simply checks the button status repeatedly and forever or you could write an interrupt service routine (ISR) to respond to the doorbell. The processor would be free to get on with other things until the doorbell was pushed when it would stop what it was doing and transfer its attention to the ISR.

How good a design this is depends on how much the doorbell has to interact with the rest of the program and how many doorbell pushes you are expecting. It takes time to respond to the doorbell push and then the ISR has to run to completion - what is going to happen if another doorbell push happens while the first push is still being processed? Some processors have provision for forming a queue of interrupts, but that doesn't help with the fact that the process can only handle one interrupt at a time. Of course, the same is true of a polling loop, but if you can't handle the throughput of events with a polling loop, you can't handle it using an interrupt either, because interrupts add the time to transfer to the ISR and back again.

Finally, before you dismiss the idea of having a processor do nothing but ask repeatedly "is the doorbell pressed", consider what else it has to do. If the answer is "not much" then a polling loop might well be your simplest option. Also, if the processor has multiple cores, then the fastest way of dealing with any external event is to use one of the cores in a fast polling loop. This can be considered to be a software emulation of a hardware interrupt – not to be confused with a software interrupt or trap, which is a hardware interrupt triggered by software.

If you are going to use interrupts to service input then a good design is to use the interrupt handler to feed an event queue. This at least lowers the chance that input will be missed.

Despite their attraction, interrupts are usually a poor choice for anything other than low-frequency events that need to be dealt with quickly.

Interrupts

The ESP32 supports 32 distinct interrupts, but only 26 can be associated with GPIO lines – the others are used internally or for timers. You can set an interrupt service routine (ISR) for each GPIO line independently and the GPIO line events that you can use to trigger an interrupt are:

```
Pin.IRQ_FALLING
Pin.IRQ_RISING
```

You can also use:
```
Pin.IRQ_FALLING | Pin.IRQ_RISING
```

to set an interrupt on both rising and falling edges. In this case finding out which event caused the interrupt is difficult. Notice that MicroPython for the ESP32 doesn't support level interrupts, even though the hardware does.

MicroPython provides a simple method for working with GPIO interrupts:

```
pin.irq(ISR, trigger)
```

This sets `ISR` as the interrupt service handler for the event. This is a very simplified version of what happens at a lower level. The `ISR` function has to accept a single parameter, which is a `Pin` object associated with the GPIO line that caused the event. You can use a lambda function to define the ISR. To know how see ***Programmer's Python: Async***, ISBN:978-1871962765.

There are, in fact, two distinct implementations of an interrupt system within general MicroPython. The first is the default and the only one that the ESP32 supports. It seems to be a full interrupt queue implementation, which is good if you don't want to miss an interrupt, but not so good for timing. The second, which the ESP currently doesn't support, is a lighter wrapping of the interrupt mechanism which doesn't allow an interrupt to occur within the interrupt handler and is more accurate from the point of view of timing. To use the lighter interrupt handling you have to add `hard = True` to the `irq` method:

```
pin.irq(ISR, trigger, hard = True)
```

Unfortunately, neither form of interrupt returns a timestamp for when the interrupt occurs, which limits their usefulness.

The `ISR` will still be called even if your MicroPython program has come to an end:

```
def HelloIRQ(pin):
    print("IRQ")

pin=Pin(4,Pin.IN,Pin.PULL_DOWN)
pin.irq(HelloIRQ,Pin.IRQ_RISING)
```

You will see `IRQ` printed whenever GPIO4 has a rising edge, even after the program has finished.

This seems very strange but you need to see it in terms of *"my program has finished but the MicroPython interpreter is still active and will run any program when it is told to"*. Setting an IRQ handler tells the MicroPython interpreter to run the function whenever the event occurs.

You can associate a different ISR to each GPIO line. For example:

```
from machine import Pin
def HelloIRQ1(pin):
    print("IRQ1")

def HelloIRQ2(pin):
    print("IRQ2")

pin1=Pin(4,Pin.IN,Pin.PULL_DOWN)
pin2=Pin(5,Pin.IN,Pin.PULL_DOWN)
pin1.irq(HelloIRQ1,Pin.IRQ_RISING)
pin2.irq(HelloIRQ2,Pin.IRQ_RISING)
```

You will see `IRQ1` or `IRQ2` printed depending on which pin the interrupt occurred on. Alternatively you can set a single ISR and work out what to do depending on the pin passed in:

```
def HelloIRQ(pin):
      def HelloIRQ1(pin):
    if str(pin) == "Pin(4)":
        print("IRQ1")
    else:
        print("IRQ2")

pin1=Pin(4,Pin.IN,Pin.PULL_DOWN)
pin2=Pin(5,Pin.IN,Pin.PULL_DOWN)
pin1.irq(HelloIRQ,Pin.IRQ_RISING)
pin2.irq(HelloIRQ,Pin.IRQ_RISING)
```

The Interrupt Queue

The interrupt as implemented in MicroPython isn't like the raw hardware interrupt produced by the ESP32. It differs in that interrupts are buffered rather than turned off in the interrupt routine. The problem is that interrupts can occur during the execution of an interrupt handler and this can cause problems. It is usual for interrupt handlers to disable interrupts while they are running to simplify things, but this isn't how MicroPython's interrupts work. What happens is that the interrupt system is kept enabled during an interrupt routine but if an interrupt occurs it is simply added to a queue. The interrupt routine then finishes and the interrupt system immediately calls it again so that no interrupt is missed. This is exactly the advantage of this approach – no interrupt is missed, but from a realtime point of view it isn't always what you want. Often the time that the interrupt occurred is important and having a queue of pending interrupts spoils this.

To see how all this works and what effect it has consider this simple example. An interrupt signal is applied to GPIO4 that provides a rising edge every second, i.e. it is a 1Hz square wave. The interrupt handler records the time of the interrupt and prints the difference between this time and the previous interrupt time. If no interrupts are missed this should always be a little more than 1 second. However, there is a sleep for 1.5 seconds at the end of the interrupt routine and so it should miss the next rising edge but get the following one. This means that the time should be reported as 2 seconds:

```
import time
from machine import Pin
t = 0
def myHandler(pin):
    global t
    temp = time.ticks_us()
    print(time.ticks_diff(temp,t))
    t = temp
    time.sleep(1.5)
    return


pin = Pin(4, Pin.IN, Pin.PULL_DOWN)
pin.irq(myHandler, Pin.IRQ_FALLING)
```

If you try this program you will find that it prints a little more than 1.5 seconds. The reason is that the supposedly missed interrupt event is added to a queue and as soon as the interrupt handler is finished it is called again – hence the supposed 1.5 seconds between interrupts.

You can clear the queue of interrupts waiting to be handled by disabling interrupts within the interrupt handler and then turning them back on again:

```
import time
from machine import Pin
t = 0
def myHandler(pin):
    global t
    pin.irq(None, Pin.IRQ_FALLING)
    temp = time.ticks_us()
    print(time.ticks_diff(temp,t))
    t = temp
    time.sleep(1.5)
    pin.irq(myHandler, Pin.IRQ_FALLING)
    return
pin = Pin(4, Pin.IN, Pin.PULL_DOWN)
pin.irq(myHandler, Pin.IRQ_FALLING)
```

With this change the interrupt handler does miss the very next edge and the time displayed is slightly more than 2 seconds.

Notice the use of None as an interrupt handler to turn interrupts off. How to deal with missing interrupts is a matter of what is most important – responding to all interrupts or responding at the time that the interrupt occurred.

Interrupt Service Routine Restrictions

There are other restrictions on writing an ISR. Firstly, it should only run for a short time because while the ISR is running the main Python thread is suspended and cannot service any other peripheral. A long-running ISR not only blocks the main thread, but also other interrupts. In most cases the best design is to allow the ISR to set status indicators and then to hand off and allow the main thread to react to the new status.

For example, if an ISR is called to collect data from a sensor it should simply acquire the data and store it in a shared variable. It should avoid trying to process the data. Instead it should set a flag that signals to the main thread that new data is available and that it should process it.

Another problem is that ISRs shouldn't allocate memory, i.e. create or extend objects. The reason is that an ISR can interrupt the Python main thread at a point that is part way though an operation. This means that the Python heap might well be locked when the ISR runs and so cannot create anything new without risking an exception. There are a number of possible solutions. The simplest is to create all objects that the ISR needs to use before it runs and, if you need to add to an object, find a representation that allows you to allocate the space needed before using it.

For example, prefer an Array.array object to a List or Dictionary object as an Array.array object is pre-allocated at its initialized size. To know more about this and about how appending data to a List or adding to a Dictionary causes memory to be allocated see **Programmer's Python: Everything Is Data**, ISBN:9781871962598.

Things are actually more subtle as there are actions which create objects on the heap that you might not expect to do so. For example, creating a reference to a method causes an object to be created on the heap. Equally using floats in an ISR is a problem as these are allocated on the heap.

Another consequence of not being able to allocate memory is that an ISR can't raise an exception as this requires memory allocation. The solution is to add:

```
micropython.alloc_emergency_exception_buf(100)
```

to the main program.

An alternative to having to avoid allocating memory in general is to hand it off to a non-interrupt routine using the `micropython.schedule` function:

`schedule(function, arg)`

This will call `function(arg)` at the first possible moment after the ISR terminates. The "first possible moment" is determined by when the main thread is between complete Python instructions. That is, an ISR can be called in the middle of a Python instruction, but the schedule function is always called between Python instructions and so it can always access the heap. The exception to this is if the function passed to schedule is an object method – this requires the ISR to allocate memory and so it fails. Notice that you can use an object method as an ISR because the reference is created before the ISR is called. As long as you only pass a standard unbound function to schedule it all should work. A schedule function will also run to completion without being interrupted by another schedule function, but it can be suspended by an interrupt.

This is all there is to using GPIO to generate an interrupt and handling it. In practice, things are more difficult to get right than you might expect. In particular, access to shared resources presents a problem. A Python program can share data with an ISR by declaring a variable to be global.

Race Conditions and Starvation

Implementing an ISR is a step into the complex world of asynchronous programs and if this is something of interest see **Programmer's Python: Async**, ISBN:978-1871962765. The biggest new problem that asynchronicity introduces is the possibility of race conditions. A race condition occurs when two sections of code modify a shared resource in such an uncontrolled way that the final outcome depends on the timing of the code execution. Race conditions are particularly difficult to debug because they look random and the tendency is to think that they are due to faulty hardware and, worse, an intermittent fault.

It is difficult to provide a clear and simple example of a race condition for the ESP32 because real time programming is inherently difficult to test. In addition, the implementation of interrupt handling in the ESP32 is at a higher level than raw interrupts in the sense that an ISR, once started, runs to completion. That is, ISRs are not interrupted. This means that it is the code in the main thread of execution which is interrupted and is the source of any race conditions. So while race conditions happen, they are difficult to demonstrate.

Consider the problem of setting a byte array to either all ones or all zeros. In an ideal world this data structure would always be in either one of the two states – the setting would be atomic and not interruptible. However, the main thread can be interrupted both within and between MicroPython instructions. The following program uses an interrupt on GPIO4 to set a byte array to zero and a `while` loop in the main program to set it to all ones:

```
import time
from machine import Pin

data = bytearray(b'\xf0\xf1\xf2')

def myHandler(pin):
    global data
    for i in range(3):
        data[i]=0

pin = Pin(4, Pin.IN, Pin.PULL_DOWN)
pin.irq(myHandler, Pin.IRQ_RISING)

while True:
    for i in range(3):
        data[i] = 255
    if data[0]!=data[1] or data[1]!=data[2] or data[2]!=data[0]:
        print(data)
```

If you run this program you will discover that the byte array is often in a state that is a mix of the two:

```
bytearray(b'\x00\x00\xff')
bytearray(b'\x00\xff\xff')
bytearray(b'\x00\xff\xff')
bytearray(b'\x00\xff\xff')
bytearray(b'\x00\xff\xff')
bytearray(b'\x00\x00\xff')
```

This occurs frequently even with interrupts occurring at ten per second. What happens is that the `for` loop starts to set the byte array to all ones a byte at a time. If an interrupt occurs during this process then the bytes are set to zero and when the loop restarts only the remaining bytes are set to all ones.

If you don't want the byte array to be in an inconsistent state then you need to disable the ISR while the main thread is using it:

```
from machine import Pin

data=bytearray(b'\xf0\xf1\xf2')
def myHandler(pin):
    global data
    for i in range(3):
        data[i] = 0
    print(data)

pin = Pin(4, Pin.IN, Pin.PULL_DOWN)
pin.irq(myHandler, Pin.IRQ_RISING)
while True:
    pin.irq(None, Pin.IRQ_RISING)
    for i in range(3):
        data[i] = 255

    if data[0]!=data[1] or data[1]!=data[2] or data[2]!=data[0]:
        print(data)
    pin.irq(myHandler, Pin.IRQ_RISING)
```

This now works and you never see an inconsistent state for the byte array but now the ISR hardly ever gets to run. It only gets called once per while loop iteration and this severely limits its responsiveness. This is an example of "starvation" where one process hogs the CPU for so much of the time other processes fail to make much progress. In this case it is the ISR that is slowed down but a CPU hogging ISR can slow the main program down in exactly the same way. Notice the way that we set None as an ISR to disable the interrupt. In theory you can use:

```
s=machine.disable_irq()
print("doing something useful")
machine.enable_irq(s)
```

to create sections of code where interrupts cannot occur, but notice that this disables all interrupts, including timer ticks and this generally causes the ESP32 to crash.

Measuring Pulse Width

In Chapter 6 we saw how to use polling to measure pulse widths. You can do the same job with interrupts – simply detect a rising and then a falling edge. At this point it is tempting to get the ISRs to do all of the task of measuring the temperature, but again a state machine approach is much better. In general, it is nearly always a good idea to get the ISRs to set the value of a state variable and then return as soon as possible. This approach reduces the

ISRs to their minimum and makes the program work faster and more reliably. For example:

```
import time
from time import sleep
from machine import Pin

pin=Pin(4,Pin.IN,Pin.PULL_DOWN)

event=0
def rise(pin):
    global event
    event=1

def fall(pin):
    global event
    event=2

while True:
    pin.irq(rise, Pin.IRQ_RISING)
    while  not(event==1):
        pass
    t=time.ticks_us()
    pin.irq(fall, Pin.IRQ_FALLING)
    while  not(event==2):
        pass
    t=time.ticks_diff(time.ticks_us(),t)
    print(t)
    sleep(1)
```

The main program simply tests the state variable, event, and reacts accordingly. The only global variable needed is event and the ISRs do nothing but set its value and return – what could be simpler.

If you try this out, you will find that the pulse measurements are reasonably accurate down to 125µs, after which the next falling edge is missed and the second falling edge is detected. This compares poorly with the 12µs a direct polling approach can provide.

Timers

A very common use of interrupts is to run a function after a delay or run one regularly every so often. The ESP32 has four hardware timers that can be used to do just this.

To create a Timer object use its constructor:

```
timer=Timer(n)
```

where n is the number of the hardware timer, 0 to 3, you want to use.

Once you have a `Timer` object you can use its `init` method to set up either a periodic callback or a one-off callback, a one-shot:

`Timer.init(mode = mode, period = - 1, callback = None)`

Mode can be either of:

- `Timer.ONE_SHOT`   The timer runs once and the callback is called when the period is up
- `Timer.PERIODIC`   The timer runs repeatedly calling the callback each time the period is up.

When you are finished with a timer you can use `Timer.deinit()` to free the hardware and stop any periodic callback.

Notice that the callback function is an interrupt handler and is subject to all of the restrictions and cautions that apply to a general interrupt handler. The callback accepts a single parameter which is the `Timer` object that called it.

Responding to Input

This look at methods of dealing with the problems of input isn't exhaustive - there are always new ways of doing things, but it does cover the most general ways of implementing input. As already mentioned, the problem with input is that you don't know when it is going to happen. What generally matters is speed of response.

For low-frequency inputs, interrupts are worthwhile. They can leave your program free to get on with other tasks and simplify its overall structure. For high-frequency inputs that need to be serviced regularly, a polling loop is still the best option for maximum throughput. How quickly you can respond to an input depends on how long the polling loop is and how many times you test for it per loop.

Summary

- You can use edge events to generate an interrupt and call an interrupt handler.

- MicroPython has two interrupt implementations, but the ESP32 only uses the default which allows interrupts to occur during the interrupt handler and a queue of interrupts is formed.

- The ESP32 runs ISRs to completion, i.e. they are not interrupted once started.

- The queuing of interrupts means that an interrupt is never missed, but the lack of a timestamp means that you cannot know when the queued interrupt occurred.

- You can turn interrupts off and clear that queue by setting the ISR to None.

- ISRs are subject to a range of restrictions – in particular they cannot reliably create objects on the heap.

- If you need an ISR to use the heap delegate the task to a function run using schedule.

- Race conditions can occur if the update of shared resources isn't atomic. You can make an update atomic by disabling interrupts.

- Do not use machine.disable_irq and machine.enable_irq as they tend to crash the machine. Timers can also be used to schedule the running of a function after a delay or at a regular interval.

- The overhead in using an interrupt is quite large.

- Whenever possible, avoid using interrupts.

Chapter 8

Pulse Width Modulation

One way around the problem of getting a fast response from a microcontroller is to move the problem away from the processor. In the case of the ESP32 there are some built-in devices that can use GPIO lines to implement protocols without the CPU being involved. In this chapter we take a close look at the use of Pulse Width Modulation (PWM) including generating sound, driving LEDs and servos.

When performing their most basic function, i.e. output, the GPIO lines can be set high or low by the processor. How fast they can be set high or low depends on the speed of the processor.

Using the GPIO line in its Pulse Width Modulation (PWM) mode you can generate pulse trains up to 40 MHz. The reason for the increase in speed is that the GPIO is connected to a pulse generator and, once set to generate pulses of a specific type, the pulse generator just gets on with it without needing any intervention from the GPIO line or the processor. In fact, the pulse output will continue after your program has ended. Of course, even though the PWM line can generate very fast pulses, usually what you want to do is change the nature of the pulses and this is a slower process involving the processor.

Some Basic PWM Facts

There are some facts worth getting clear right from the start, although some of their significance will only become clear as we progress.

First, what is PWM? The simple answer is that a pulse width modulated signal has pulses that repeat at a fixed rate, say one pulse every millisecond, but the width of the pulse can be changed. There are two basic things to specify about the pulse train that is generated, its repetition rate and the width of each pulse. Usually the repetition rate is set as a simple repeat period and the width of each pulse is specified as a percentage of the repeat period, referred to as the duty cycle. So, for example, a 1ms repeat and a 50% duty cycle specifies a 1ms period, which is high for 50% of the time, i.e. a pulse width of 0.5ms. The two extremes are 100% duty cycle, i.e. the line is always high, and 0% duty cycle, i.e. the line is always low.

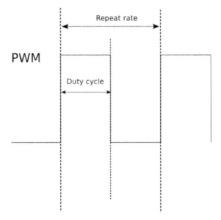

Notice it is the duty cycle that carries the information in PWM and not the frequency. What this means is that, in general, you select a repeat rate and stick to it and what you change as the program runs is the duty cycle.

In many cases PWM is implemented using special PWM-generator hardware that is either built into the processor chip or provided by an external chip. The processor simply sets the repeat rate by writing to a register and then changing the duty cycle by writing to another register. This provides the ideal sort of PWM with no load on the processor and glitch-free operation. You can even buy add-on boards that will provide additional channels of PWM without adding to the load on the processor.

The alternative to dedicated PWM hardware is to implement it in software. You can work out how to do this quite easily. All you need is a timing loop to set the line high at the repetition rate and then set it low again according to the duty cycle. You can implement this using either interrupts or a polling loop and in more advanced ways, such as using a DMA (Direct Memory Access) channel.

ESP32 PWM

The ESP32 has two PWM hardware implementations. One is intended for use in motor control and has extra features such as a dead zone and autobraking. This isn't supported by MicroPython and if you want to make use of it then you have to move to C. The second, LEDC, is specifically designed to drive LEDs with facilities such as auto-dimming plus more exotic features. While MicroPython does support the basic LEDC operations it doesn't provide access to all its additional features.

A PWM generator can be assigned to any GPIO pin. The number of PWM generators an ESP32 has depends on its exact model. They come in two groups – fast and slow. The fast type has the autodimming features and is able to smoothly change frequency and duty cycle. The slow type lacks these features and it is up to software to change its frequency and duty cycle. Each group also has a set number of timers which determine how many different frequencies can be generated and a given number of channels.

The most common development board using an EP32 has two groups, one fast and one slow, of PWM with eight channels in each group. The ESP32-S2 only has one fast group, but is otherwise identical. The ESP32-C3, which is RISC based, is the same as the ESP32-S2, but with only six channels. All ESP32 devices have four timers in each group, meaning you can set four different frequencies.

The distinction between the two groups is irrelevant from the point of view of MicroPython as it doesn't make use of the extra features in the fast group. What this means is that, from the point of view of MicroPython, an ESP32 has 16 PWM channels which can work at eight different frequencies. All of the channels can work at different duty cycles.

You don't have to know about how the PWM hardware works, but it helps with understanding some of the restrictions.

To create a `PWM` object you have to pass its constructor a `Pin` object. For example:

```
pwm1 = PWM(Pin(4))
```

creates a `PWM` object associated with GPIO4. You can set the frequency using:

```
pwm1.freq(500)
```

which sets the frequency in Hz. The PWM hardware isn't enabled at this point. To start it generating a signal you have to set the duty cycle. This is done using:

```
pwm1.duty_u16(duty)
```

where `duty` is a value in the range 0 to 65,535 corresponding to 0 to 100%.

There is also:

```
pwm1.duty_ns(ns)
```

which sets the time the line is high in nanoseconds. This isn't as useful for general use and if you specify a time that is greater than the set period you will generate an exception.

Alternatively you can use the constructor to specify all of the characteristics of the PWM:

```
machine.PWM(dest, freq=f, duty_u16=d, duty_ns=t)
```

The MicroPython implementation of PWM allocates timers to channels in an intelligent way. If you create a PWM object working at a particular frequency it first looks to see if there is a timer in the same group working at that frequency. If there is, it allocates it to the PWM object. If there isn't an existing timer working at that frequency then a free one is allocated and set to work at the new frequency. If there are no free timers left and none are running at the frequency required then an exception is thrown. What this means is that you can allocate frequencies without worrying until you have used up all of the timers and then you have to set frequencies you have already used. This means that for an ESP32 you can set up to eight different frequencies for the 16 different channels.

You can easily create your own duty cycle methods that work in terms of percentages or whatever way you want to specify the duty cycle. For example, you can create a new class which has a duty cycle set as a percentage:

```
class myPWM(PWM):
    def __init__(self, pin: Pin):
        super().__init__(pin)
    def duty(self,d):
        print(65535*d//1000)
        super().duty_u16(65535*d//1000)
```

In this case the percentage is specified multiplied by 10. For example, to set a 50% duty cycle you would use:

```
pwm1 = myPWM(Pin(4),freq=250)
pwm1.duty(500)
```

Once you have set the duty cycle the PWM generator starts to output the specified PWM signal on the pin. Notice that this works even after your program has completed. To stop the PWM signal use:

```
pwm16.deinit()
```

You can change the frequency or duty cycle at any time. For example:

```
from machine import Pin, PWM
pwm1 = PWM(Pin(4),freq=250)
pwm2 = PWM(Pin(2),freq=250)
pwm1.duty_u16(65535//2)
pwm2.duty_u16(65535//4)
```

produces a PWM signal on GPIO2 and GPIO4 at the same frequency of 250Hz and duty cycles of 50% and 25% respectively.

You can see the result in this logic analyzer display:

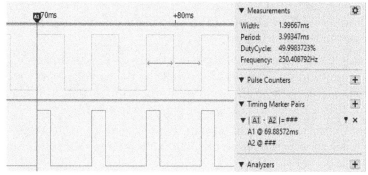

You can see from this trace that the pulses on each line start their duty cycle at exactly the same time.

Changing The Duty Cycle

For reasons that will be discussed later, most applications of PWM vary the duty cycle or the period of the pulse train while the frequency remains fixed. This raises the next question, how fast can you change the duty cycle? There is no easy way to give an exact answer and, in most cases, an exact answer isn't of much value. The reason is that for a PWM signal to convey information it generally has to deliver a number of complete cycles with a given duty cycle. This is because of the way pulses are often averaged in applications. We also have another problem – synchronization. This is more subtle than it first seems. The hardware won't change the duty cycle until the current pulse is complete. You might think that the following program works to switch between two duty cycles on a per pulse basis:

```
import time
from machine import Pin, PWM
pwm1 = PWM(Pin(4),freq = 50)
while True:
    pwm1.duty_u16(65535//2)
    time.sleep_ms(19)
    pwm1.duty_u16(65535//4)
    time.sleep_ms(19)
```

However, if you try this out on an ESP32 the result isn't what you might expect on a first analysis:

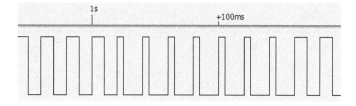

117

You don't get one 25% pulse followed by one 50% pulse, but a varying number of each in turn. The reason is, of course, that the duty cycle is being set asynchronously. The time that the duty cycle changes drifts in time and produces an interference pattern.

However if you try the same program out on an ESP32 S3 the results are what you are intending. The reason is that the duty cycle is only set when the counter rolls over providing a simple synchronization. At higher frequencies this too fails to change the duty cycle accurately.

If you want to create a PWM bitstream that varies duty cycle accurately on a per pulse basis then you need to use RMT, the remote controller introduced in Chapter 4.

Pulse Coding Using RMT

RMT can be used to send a bitstream with accurately specified duty cycles. All you have to do is construct a list with the correct timings for the high and low portions of each pulse:

```
import esp32
from machine import Pin
import machine
pin=Pin(4,Pin.OUT,value=0)
rmt=esp32.RMT(0,pin=pin)
t=20000000 # pulse repetition in us
d=[10,20,30,40,50] #duty cycles in percent

times=[]
for p in d:
    times.append(int(t*p/100))
    times.append(int((t*(100-p)/100)))

rmt.loop(True)
rmt.write_pulses(times,1)
```

The frequency is specified as a time in μs to make the math easier. All we have to do is multiply up the list of duty cycles to get the high and low times for each pulse and then use this to send a bitstream from GPIO4. Notice that the loop method is used to repeat the same duty cycle over and over.The logic analyzer trace reveals that the pulses really do have duty cycles of 10,20,30,40 and 50%. This technique can be used to create precise codes like PCM, Pulse Code Modulation.

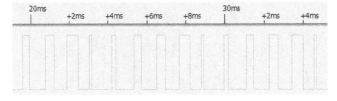

Duty Cycle Resolution

It seems as if you can set the duty cycle to a 16-bit value giving you 65535 different settings, however, this is only true in a few cases.

The PWM hardware implements the following algorithm (in pseudo code):

```
wrap = clock_frequency/PWM_frequency
level = wrap*duty%/100
set GPIO line high
for count in range(wrap):
      wait one clock cycle
      if count > level:
            set GPIO line low
```

In other words, the frequency of the PWM signal depends on the value of wrap and the duty cycle depends on level. For example, if clock_frequency is 100MHz, PWM_frequency is 10MHz and duty% is 50% then:

```
wrap = 10
```

```
level = 5
```

The for loop runs for 10 clock pulses and the line is high for 5 clock pulses. You can see that this does produce the required frequency and duty cycle.

When you select a PWM_frequency this gives the total number of clock pulses counted in a pulse width modulation cycle. Clearly you can only set the level and hence the duty cycle between 0 and wrap and this can limit the precision that you can set. For example, as the clock frequency is set to 40MHz setting a PWM_frequency of 20MHz gives wrap = 2 and, given the duty cycle resolution is just two bits, level can only be 0, 1, 2, 3 which is a duty cycle of 0%, 25%, 75% and 100%.

In other words, the PWM_frequency you select affects the accuracy of the setting of the duty cycle. In most cases the wrap value is large enough to ignore the problem, but sometimes it is important. You can see that this is the case in the following example:

```
import time
from machine import Pin, PWM
pwm1 = PWM(Pin(4),freq = 20000000)
pwm1.duty_u16(65535//2+2)
```

This produces a duty cycle of 50% as you would expect, but if you change the duty cycle to 65535//4*n+2 for n = 0, 1, 2, 3 you get duty cycles of approximately 0%, 25%, 50%, and 75% and these are the only duty cycles you can get, no matter what you try to set it to.

You can discover the duty cycle resolution for any given frequency by printing the PWM instance:

```
print(pwm1)
```

which displays:

```
PWM(Pin(4), freq=20000000, duty_u16=16384, resolution=2,
   (duty=25.00%, resolution=25.000%), mode=0, channel=0, timer=0)
```

You can see that the resolution is reported as 2 bits or 25%.

At lower frequencies the duty cycle precision is usually closer or greater than 16-bits and we tend to ignore any restrictions. For example, at 50Hz the frequency used for controlling servo motors the resolution is 20 bits which is more than you can specify using a 16-bit parameter!

Uses of PWM – Digital to Analog

What sorts of things do you use PWM for? There are lots of very clever uses for PWM. However, there are two applications which account for most PWM applications - voltage or power modulation and signaling to servos.

The amount of power delivered to a device by a pulse train is proportional to the duty cycle. A pulse train that has a 50% duty cycle is delivering current to the load only 50% of the time and this is irrespective of the pulse repetition rate. So the duty cycle controls the power, but the period still matters in many situations because you want to avoid any flashing or other effects. A higher frequency smooths out the power flow at any duty cycle.

If you add a low-pass filter to the output of a PWM signal then what you get is a voltage that is proportional to the duty cycle. This can be looked at in many different ways, but again it is the result of the amount of power delivered by a PWM signal. You can also think of it as using the filter to remove the high-frequency components of the signal, leaving only the slower components due to the modulation of the duty cycle.

How fast you can work depends on the duty cycle resolution. If you work with 8-bit resolution your D-to-A conversion will have 256 steps, which at 3.3V gives a potential resolution of 3.3/256 or about 13mV. This is often good enough. If you understand the previous section on duty cycle resolution this means that the PWM frequency has to be 125000000//256 to give a wrap of 256. The PWM output in this configuration mimics the workings of an 8-bit D-to-A converter.

To demonstrate the sort of approach that you can take to D-to-A conversion, the following program creates a sine wave. To do this we need to compute the duty cycle for 256 points in a complete cycle. We could do this each time a value is needed, but to make the program fast enough we have to compute the entire 256 points and store them in an array. While there are fixed-point arithmetic ways of computing the sine or the cos of an angle, it is simpler to use MicroPython's floating-point software. Notice that the ESP32 S2 doesn't have floating-point arithmetic implemented in hardware but the original ESP32 and S3 do support hardware floating point but it isn't very fast.

The program is:

```
from machine import Pin, PWM
import array
import math

wave = array.array('H', [0]*256)
for i in range(256):
    wave[i] = int(65535//2 +
                (math.sin(i * 2.0 * 3.14159 / 256.0) * 65535//2))

pwm1 = PWM(Pin(4),freq=300000)
print(pwm1)
while(True):
    for i in range(256):
        pwm1.duty_u16(wave[i])

print(pwm_get_wrap(0))
while(True):
    for i in range(256):
        pwm16.duty_u16(wave[i])
```

The 16-bit duty cycle values needed are computed and stored in the wave array. Then the PWM is set up with the highest frequency that will provide 256 levels of duty cycle. Finally, a for loop is used to set the duty cycle from the array. Notice that there is no attempt at synchronizing when the duty cycle update will occur – it happens as fast as possible.

The waveform repeats after around 5ms, which makes the frequency around 200Hz.

To see the analog waveform, we need to put the digital output into a low-pass filter. A simple resistor and capacitor work reasonably well:

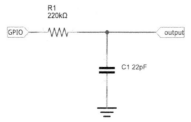

The filter's cutoff is around 33kHz and might be a little on the high side for this low-frequency, 200Hz, output, but it produces a reasonable waveform:

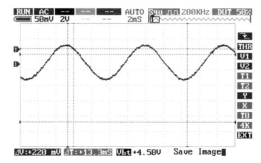

You can use this technique to create a sine wave, or any other waveform you need, but for high-quality audio you need a higher sampling rate.

Frequency Modulation

Using PWM to create musical tones, and sound effects in general, is a well-explored area which is too wide to cover in this book. In most cases we choose to vary the duty cycle at a fixed sample rate, but an alternative is to leave the duty cycle fixed at, say, 50% and modulate the frequency. You can use this approach to create simple musical tones and scales.

As the frequency of middle C is 281.6Hz, to generate middle C you could use:

```
from machine import Pin, PWM
pwm1 = PWM(Pin(4),freq=282)
pwm1.duty_u16(65535//2)
```

The resulting output is a square wave with a measured frequency of 282.04Hz which isn't particularly nice to listen to. You can improve it by feeding it through a simple low-pass filter like the one used above for waveform synthesis. You can look up the frequencies for other notes and use a table to generate them.

Controlling an LED

You can also use PWM to generate physical quantities such as the brightness of an LED or the rotation rate of a DC motor. The only differences required by these applications are to do with the voltage and current you need and the way the duty cycle relates to whatever the physical effect is. In other words, if you want to change some effect by 50%, how much do you need to change the duty cycle? For example, how do we "dim" an LED?

The simplest example is to drive the on-board LED using a PWM signal:

```
from machine import Pin, PWM
from time import sleep_ms
pwm1 = PWM(Pin(4),freq=2000)

while True:
    for d in range(0,65535,655):
        pwm1.duty_u16(d)
        sleep_ms(50)
```

If you try this out you will see the LED slowly increase in brightness, but it seems to be a longer time at maximum brightness than at any other value. This is a consequence of the non-linear relationship between duty cycle and perceived brightness.

By changing the duty cycle of the PWM pulse train you can set the amount of power delivered to an LED, or any other device, and hence change its brightness. If you use a 50% duty cycle, the LED is on 50% of the time and it has been determined that this makes it look as if it is half as bright. However, this is not the end of the story as humans don't respond to physical brightness in a linear way. The Weber-Fechner law gives the general relationship between perceived intensity and physical stimulus as logarithmic.

In the case of an LED, the connection between duty cycle and brightness is a complicated matter, but the simplest approach uses the fact that the perceived brightness is roughly proportional to the cube root of the physical brightness. The exact equations, published as CIE 1931, are:

$L = 903.3 \cdot (Y / Y_n)$ $\qquad$ $(Y / Y_n) \leq 0.008856$

$L = 116 \cdot (Y / Y_n)^{1/3} - 16$ $\qquad$ $(Y / Y_n) > 0.008856$

where L is the perceived brightness and Y / Y_n is a measure of physical brightness.

The exact relationship is complicated, but in most cases a roughly cubic law, obtained by inverting the CIE relationship, can be used:

$$d=kb^3$$

where b is the perceived brightness and d is the duty cycle. The constant k depends on the LED. The graph below shows the general characteristic of the relationship for a duty cycle of 0 to 100% on the y-axis and arbitrary, 0 to 100, perceived brightness units on the x-axis.

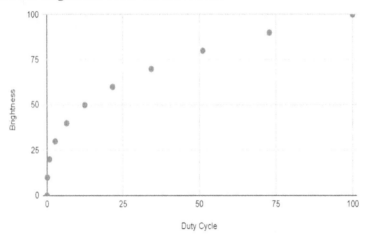

Notice that, as the LED when powered by a PWM signal is either full on or full off, there is no effect in the change in LED light output with current - the LED is always run at the same current. What all of this means is that if you want an LED to fade in a linear fashion you need to change the duty cycle in a non-linear fashion. Intuitively it means that changes when the duty cycle is small produce bigger changes in brightness than when the duty cycle is large.

A program to implement cubic dimming is:

```
from utime import sleep_ms
from machine import Pin, PWM

pwm1 = PWM(Pin(4),freq=2000)

while True:
    for b in range(0,100):
        pwm1.duty_u16(int(65535*b*b*b/1000000))
        sleep_ms(50)
```

If you try this out you should notice that the LED changes brightness more evenly across its range. The only problem is that now 100 steps are insufficient to mask the steps in brightness at the lower level. The solution is to work with a more precise specification of duty cycle.

In most cases it is irrelevant exactly how linear the response of the LED is - a rough approximation looks as smooth to the human eye. You can even get away with using a square law to dim the LED. The only exception is when you are trying to drive LEDs to create a gray-level or color display when color calibration is another level of accuracy.

There is also the question of what frequency we should use. Clearly it has to be fast enough not to be seen as flickering and this generally means it has to be greater than 80Hz, the upper limit for human flicker fusion, but, because of the strobe effect, flickering becomes more visible with moving objects. The faster the LED switches on and off, the less flicker should be visible, but before you select frequencies in the high kHz range it is worth knowing that an LED has a minimum time to turn on and so frequencies at low kHz work best.

If you want to dim something other than the on-board LED, you will, in many cases, need a driver to increase the brightness. For a simple example, consider connecting a standard LED to the PWM line and using the BJT driver circuit introduced in Chapter 5.

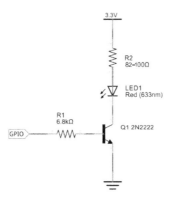

What Else Can You Use PWM For?

PWM lines are incredibly versatile and it is always worth asking the question "could I use PWM?" when you are considering almost any problem. The ESP32's PWM generator is particularly versatile. For example, it has an option to vary the brightness of an LED without the CPU getting involved. However, MicroPython doesn't support this and other of its more advanced features.

The LED example suggests how you can use PWM as a power controller. You can extend this idea to a computer-controlled switch-mode power supply. All you need is a capacitor to smooth out the voltage and perhaps a transformer to change the voltage. You can also use PWM to control the speed of a DC motor and, by adding a simple bridge circuit, you can control its direction and speed.

Finally, you can use a PWM signal as a modulated carrier for data communications. For example, most infrared controllers make use of a 38kHz carrier, which is roughly a $26\mu s$ pulse. This is switched on and off for 1ms and this is well within the range that the PWM can manage. So all you have to do is replace the red LED in the previous circuit with an infrared LED and you have the start of a remote control, or data transmission, link. Of course the RMT hardware discussed in Chapter 4 also does this job and it does it better, but it is only in beta at the moment.

One big area of use is in controlling motors, and servo motors in particular, and this is the subject of the next chapter.

Summary

- PWM, Pulse Width Modulation, has a fixed repetition rate but a variable duty cycle, i.e. the amount of time the signal is high or low changes.

- PWM can be generated by software simply by changing the state of a GPIO line correctly, but it can also be generated in hardware so relieving the processor of some work.

- As well as being a way of signaling, PWM can also be used to vary the amount of power or voltage transferred. The higher the duty cycle, the more power/voltage.

- The ESP32 has 16 hardware PWM generators and these can be used with any of the GPIO lines capable of output.

- There are only eight timers which determine the frequency that the PWM lines work at. These are allocated as needed as you setup PWM lines.

- You cannot change the duty cycle of a PWM signal in a precisely timed way unless you use the RMT hardware instead.

- The higher the frequency the lower the duty cycle resolution.

- You can find the frequency and resolution by printing the PWM object.

- PWM can be used to implement digital to analog conversion simply by varying the duty cycle. In the same way, by varying the duty cycle, you can dim an LED.

Chapter 9

Controlling Motors And Servos

Controlling motors is an obvious use for the ESP32, but it is important to understand the different types of motor that you can use and exactly how to control them using PWM. In addition to PWM control, we also look at the very useful stepper motor which doesn't make use of PWM.

The ESP32 has a PWM generator which is specifically targeted at motor control. Unfortunately MicroPython doesn't support its use and it is fairly complicated. It includes the ability to set dead-time, synchronize PWM output with external events and detect faults. It is well worth using for motor control but to do so you would have to move to C.

The simplest division among types of motor is AC and DC. AC motors are generally large and powerful and run from mains voltage. As they are more difficult to work with, and they work at mains voltages, these aren't used much in IoT applications. DC motors generally work on lower voltage and are much more suitable for the IoT. In this chapter we will only look at DC motors and how they work thanks to pulse width modulation. The parts used are listed in the Resources section of the book's webpage at www.iopress.info.

DC Motor

There are two big classes of DC motor – brushed and brushless. All motors work by using a set of fixed magnets, the stator, and a set of rotating magnets, the rotor. The important idea is that a motor generates a "push" that rotates the shaft by the forces between the magnet that makes up the stator and the magnet that makes up the rotor. The stronger these magnets are, the stronger the push and the more torque (turning force) the motor can produce. To keep the motor turning, one of the two magnetic fields has to change to keep the rotor being attracted to a new position.

DC motors differ in how they create the magnetism in each component, either using a permanent magnet or an electromagnet.

This means there are four possible arrangements:

	1	2	3	4
Stator	Permanent	Permanent	Electromagnet	Electromagnet
Rotor	Permanent	Electromagnet	Permanent	Electromagnet
Type	Can't work	Brushed DC	Brushless DC	Series or shunt

Arrangement 1 can't produce a motor because there is no easy way of changing the magnetic field. Arrangement 4 produces the biggest and most powerful DC motors used in trains, cars and so on. Arrangement 2, Brushed DC, is the most commonly encountered form of "small" DC motor. However, arrangement 3, brushless DC, is becoming increasingly popular.

Different arrangements produce motors which have different torque characteristics, i.e. how hard they are to stop at any given speed. Some types of motor are typically low torque at any speed, i.e. they spin fast but are easy to stop.

Low torque motors are often used with gearboxes, which reduce the speed and increase the torque. The big problem with gearboxes, apart from extra cost, is backlash. The gears don't mesh perfectly and this looseness means that you can turn the input shaft and at first the output shaft won't move. Only when the slack in the gears has been taken up will the output shaft move. This makes a geared motor less useful for precise positioning, although there are ways to improve on this using feedback and clever programming.

Brushed Motors

To energize the electromagnets, a brushed motor supplies current to the armature via a split ring or commutator and brushes. As the rotor rotates, the current in the coil is reversed and it is always attracted to the other pole of the magnet.

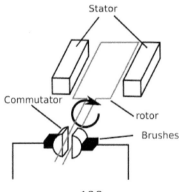

The only problem with this arrangement is that, as the brushes rub on the slip ring as the armature rotates, they wear out and cause sparks and hence RF interference. The quality of a brushed motor depends very much on the design of the brushes and the commutator.

Very small, cheap, brushed DC motors, of the sort in the picture below, tend to not have brushes that can be changed and when they wear out the motor has to be replaced. They also tend to have very low torque and high speed. This usually means that they have to be used with a gearbox. If you overload a brushed motor then the tendency is to demagnetize the stator magnets. The cheapest devices are basically toys.

Higher quality brushed motors are available and they also come in a variety of form factors. For example, the 775 motor is 66.7 by 42mm with a 5mm shaft:

Even these motors tend not to have user-serviceable brushes, but they tend to last a long time due to better construction.

Unidirectional Brushed Motor

A brushed motor can be powered by simply connecting it to a DC supply.
Reversing the DC supply reverses the direction of the motor. The speed is
simply proportional to the applied voltage. If all you want is a unidirectional
control then all you need is a PWM driver that can supply the necessary
current and voltage.

A single transistor solution is workable as long as you include a diode to
allow the energy stored in the windings to discharge when the motor is
rotating, but not under power:

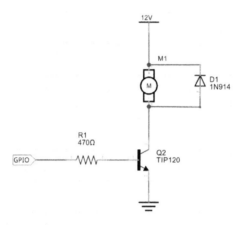

This circuit is simple and will work with motor voltages up to 40V and
motor currents up to 5A continuous, 8A peak. The only small point to note
is that the TIP120 is a Darlington pair, i.e. it is two transistors in the same
case, and as such the base voltage drop is twice the usual 0.6V, i.e. 1.2V, and
this has to be taken into account when calculating the current-limiting
resistor.

It is sometimes said that the TIP120 and similar are inefficient power
controllers because, comprising two transistors, they have twice the emitter-
collector voltage you would expect, which means they dissipate more power
than necessary.

If you are running a motor from a battery you might want to use a MOSFET, but, as described earlier, 3.3V is low to switch a MOSFET on and off. One solution is to use a BJT to increase the voltage applied to the gate:

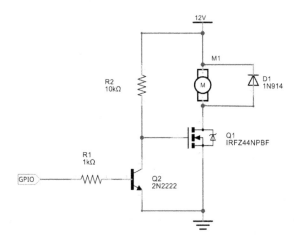

The BJT connects the gate to 12V. As the IRFZ44NPBF has a threshold voltage between 2V and 4V, devices should work at 5V and sometimes at 3.3V without the help of the BJT, but providing 12V ensures that the MOSFET is fully on. One problem with the circuit is that the use of the BJT inverts the signal. When the GPIO line is high the BJT is on and the MOSFET is off and vice versa. In other words, GPIO line high switches the motor off and low switches it on. This MOSFET can work with voltages up to 50V and currents of 40A. The 2N2222 can only work at 30V, or 40V in the case of the 2N2222A.

A third approach to controlling a unidirectional motor is to use half an H-bridge. Why this is so-called, and why you might want to do it, will become apparent in the next section on bidirectional motors. Half an H-bridge makes use of two complementary devices, either an NPN and a PNP BJT or an N- and P-type MOSFET.

133

For example:

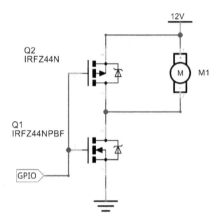

If the GPIO line is high then Q1 is on and Q2 off and the motor runs. If the GPIO line is low then Q1 is off and Q2 is on and the motor is braked – it has a resistance to rotating because of the back electromotive force (EMF) generated when the rotor turns. You probably need a BJT to feed the MOSFETs as selected.

Unidirectional PWM Motor Controller

A function to control the speed of a unidirectional motor is very simple. The speed is set by the duty cycle – the only parameter you have to choose in addition is the frequency. If you want an optimal controller then setting the frequency is a difficult task. Higher speeds make the motor run faster and quieter – but too high a frequency and the motor loses power and the driving transistor or MOSFET becomes hot and less efficient. The determining factor is the inductance of the motor's coil and any other components connected to it such as capacitors. In practice, PWM frequencies from 100Hz to 20kHz are commonly used, but in most cases 1kHz to 2kHz is a good choice.

How should we implement code to make motor control easy? A good pattern is to create an object which has fields that represent the state of the entity and methods to control it. For example, to implement a unidirectional motor we can create a Motor class:

```
class Motor:
    def __init__(self, pinNo):
        self.pwm1 = PWM(Pin(pinNo), freq=2000, duty_u16=0)
        self.gpio = pinNo
        self._on = False
        self.speed=0
```

134

You can see that this has all of the information needed to define the current state of a motor. All we need now are some functions to modify the fields and implement the changes to the state.

First we need a function to set the speed:

```
def setSpeed(self,s):
    self._on=True
    self.speed=s
    self.pwm1.duty_u16(int(65535*s/100))
```

and two functions to turn the motor on and off:

```
def off(self):
    self._on=False
    self.pwm1.duty_u16(0)
def on(self):
    self._on=True
    self.pwm1.duty_u16(int(65535*self.speed/100))
```

After this we can create and use a motor very easily. A full program complete with a demonstration is:

```
from machine import Pin, PWM
from time import sleep
class Motor:
    def __init__(self, pinNo):
        self.pwm1 = PWM(Pin(pinNo), freq=2000, duty_u16=0)
        self.gpio = pinNo
        self._on = False
        self.speed=0
    def setSpeed(self,s):
        self._on=True
        self.speed=s
        self.pwm1.duty_u16(int(65535*s/100))
    def off(self):
        self._on=False
        self.pwm1.duty_u16(0)
    def on(self):
        self._on=True
        self.pwm1.duty_u16(int(65535*self.speed/100))

motor=Motor(4)
sleep(1)
motor.setSpeed(50)
sleep(1)
motor.off()
sleep(1)
motor.setSpeed(90)
sleep(1)
motor.off()
```

This sets up a motor connected to GPIO4, sets it to 50% speed, pauses, turns it off, then on again at 90% and finally off.

Bidirectional Brushed Motor

If you want bidirectional control then you need to use an H-bridge:

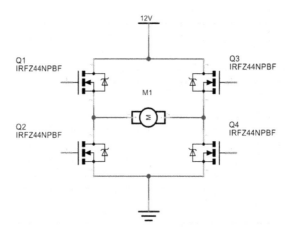

It is easy to see how this works. If Q1 and Q4 are the only MOSFETs on the motor, + is connected to 12V and – to ground. The motor runs in the forward direction. If Q2 and Q3 are the only MOSFETs on the motor, + is connected to ground and – is connected to 12V. The motor runs in the reverse direction. Of course, if none or any single one is on the motor is off. If Q1 and Q3, or Q2 and Q4, are on then the motor is braked as its windings are shorted out and the back EMF acts as a brake.

You can arrange to drive the four MOSFETs using four GPIO lines - just make sure that they switch on and off in the correct order. To make the bridge easier to drive, you can add a NOT gate to each pair so that you switch Q1/Q2 and Q3/ Q4 to opposite states.

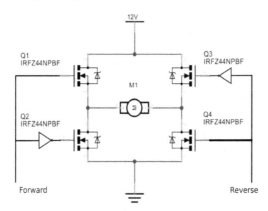

An alternative design is to use complementary MOSFETs:

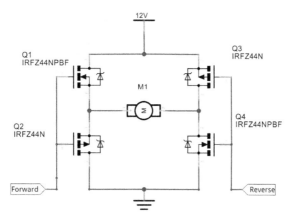

In this configuration, the first GPIO line drives the motor forward and the second drives it in reverse. The effect of setting the two lines is:

Forward	Reverse	Motor
Low	Low	Off
Low	High	Reverse
High	Low	Forward
High	High	Braked

You can also drive the GPIO lines for Forward/Reverse with a PWM signal and control the motor's speed as well as direction. If you use the MOSFETs shown in the diagram then you would also need a BJT to increase the drive voltage to each MOSFET, as in the unidirectional case. You also need to include diodes to deal with potential reverse voltage on each of the MOSFETs. The most important thing about an H-bridge is that Q1/Q2 and Q3/Q4 should never be on together – this would short circuit the power supply.

If working with four power BJTs or MOSFETs is more than you want to tackle, the good news is that there are chips that implement two H-bridges per device. You can also buy low-cost ready-made modules with one or more H-bridges. One of the most used devices is the L298 Dual H-bridge which works up to 46V and total DC current of 4A.

The block diagram of one of the two H-bridges shows exactly how it works:

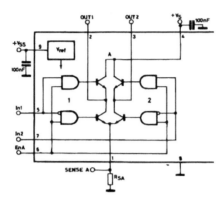

You can see that the bridge is made up of four BJTs and there are logic gates to allow IN1 and IN2 to select the appropriate pairs of devices. The only extras are AND gates and that the ENA (enable) line is used to switch all of the transistors off. The line shown as SENSE A can be used to detect the speed or load of the motor, but is rarely used.

A typical module based on the L298 can be seen below.

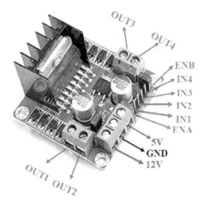

It is easier to describe how to use this sort of module with a single motor. The motor is connected to OUT1 and OUT2. Three GPIO lines are connected to ENA, IN1 and IN2. ENA is an enable line, which has to be high for the motor to run at all. IN1 and IN2 play the role of direction control lines – which one is forward and which is reverse depends on which way round you connect the motor. Putting a PWM signal onto ENA controls the speed of the motor and this allows IN1 and IN2 to be simple digital outputs.

Notice that the power connector shows 5V and 12V supplies, but most of these modules have a voltage regulator which will reduce the 12V to 5V.

In this case you don't have to supply a 5V connection. If you want to use more than 12V then the regulator has to be disconnected and you need to arrange for a separate 5V supply – check with the module's documentation. Notice that the transistors in the H-bridge have around a 2V drop, so using 12V results in just 10V being applied to the motor.

Another very popular H-bridge device is the SN754410 driver. This is suitable for smaller, lower-powered, motors and has two complete H-bridges. It can supply up to 1A per driver and work from 4.5 to 36V. It has the same set of control lines as the L298, i.e. each motor has a forward/reverse control line and an enable line. You don't have to use the enable line - it can be connected to +5V to allow PWM to be applied on the forward/reverse lines.

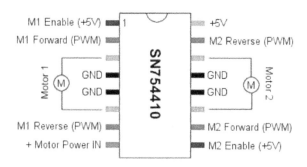

Bidirectional Motor Software

We can easily extend the Motor class and its methods to work with a bidirectional motor. The only real difference is that now we have to use two GPIO lines. For forward we activate the first GPIO line and for reverse we activate the second:

```
class BiMotor(Motor):
    def __init__(self, pinNo1,pinNo2):
        super().__init__(pinNo1)
        self.forward = True
        self.pwm2 = PWM(Pin(pinNo2),freq=2000,duty_u16=0)

    def setForward(self, forward):
        if self.forward == forward:
            return
        self.pwm1.duty_u16(0)
        self.pwm1, self.pwm2 = self.pwm2, self.pwm1
        self.forward = forward
        self.pwm1.duty_u16(int(65535 * self.speed / 100))
```

```
motor = BiMotor(2,4)
sleep(1)
motor.setSpeed(50)
sleep(1)
motor.setForward(False)
sleep(1)
motor.setSpeed(90)
sleep(1)
motor.setForward(True)
motor.off()
```

Notice that changing direction is just a matter of swapping pwm1 and pwm2 – only pwm1 is active and driving the motor.

This is a very basic set of functions, you can add others to improve motor control according to how sophisticated you want it to be. For example, a brake function would set both lines high for brake mode, or you could introduce limits on how fast the speed can be changed.

There are H-bridges that use two lines to control Phase and Enable (PWM). These map to the usual Forward, Reverse and Enable as shown below:

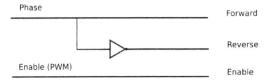

The disadvantage of this arrangement is that you cannot set Forward and Reverse to put the motor into brake mode. If you do have this sort of controller, anything based on the MAX14870/2 for example, then you can modify the functions to use a single PWM line and one standard GPIO line for speed and direction.

Using A Single Full H-Bridge As Two Half H-Bridges

It is easy to think of an H-bridge as being only for bidirectional control, but each full bridge is composed of two half bridges and this means a typical dual full H-bridge can control four unidirectional motors:

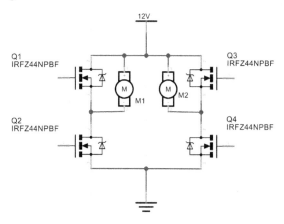

In this case Forward is now MotorM1 speed control and Reverse is now MotorM2 speed control. Any enable line has to be set high to allow the two motors to be controlled. You can make use of this arrangement with the unidirectional software given earlier.

Controlling a Servo

Hobby servos, of the sort used in radio control models, are very cheap and easy to use and they connect via a standard PWM protocol. Servos are not drive motors, but positioning motors. That is, they don't rotate at a set speed, they move to a specified angle or position.

A servo is a motor, usually a brushed DC motor, with a feedback sensor for position, usually a simple variable resistor (potentiometer) connected to the shaft. The output is usually via a set of gears which reduces the rotation rate and increases the torque. The motor turns the gears, and hence the shaft, until the potentiometer reaches the desired setting and hence the shaft has the required angle/position.

A basic servo has just three connections, ground, a power line and a signal line. The colors used vary, but the power line is usually red, ground is usually black or brown and the signal line is white, yellow or orange. If a standard J-connector is fitted then the wire nearest the notch, pin 3, is Signal, the middle wire, pin 2, is 5V and outer wire, pin 1, is Ground.

The power wire has to be connected to a 5V supply capable of providing enough current to run the motor - anything up to 500mA or more depending on the servo. The good news is that the servo's signal line generally needs very little current, although it does, in theory, need to be switched between 0V and 5V using a PWM signal.

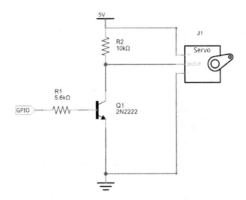

You can assume that the signal line needs to be driven as a voltage load and so the appropriate way to drive the servo is:

◆   The servo's + line needs to be connected to an external 5V power supply.

◆   The 10K resistor R1 can be a lot larger for most servos - 47K often works. The 5.6K resistor limits the base current to slightly less than 0.5mA.

Notice, however, that if you are using a single BJT driver, like the one shown above, the input is inverted.

This is the correct way to drive a servo, but in nearly all cases you can drive the servo signal line directly from the 3.3V GPIO line with a 1K resistor to limit the current if anything goes wrong with the servo. Some servos will even work with their motor connected to 3.3V, but at much reduced torque.

Now all we have to do is set the PWM line to produce 20ms pulses with pulse widths ranging from 0.5ms to 2.5ms – i.e. a duty cycle of 2.5 to 12.5%.

Once again, it is easier to use a class to represent the current state of a servo and create methods to change the state:

```
from machine import Pin, PWM
from time import sleep
class Servo:
    def __init__(self, pinNo):
        self.pwm = PWM(Pin(pinNo),freq=50,
                             duty_u16= int(65535*2.5/100))
    def setPosition(self, p):
        self.position = p
        self.pwm.duty_u16(int(65535*p/1000 + 65535*2.5/100))
    def off(self):
        self.pwm.deinit()
servo=Servo(4)
sleep(1)
servo.setPosition(100.0)
sleep(1)
servo.setPosition(50.0)
sleep(1)
servo.setPosition(0)
sleep(1)
servo.off()
```

Notice that we set the frequency to 50Hz. If you want to work with a non-standard servo you can change this or make it settable. The setPosition function sets the position in terms of percentages. That is, setPosition(50) sets the servo to the middle of its range. This assumes that the servo has a standard positioning range and most don't. In practice, to get the best out of a servo you need to calibrate each servo and discover what range of movement is supported. The main program creates a Servo object on GPIO4 and then moves the servo to its maximum, middle and minimum positions.

If you run the program using the transistor circuit given earlier, you will discover that the servo does nothing at all, apart perhaps from vibrating. The reason is that the transistor voltage driver is an inverter. When the PWM line is high, the transistor is fully on and the servo's pulse line is effectively grounded. When the PWM line is low, the transistor is fully off and the servo's pulse line is pulled high by the resistor. The solution is to invert the duty cycle from 2.5 to 12.5% to 100-2.5% to 100-12.5%:

```
 self.pwm.duty_u16(int(65535-65535*p/1000 - 65535*2.5/100))
```

It is worth mentioning that servos make good low-cost DC motors, complete with gearboxes. All you have to do is open the servo, unsolder the motor from the control circuits and solder two wires to the motor. If you want to use the forward/reverse electronics you can remove the end stops on the gearbox, usually on the large gearwheel, and replace the potentiometer with a pair of equal value resistors, 2.2kΩ, say.

Brushless DC Motors

Brushless DC motors are more expensive than brushed DC motors, but they are superior in many ways. They don't fail because of commutator or brush wear and need no maintenance. They provide maximum rotational torque at all points of the rotation and generally provide more power for the same size and weight. They can also be controlled more precisely. The only negative points are higher cost and slightly more complex operation. In practice, it is usually better to use a brushed DC motor unless you really need something extra.

A brushless DC motor is basically a brushed motor turned inside out – the stator is a set of electromagnets and the rotor is a set of permanent magnets. In some designs the permanent magnets are inside the stator in the manner of a brushed motor, an inrunner, and sometimes the magnets are outside of the stator, an outrunner.

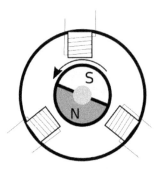

An inrunner – the permanent magnets form the rotor and the coils are switched to attract.

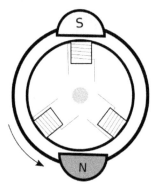

An outrunner – the permanent magnets are on the outside of the stator and the whole cover rotates.

A brushless motor works in exactly the same way as a brushed motor. As the coils are stationary there is no need for a mechanical commutator, but there is still need for commutation – the coils have to be switched on in sequence to create a rotating magnetic field which pulls the rotor around with it. This means that you have to implement an electronic commutator, which is another name for a brushless DC motor.

An electronic commutator has to sense the position of the rotor and change the magnetic field generated by the stator to keep the rotor moving. Brushless motors differ in the number of magnets they have and the number of phases. The most common is a three-phase motor as these are used in radio control modeling. Essentially you need at least a driver for each of the phases and a GPIO line to generate the signal. In practice, you need two drivers for each phase and they have to be driven from a dual supply so that the magnetic field can be positive, zero or negative.

This would be possible to do with software, but it isn't easy and a more reasonable alternative is to buy a ready-built controller. There are two types of brushless motor – with Hall sensors and without. The former are more expensive, but easier to control because the electronics always knows where the rotor is and can apply the correct drive. The ones without sensors are controlled by measuring the back EMF from the motor and this is much harder. Most of the lower-cost speed controllers need motors with Hall sensors.

The radio control community has taken to using three-phase brushless motors and this has resulted in a range of motors and controllers at reasonable prices intended as high-power, high-speed, unidirectional motors for use in quadcopters and model planes.

If you can live with their limitations they provide a good way to couple the ESP32 to a brushless motor. In this case all you need is a three-phase brushless motor of the sort used in RC modeling and an ESC (Electronic Speed Controller) of the sort shown below:

The three leads on the left go to the three phases of the motor and the red and black leads on the right go to a power supply – often a LiPo battery. The small three-wire connector in the middle is a standard servo connector and you can use it exactly as if the brushless motor was a servo, with a few exceptions. The first is that pin 2 supplies 5V rather than accepts it. Don't connect this to anything unless you want a 5V supply. The second problem is that ESCs are intelligent. When you first apply power they beep and can be programmed into different modes by changing the PWM signal from Max to Min. Also, to use an ESC you have to arm it. This is to avoid radio control modelers from being injured by motors that start unexpectedly when the power is applied. The most common arming sequence is for the ESC to beep when power is applied. You then have to set the PWM to Min, when the ESC will beep again. After a few moments you will have control of the motor.

The need for an arming procedure should alert you to the fact that these model motors are very powerful. Don't try working with one loose on the bench as it will move fast if switched on and at the very least make a twisted mess of your wires. Most importantly of all, don't run a motor with anything attached to it until you have everything under control.

Stepper Motors

There is one sort of brushless motor that is easy to use and low cost – the stepper motor. This differs from a standard brushless motor in that it isn't designed for continuous high-speed rotation. A stepper motor has an arrangement of magnets and coils such that powering some of the coils holds the rotor in a particular position. Changing which coils are activated makes the rotor turn until it is aligned with the coils and stops moving. Thus the stepper motor moves the rotor in discrete steps. This makes driving it much simpler, but note it doesn't use PWM for speed control.

Stepper motors have no brushes and so don't wear out as fast as brushed motors. They also have roughly the same torque at any speed and can be used at low speeds without a gearbox. They can remain in a fixed position for a long time without burning out, as DC motors would. Unlike a servo, however, if a stepper motor is mechanically forced to a new position, it will not return to its original position when released. The only disadvantage of a stepper motor is that the continuous rotation produced by repeated stepping can make the motor vibrate.

Stepper motors vary in the size of step they use – typically 1.8 degrees giving 200 steps per rotation, although gearing can be used to reduce the step size. Another big difference is that the rotor is made up of either permanent magnets or soft iron. The first type is called a Permanent Magnet or PM stepper and the second is called a Variable Reluctance or VR and they differ in how you drive them with PM steppers being easier to understand. There are also hybrid steppers which share the good characteristics of both PM and VR stepper motors. These are more expensive and are generally only used where accuracy of positioning is important. They also differ in the number of phases, i.e. independent banks of coils, they have.

The diagram below shows a two-phase PM motor with Phase 1 activated:

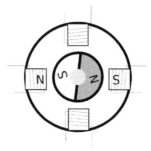

If Phase two is activated, the rotor turns through 90 degrees. This is the simplest stepper motor you can make.

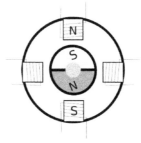

A typical stepper motor will have many more coils than four, but they are usually connected into two or three phases.

Another big difference is bipolar versus unipolar. A bipolar motor is like the one shown in the diagram. To generate a north pole the current has to flow in the opposite direction to when you want to create a south pole. This means you have to drive each bank of coils with a bidirectional driver, e.g. an H-bridge. A unipolar motor has two windings, one in each direction, and both windings can be driven by a unidirectional driver – one giving a north pole and the other a south pole. Notice that a unipolar motor has twice the number of coils to drive and the switching sequence is slightly different.

A two-phase bipolar motor with Phases A and B would switch on in the sequence:

A → B → A- → B- → A etc

where the minus sign means the current flows the other way.

A two-phase unipolar motor has two coils per phase, A1, A2 and B1, B2 with the 1 and 2 windings creating opposite magnetic fields for the same current flow. Now the sequence is:

A1 → B1 → A2 → B2 → A1 etc

and all driven in the same direction.

Switching single phases fully on and off in sequence makes the motor make repeated steps. You can also switch on more than one phase at a time to generate micro-steps. For example, in our two-phase example, switching on two phases makes the rotor settle between the two, so producing a half micro-step:

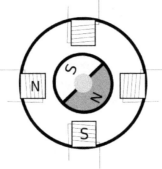

The driving sequence for a two-phase bipolar motor is:

A → AB →B → BA- → A- → A- B- → B- → AB- → A

with minus indicating that the coil is energized in the opposite direction, giving a total of eight, rather than four, steps.

You can even vary the current through the coils and move the rotor to intermediate positions. At the extreme limit you can vary the current sinusoidally and produce a smooth rotation. Micro-stepping is smoother and can eliminate buzzing. For high accuracy positioning, micro-stepping is a poor performer under load.

Stepper Motor Driver

How best to drive a stepper motor using an ESP32? There are some specialized chips that work with unipolar and bipolar stepper motors. However, you can easily control a bipolar stepper motor using one the H-bridges described in the section on directional motor control.

For example, using complementary MOSFETS:

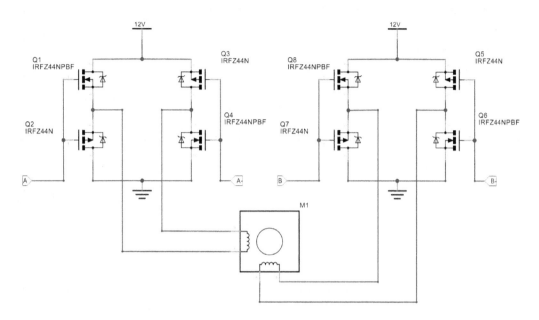

You can use a dual H-bridge module in the same way if you don't want to build it from scratch. The motor has to be a bipolar two-phase motor, often called a four-wire stepper motor. You can see that for this arrangement you need four GPIO lines, A, A-, B and B-.

What about driving the dual H-bridge using software? You need four GPIO lines and you need to pulse them in a specific phase to make the motor rotate. The first question to answer is how to specify the four GPIO lines to be used. As we will see, there is a big advantage and simplification in using a block of four consecutive lines. The reason is that we can easily set the bits corresponding to these lines in a mask and so set them in a single operation. In this case we simply record the number of the numerically lowest GPIO line GPIOn and assume that a block of four GPIO lines are allocated

GPIOn → A, GPIOn+1 → A-, GPIOn+2 → B and GPIOn+3 → B-.

As before, we use a class to record the current state of the motor and its methods:

```python
from machine import Pin, mem32
from time import sleep_ms
class StepperBi4():
    def __init__(self, pinA):
        self.phase = 0
        self.pinA = pinA
        self.gpios = tuple([Pin(pinA, Pin.OUT),
                            Pin(pinA + 1, Pin.OUT),
                            Pin(pinA + 2, Pin.OUT),
                            Pin(pinA + 3, Pin.OUT)])
        self.gpios[0].on()
        self.gpioMask = 0xF << self.pinA
        self.halfstepSeq = [0x1, 0x5, 0x4, 0x6, 0x2, 0xA, 0x8, 0x9]

    #   [           B- B -A  A
    #              [0, 0, 0, 1],
    #              [0, 1, 0, 1],
    #              [0, 1, 0, 0],
    #              [0, 1, 1, 0],
    #              [0, 0, 1, 0],
    #              [1, 0, 1, 0],
    #              [1, 0, 0, 0],
    #              [1, 0, 0, 1]
    #   ]
    #   change 0x3FF44004 to 0x60004004 for an S3
    def _gpio_set(self, value, mask):
        mem32[0x3FF44004] = mem32[0x3FF44004] & ~mask | \
                                                value & mask

    def setPhase(self, phase):
        value = self.halfstepSeq[phase] << self.pinA
        self._gpio_set(value, self.gpioMask)
        self.phase = phase

    def stepForward(self):
        self.phase = (self.phase + 1) % 8
        self.setPhase(self.phase)

    def stepReverse(self):
        self.phase = (self.phase - 1) % 8
        self.setPhase(self.phase)

step = StepperBi4(16)
step.setPhase(0)

while True:
    step.stepForward()
    sleep_ms(1)
```

You can see that the List halfstepSeq is just the hex value corresponding to the binary representation of which line is high and which is low in each state. The bits correspond to the GPIO lines such that the low order bits control the lowest numbered GPIO line.

The setPhase function uses the _gpio_set function given earlier to change only the GPIO lines we are using to the bit pattern in the stepTable for the specified phase. Remember to change 0x3FF44004 to 0x60004004 for an S3 The stepForward and stepReverse simply move down or up in the phase table, making sure to go back to the start when the end is reached. This is what the modulus operator, %, does for us and phase follows the sequence 0,1,2,3,4,5,6,7,0,1 and so on.

You can see that if GPIO16 is A, GPIO17 is A-, GPIO18 is B and GPIO19 is B- and stepping through the stepTable gives the sequence given earlier:

A → AB → B → BA- → A- → A-B- → B- → AB- → A

If you are using the Arduino Nano ESP32 then use pins GPIO5 to GPIO8.

You can use a full step table if you want to as long as you remember to work in mod 4 rather than 8:

```
self.stepSeq =[0x1,0x2,0x4,0x8]
    #    [              B- B -A  A
    #                  [0, 0, 0, 1],
    #                  [0, 1, 0, 0],
    #                  [0, 0, 1, 0],
    #                  [1, 0, 0, 0],
    #    ]
```

Of course, these are identical to the odd elements of the half step table so we can achieve the same result by using that table but increasing the increment by 2 instead of 1:

```
    def stepForward(self):
        self.phase=(self.phase+2) % 8
        self.setPhase(self.phase)

    def stepReverse(self):
        self.phase=(self.phase-2) % 8
        self.setPhase(self.phase)
```

To try either version of the program you need an H-bridge connected so that GPIO16 is A, GPIO17 is A-, GPIO18 is B and GPIO19 is B-. The maximum stepping speed, i.e. with no timer delay, is such that a 200-step motor, i.e. 400 half steps, will rotate in 400*0.06 ms= 0.024 s, i.e. 2500rpm, which is too fast for most stepper motors. In practice include delays to slow things down to a few hundred rpm.

If you are using one of the many dual H-bridge modules then the wiring is as shown below:

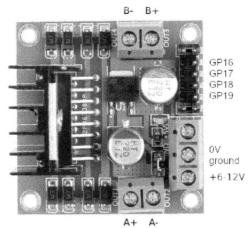

If you are using the Arduino Nano ESP32 then use pins GPIO5 to GPIO8.

Notice that you have to connect the ground of the power supply and the ESP32's ground together. It is also a good idea to use a power supply with a current trip when first trying things out.

The outputs are as you would expect for a half-stepping motor:

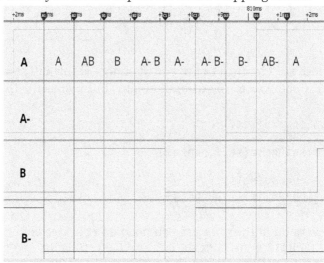

Stepper Motor Rotation – Using Timers

Most of the time you use a stepper motor to move to a given position by executing an exact number of steps. If you do want to make a stepper motor rotate then you need to arrange to step at a regular rate. The simplest way to do this is to use a timer interrupt.

To make the motor rotate on its own we need a timer interrupt handler:

```
def _doRotate(self,timer):
    if self.forward:
        self.stepForward()
    else:
        self.stepReverse()
```

You can see that this function simply steps the motor forward or backward depending on the setting of the forward attribute.

To make this work we need a function to set up the timer interrupt:

```
def rotate(self, forward, speed):
    self.forward = forward
    self.speed = speed
    if speed == 0:
        self.timer.deinit()
        self.timer = None
        return
    if self.timer == None:
        self.timer = Timer(0)
    self.timer.init(freq=speed, mode=Timer.PERIODIC,
                                callback=self.doRotate)
```

The speed is specified in half steps per second. So setting speed to 200 gives a step rate of 200 half steps per second, i.e. 5ms per step or a rotation of 30rpm. Notice that we have to deal with a speed of zero differently by removing the timer. We also have to check that there isn't already a timer allocated – if there is we just use it. We also need some additional attributes:

```
self.forward = True
self.speed = 0
```

A main program to rotate the motor for 500ms at 10ms per step, i.e. 0.25rpm and then stop it for another 500ms is:

```
step = StepperBi4(16)
step.setPhase(0)
while True:
    step.rotate(True,100)
    sleep_ms(500)
    step.rotate(True,0)
    sleep_ms(500)
```

153

Notice that when the motor is stopped the phase is still active and so the motor holds its position under power:

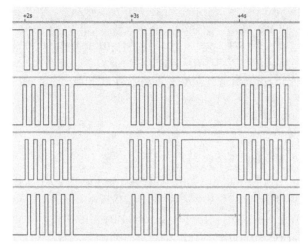

You can elaborate on this basic scheme to include more complex controls on the motor's behavior, including things like allowing it to freewheel and selecting full or half stepping.

The complete program including the timer interrupt handling is:

```
from machine import Pin, mem32, Timer
from time import sleep_ms
class StepperBi4():
    def __init__(self, pinA):
        self.phase = 0
        self.pinA = pinA
        self.gpios = tuple([Pin(pinA, Pin.OUT),
                            Pin(pinA + 1, Pin.OUT),
                            Pin(pinA + 2, Pin.OUT),
                            Pin(pinA + 3, Pin.OUT)])
        self.gpios[0].on()
        self.gpioMask = 0xF << self.pinA
        self.halfstepSeq = [0x1, 0x3, 0x2, 0x6, 0x4, 0xC, 0x8, 0x9]
        self.timer = None
        self.forward = True
        #    [
        #                [0,0,0,1],
        #                [0,0,1,1],
        #                [0,0,1,0],
        #                [0,1,1,0],
        #                [0,1,0,0],
        #                [1,1,0,0],
        #                [1,0,0,0],
        #                [1,0,0,1]
        #    ]
```

```
        #   change 0x3FF44004 to 0x60004004 for an S3
        def _gpio_set(self,value, mask):
            mem32[0x3FF44004] = mem32[0x3FF44004] & ~mask |
                                               value & mask

        def setPhase(self, phase):
            value = self.halfstepSeq[phase] << self.pinA
            self._gpio_set(value, self.gpioMask)
            self.phase = phase


        def stepForward(self):
            self.phase = (self.phase + 1) % 8
            self.setPhase(self.phase)


        def stepReverse(self):
            self.phase = (self.phase - 1) % 8
            self.setPhase(self.phase)

        def doRotate(self, timer):
            if self.forward:
                self.stepForward()
            else:
                self.stepReverse()

        def rotate(self, forward, speed):
            self.forward = forward
            self.speed = speed
            if speed == 0:
                self.timer.deinit()
                self.timer = None
                return
            if self.timer == None:
                self.timer = Timer(0)
            self.timer.init(freq = speed, mode = Timer.PERIODIC,
                                        callback = self.doRotate)


step=StepperBi4(16)
step.setPhase(0)
while True:
    step.rotate(True,100)
    sleep_ms(500)
    step.rotate(True,0)
    sleep_ms(500)
```

Summary

- There are a number of different types of electric motor, but DC brushed or brushless motors are the most used in the IoT.

- Brushed motors can be speed controlled using a single transistor driver and a PWM signal.

- For bidirectional control you need an H-bridge. In this case you need two PWM signals.

- Servo motors set their position in response to the duty cycle of a PWM signal.

- Brushless DC motors are very powerful and best controlled using off-the-shelf electronic modules. They are very powerful and thus dangerous if used incorrectly. They can be driven using a simple PWM signal.

- Stepper motors are a special case of a Brushless DC motor. They move in discrete steps in response to energizing different coils.

- A unipolar motor has coils that can be driven in the same direction for every step. A bipolar motor has coils that need to be driven in reverse for some steps.

- Bipolar motors need two H-bridges to operate and four GPIO lines.

- You can easily create a stepper motor driver using four GPIO lines.

Chapter 10

Getting Started With The SPI Bus

The Serial Peripheral Interface (SPI) bus can be something of a problem because it doesn't have a well-defined standard that every device conforms to. Even so, if you only want to work with one specific device it is usually easy to find a configuration that works - as long as you understand what the possibilities are.

SPI Bus Basics

The SPI bus is commonly encountered as it is used to connect all sorts of devices from LCD displays, through realtime clocks to A-to-D converters, but as different companies have implemented it in different ways, you have to work harder to implement it in any particular case. However, it does usually work, which is a surprise for a bus with no standard, or clear, specification.

The reason it can be made to work is that you can specify a range of different operating modes, frequencies and polarities. This makes the bus slightly more complicated to use, but generally it is a matter of looking up how the device you are trying to work with implements the SPI bus and then getting the ESP32 to work in the same way.

The SPI bus is odd in another way - it does not use bidirectional serial connections. There is a data line for the data to go from the master to the slave and a separate data line from the slave back to the master. That is, instead of a single data line that changes its transfer direction, there is one for data going out and one for data coming in. It is also worth knowing that the drive on the SPI bus is push-pull and not open-collector/drain. This provides higher speed and more noise protection as the bus is driven in both directions.

In the configuration most used for the ESP32, there is a single master and, at most, two slaves. The signal lines are:

- ◆ MOSI (Master Output Slave Input), i.e. data to the slave
- ◆ MISO (Master Input Slave Output), i.e. data to the master
- ◆ SCLK (Serial Clock), which is always generated by the master

In general, there can also be any number of SS (Slave Select), CE (Chip Enable) or CS (Chip Select) lines, which are usually set low to select which slave is being addressed. Notice that unlike other buses, I2C for example, there are no SPI commands or addresses, only bytes of data. However, slave devices do interpret some of the data as commands to do something or send some particular data.

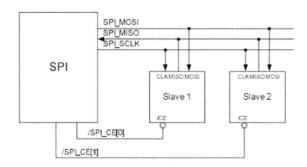

There are two other modes of operation of the SPI interface – bidirectional and LoSSI mode. The bidirectional mode simply uses a single data line, MIMO, for both input and output. The direction of the line is determined by writing a command to the slave. LoSSI mode is used to communicate with sophisticated peripherals such as LCD panels. Both of these are unsupported and beyond the scope of this chapter. However, once you know how standard mode works, the other two are simple variations.

The data transfer on the SPI bus is also slightly odd. What happens is that the master pulls one of the chip selects low, which activates a slave. Then the master toggles the clock SCLK and both the master and the slave send a single bit on their respective data lines. After eight clock pulses, a byte has been transferred from the master to the slave and from the slave to the master. You can think of this as being implemented as a circular buffer, although it doesn't have to be.

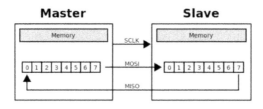

This full-duplex data transfer is often hidden by the software and the protocol used. For example, there is a read function that reads data from the slave and sends zeros or data that is ignored by the slave. Similarly, there is

158

a write function that sends valid data, but ignores whatever the slave sends. The transfer is typically in groups of eight bits, usually most significant bit first, but this isn't always the case. In general, as long as the master supplies clock pulses, data is transferred.

Notice this circular buffer arrangement allows for slaves to be daisy-chained with the output of one going to the input of the next. This makes the entire chain one big circular shift register. This can make it possible to have multiple devices with only a single chip select, but it also means any commands sent to the slaves are received by each one in turn. For example, you could send a convert command to each A-to-D converter in turn and receive back results from each one.

The final odd thing about the SPI bus is that there are four modes which define the relationship between the data timing and the clock pulse. The clock can be either active high or low, which is referred to as clock polarity (CPOL), and data can be sampled on the rising or falling edge of the clock, which is clock phase (CPHA).

All combinations of these two possibilities gives the four modes:

SPI Mode*	Clock Polarity CPOL	Clock Phase CPHA	Characteristics
0	0	0	Clock active high data output on falling edge and sampled on rising
1	0	1	Clock active high data output on rising edge and sampled on falling
2	1	0	Clock active low data output on falling edge and sampled on rising
3	1	1	Clock active low data output on rising edge and sampled on falling

*The way that the SPI modes are labeled is common but not universal.

There is often a problem trying to work out what mode a slave device uses. The clock polarity is usually easy and the Clock phase can sometimes be worked out from the data transfer timing diagrams and:

◆ First clock transition in the middle of a data bit means CPHA=0

◆ First clock transition at the start of a data bit means CPHA=1

So to configure the SPI bus to work with a particular slave device:

1. Select the clock frequency - anything from 125MHz to 3.8kHz

2. Determine the CS polarity - active high or low

3. Set the clock mode Mode0 thru Mode3

Now we have to find out how to do this using MicroPython.

ESP32 SPI Interfaces

The ESP32 has four SPI controllers. SPI0 is used internally for memory access and isn't available. SPI1 can act as a master and SPI2 and SPI3 can be masters or slaves. MicroPython allows you to to use SPI2 and SPI3 so you effectively have access to two SPI controllers.

To add to the confusion SPI2 and SPI3 are MicroPython's SPI channels 1 and 2 respectively. They are also called HSPI and VSPI and while they can be connected to any GPIO pins there is a speed advantage in allowing them to work with their default pins. The reason is that the SPI hardware is connected directly to the defaults but goes via a multiplexer to other GPIO lines. As a result the default pins work at higher frequencies. The default pins can work up to 80MHz but a general GPIO line can only work at 40MHz. This isn't true for the ESP32-S3.

Default GPIO Pins		
	SPI2 HSPI id=1	SPI3 VSPI id=2
SCLK	14	18
MOSI	13	23
MISO	12	19

For a full SPI interface you need to use one pin for MISO, one for MOSI and one for SCLK. The CSn lines are not really part of the SPI implementation. To make use of them you have to treat them like standard GPIO lines and set them high and low to select the device under program control. What this means is that you can use as many of the CSn lines with any SPI interface as you need.

You can make use of the hardware SPI implementation via the `machine.SPI` object.

There is also a software implementation of the SPI protocol in the form of the `machine.SoftSPI` object. This has all of the same methods as the hardware implemented SPI object. If possible make use of the hardware based SPI object as it minimizes CPU load, but if you run out of SPI controllers then you could make use of the software SPI object which works with any selection of pins. In the rest of the chapter the hardware SPI object is used, but the modifications to use `SoftSPI` are minor.

The SPI Functions

Before you can make use of the SPI methods you have to import the SPI module:

```
from machine import SPI
```

and you have to create an SPI object:

```
spi=SPI(n)
```

where n is 1 or 2 to select one of the two SPI controllers. You can also include parameters that are used in the initialization method to the constructor. If you don't, the SPI controller keeps the last configuration it was used in.

The SPI methods can be grouped into initialization and data transfer.

Initialization

There is an init method that can be used to set up the hardware:

```
SPI.init(baudrate=1000000, polarity=0, phase=0, bits=8,
            firstbit=SPI.MSB, sck=None, mosi=None, miso=None)
```

The mode is set by specifying polarity and phase using:

phase = 0   Data latched on first clock transition
phase = 1   Data latched on second clock transition
together with:

polarity = 0 Clock active high
polarity = 1 Clock active low

You have to specify the pins used for sck, mosi and miso in the constructor and these have to be Pin objects, not just GPIO numbers.

You can use the:

```
SPI.deinit()
```

function to turn off the SPI bus you have been using.

Data Transfer

Because of the way the SPI bus uses a full-duplex transfer, things are a little different from other buses when it comes to implementing functions to transfer data. The most basic transfer function is:

```
SPI.write_readinto(write_buf, read_buf)
```

The buffers are byte arrays and they have to be of the same length. The write_buf is sent byte-by-byte as data is read into the read_buf at the same time. If you don't understand this idea of a send (source) and a receive (destination) byte array then see the discussion about how SPI works given earlier.

Notice that a call to any of the transfer functions is blocking, i.e. the function doesn't return until the transfer is complete. There is also no need for a timeout as all SPI transfers end after the number of clock pulses needed to transfer the specified data. Also all of the transfer functions return the number of elements read/written.

If you are only interesting in reading or writing data then you can use:

```
SPI.read(nbytes, write = 0)
```

```
SPI.readinto(buf, write = 0)
```

The read function returns a byte array with `nbytes` elements. The `readinto` function uses the specified buffer and reads data until it is full. Both send the byte specified by `write` as the data to the slave. Finally you can send data using:

```
SPI.write(buf)
```

In the case of the write function, the received data is simply discarded.

There is one final complication that you can mostly ignore. The SPI hardware is buffered. Both the MISO and MOSI connections have an 8-deep FIFO buffer and this means that you can send and receive data faster if the buffer isn't full or empty. Unfortunately, MicroPython doesn't provide any way to find the state of the buffer.

Using the Data Transfer Functions

When you first start using SPI it can be difficult to get used to the idea that you send and receive data both at the same time. Indeed, you cannot receive data unless you send the same number of data elements.

The most basic of the transfer functions is `spi.write_readinto` and it makes the bidirectional transfer obvious. For example:

```
read = bytearray(3)
write = bytearray('ABC','utf-8')
spi.write_readinto(write,read)
```

This sends the three elements in `write` and receives back three elements in `read`. Whether the three elements in `read` make any sense is a matter of what the slave sends back and they may be of no interest at all. If this is the case, you might as well use:

```
write = bytearray('ABC','utf-8')
spi.write(write)
```

Whatever three elements the slave sends back are simply ignored.

In the same way, if what you transmit to the slave isn't of any interest, you could use:

```
read = bytearray(3)
SPI.readinto(read, write = 0)
```

This reads three bytes into read while sending three null bytes to the slave. Alternatively you could use:

```
read = spi.read(3, write = 0)
```

which returns a three-element byte array while sending null bytes to the slave.

Now we come to a subtle point. What is the difference between transferring multiple bytes and simply sending the bytes individually using multiple transfer calls? The answer is that each time you make a transfer call the chip select line should be activated, the data transferred and then deactivated. Using the buffer transfers, the chip select can be left active for the entire transfer, i.e. it isn't necessary to deactivate it between each byte. Sometimes this difference isn't important and you can transfer three bytes using three calls, or just one, to a transfer function. However, some slaves will abort the current multibyte operation if the chip select line is deactivated in the middle of a multibyte transfer. As MicroPython requires you to activate and deactivate the chip select line manually, it is up to you to make the distinction between single and multibyte transfers.

It is important to realize that the nature of the transfer is that the first element is sent at the same time that the first element is received. That is, unlike other protocols, the whole of the send buffer isn't sent before the received data comes back. The entire transfer works a data element at a time – the first element is sent while the first element is being received, then the second element is sent at the same time as the second element is being received and so on. Not fully understanding this idea can lead to some interesting bugs.

A Loopback Example

Because of the way that data is transferred on the SPI bus, it is very easy to test that everything is working without having to add any components. All you have to do is connect MOSI to MISO so that anything sent is also received in a loopback mode.

First we have to select which pins to use and, as this is fairly arbitrary at this stage, we might as well use:

```
SPI2    MISO    GPIO12
        MOSI    GPIO13
        SCLK    GPIO14
```

We can ignore the CS line at the moment as it isn't used in a loopback.

First, connect GPIO12 to GPIO13 (Nano ESP32 pins A5 and A2) using a jumper wire and start a new project.

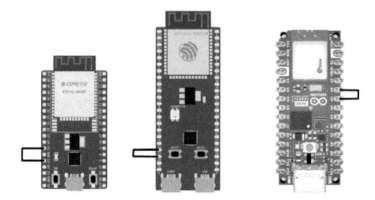

The program is very simple. First we initialize the SPI bus to use SPI1 and pins GPIO12, GPIO13 and GPIO14.

```
spi=SPI(1,sck=Pin(14),miso=Pin(12),mosi=Pin(13))
```

Next we configure the interface:

```
spi.init(baudrate=500_000,bits=8, polarity=0,
                         phase=0,firstbit=SPI.MSB)
```

We are using 8-bit data and SPI mode 0.

Check that the received data matches the sent data:

```
read = bytearray(3)
write = bytearray([0xAA,0xAA,0xAA])
spi.write_readinto(write,read)
print(read,write)
```

The hex value AA is useful in testing because it generates the bit sequence 10101010 which is easy to see on a logic analyzer. Finally we close the bus:

```
spi.deinit()
```

Putting all of this together gives us the complete program:

```
from machine import Pin, SPI
spi=SPI(1,sck=Pin(14),miso=Pin(12),mosi=Pin(13))
spi.init(baudrate=500_000,bits=8,
polarity=0,phase=0,firstbit=SPI.MSB )
read = bytearray(3)
write = bytearray([0xAA,0xAA,0xAA])
spi.write_readinto(write,read)
print(read,write)
spi.deinit()
```

If you run the program and don't get any data received back then the most likely reason is that you have connected the wrong two pins or not connected them at all.

If you connect a logic analyzer to the three GPIO lines involved you will see the data transfer:

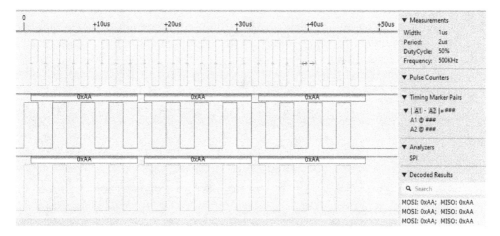

Notice that the clock is active high and the data is valid on its rising edge.

Using the CS Line

Of course there is no CS line activity on the logic analyzer because, unlike many SPI implementations, MicroPython doesn't automatically control the CS line. It is up to you to initialize a CS line as a standard GPIO line and set it as appropriate during the data transfer.

For example, let's add GPIO4:

```
SPI2    MISO    GPIO12
        MOSI    GPIO13
        SCLK    GPIO14
        CS      GPIO4
```

Notice that there is no real reason to use GPIO4 (Nano ESP32 A3), any of the output GPIO lines would do.

Using CS active low we first have to initialize the GPIO line to output and set it high:

```
CS = Pin(4,Pin.OUT)
CS.on()
```

Now we can use the CS line to activate the slave by setting it low before starting the transfer and then setting it back high again afterwards:

```
CS.off()
spi.write_readinto(write,read)
CS.on()
```

If you try this out you might notice that there is a problem if you examine what is happening. The setting of the CS line low occurs about $163\mu s$ before the first data or clock bit and the setting back to low occurs around $61\mu s$ after the final clock pulse.

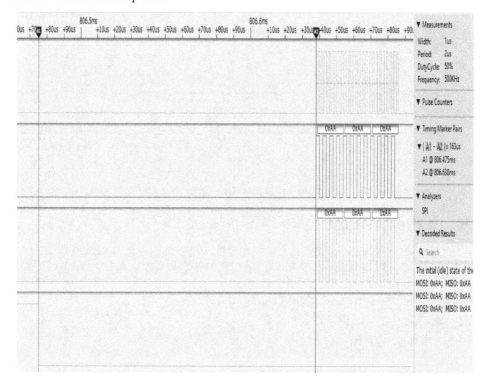

This very long delay is only on the first data sent and it represents the setup time for the SPI hardware. If you send subsequent data then the start lag is 37μs and the end lag is 47μs which is much better but still long compared to the clock speed.

For many devices this over-long CS pulse doesn't make any difference, but it slows down how fast you can send data using the Bus.

The MCP3008 SPI ADC

An alternative to using the ESP32's built-in ADC is to use an external chip. The MCP3000 family is a low-cost versatile SPI-based set of A-to-D converters. Although the MCP3008, with eight analog inputs at 10-bit precision, and the MCP3004, with four analog inputs at 10-bit precision, are the best known, there are other devices in the family, including ones with 12-bit and 13-bit precision and differential inputs, at around the same sort of cost - $1 to $2.

In this chapter the MCP3008 is used because it is readily available and provides a good performance at low cost, but the other devices in the family work in the same way and could be easily substituted.

The MCP3008 is available in a number of different packages but the standard 16-pin PDIP is the easiest to work with using a prototyping board. You can buy it from the usual sources including Amazon, see Resources on this book's webpage. Its pinouts are fairly self-explanatory:

```
CH0 ▭ 1        16 ▭ V_DD
CH1 ▭ 2        15 ▭ V_REF
CH2 ▭ 3    M   14 ▭ AGND
CH3 ▭ 4    C   13 ▭ CLK
CH4 ▭ 5    P   12 ▭ D_OUT
CH5 ▭ 6    3   11 ▭ D_IN
CH6 ▭ 7    0   10 ▭ CS/SHDN
CH7 ▭ 8    0    9 ▭ DGND
           8
```

You can see that the analog inputs are on the left and the power and SPI bus connections are on the right. The conversion accuracy is claimed as 10 bits, but how many of these bits correspond to reality and how many are noise depends on how you design the layout of the circuit.

You need to take great care if you need high accuracy. For example, you will notice that there are two voltage inputs, VDD and VREF. VDD is the supply voltage that runs the chip and VREF is the reference voltage that is used to compare the input voltage. Obviously, if you want highest accuracy, VREF, which has to be lower than or equal to VDD, should be set by an accurate low-noise voltage source. However, in most applications VREF and VDD are simply connected together and the usual, low- quality, supply voltage is used as the reference. If this isn't good enough then you can use anything from a Zener diode to a precision voltage reference chip such as the TL431. At the very least, however, you should add a $1\mu F$ capacitor to ground connected to the VDD pin and the VREF pin.

The MC3000 family is based on the same type of ADC as the ESP32's built-in device, see the next Chapter, a successive approximation converter.

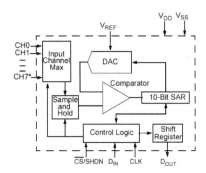

You can see that successive approximation fits in well with a serial bus as each bit can be obtained in the time needed to transmit the previous bit. However, the conversion is relatively slow and a sample-and-hold circuit has to be used to keep the input to the converter stage fixed. The sample-and-hold takes the form of a 20pF capacitor and a switch. The only reason you need to know about this is that the conversion has to be completed in a time that is short compared to the discharge time of the capacitor. So, for accuracy, there is a minimum SPI clock rate as well as a maximum.

Also, to charge the capacitor quickly enough for it to follow a changing voltage, it needs to be connected to a low-impedance source. In most cases this isn't a problem, but if it is you need to include an op amp. If you are using an op amp buffer then you might as well implement an anti-aliasing filter to remove frequencies from the signal that are too fast for the ADC to respond to. How all this works takes us into the realm of analog electronics and signal processing and well beyond the core subject matter of this book.

You can also use the A-to-D channels in pairs, i.e. in differential mode, to measure the voltage difference between them. For example, in differential mode you measure the difference between CH0 and CH1, i.e. what you measure is CH1-CH0. In most cases, you want to use all eight channels in single-ended mode. In principle, you can take 200k samples per second, but only at the upper limit of the supply voltage, i.e. VDD=5V, falling to 75k samples per second at its lower limit of VDD=2.7V.

The SPI clock limits are a maximum of 3.6MHz at 5V and 1.35MHz at 2.7V. The clock can go slower, but because of the problem with the sample-and-hold mentioned earlier, it shouldn't go below 10kHz. How fast we can take samples is discussed later in this chapter.

Connecting to the ESP32

The connection from the MCP3008 to the ESP's SPI bus is very simple and can be seen in the diagram below.

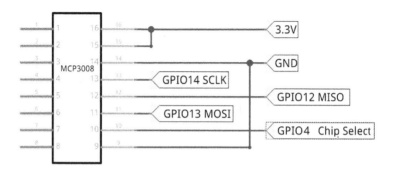

ESP32	MCP3008
GPIO12 A5 MISO	Pin 12
GPIO4 A3 Chip Select	Pin 10
GPIO14 A7 SCLK	Pin 13
GPIO13 A6 MOSI	Pin 11
3.3v	Pins 15 and 16
GND	Pins 14 and 9

The only additional component that is recommended is a $1\mu F$ capacitor connected between pins 15 and 16 to ground, which is mounted as close to the chip as possible. As discussed in the previous section, you might want a separate voltage reference for pin 15 rather than just using the 3.3V supply.

Basic Configuration

Now we come to the configuration of the SPI bus: a clock frequency of 500kHz seems a reasonable starting point.

From the datasheet, the chip select has to be active low and, by default, data is sent most significant bit first for both the master and the slave. The only puzzle is what mode to use? This is listed in the datasheet as mode 0 0 with clock active high or mode 1 1 with clock active low. For simplicity we will use mode 0 0.

We now have enough information to initialize the slave:

```
spi=SPI(1,sck=Pin(14),miso=Pin(12),mosi=Pin(13))
spi.init(baudrate=500_000, bits=8, polarity=0, phase=0,
                                    firstbit=SPI.MSB)
CS = Pin(4, Pin.OUT)
CS.on()
sleep_ms(1)
```

The Protocol

Now we have the SPI initialized and ready to transfer data, but what data do we transfer? As already discussed in the previous chapter, the SPI bus doesn't have any standard commands or addressing structure. Each device responds to data sent in different ways and sends data back in different ways. You simply have to read the datasheet to find out what the commands and responses are.

Reading the datasheet might be initially confusing because it says that you have to send five bits to the slave - a start bit, a bit that selects its operating mode single or differential, and a 3-bit channel number. The operating mode is 1 for single-ended and 0 for differential.

So to read Channel 3, i.e. 011, in single-ended mode you would send the slave:

    11011xxx

where an x can take either value. In response, the slave holds its output in a high impedance state until the sixth clock pulse, then sends a zero bit on the seventh, followed by bit 9 of the data on the eighth clock pulse.

That is, the slave sends back:

    xxxxxx0b9

where x means indeterminate.

The remaining nine bits are sent back in response to the next nine clock pulses. This means you have to transfer three bytes to get all ten bits of data. This all makes reading the data in 8-bit chunks confusing.

The datasheet suggests a different way of doing the job that delivers the data more neatly packed into three bytes. What it suggests to send a single byte is:

    00000001

At the same time, the slave transfers random data, which is ignored. The final 1 is treated as the start bit. If you now transfer a second byte with the most significant bit indicating single or differential mode, then a 3-bit channel address and the remaining bits set to 0, the slave will respond with the null and the top two bits of the conversion. Now all you have to do to get the final eight bits of data is to read a third byte:

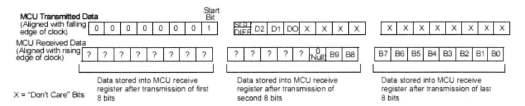

This way you get two neat bytes containing the data with all the low-order bits in their correct positions.

Using this information we can now write some instructions that read a given channel. For example, to read Channel 0 we first send a byte set to 0x01 as the start bit and ignore the byte the slave transfers. Next we send 0x80 to select single-ended and Channel 0 and keep the byte the slave sends back as the two high-order bits. Finally, we send a zero byte (0x00) so that we get the low-order bits from the slave:

```
CS.off()
write = bytearray([0x01, 0x80, 0x00])
read = bytearray(3)
spi.write_readinto(write,read)
CS.on()
```

Notice you cannot send the three bytes one at a time using transfer because that results in the CS line being deactivated between the transfer of each byte.

To get the data out of rBuff we need to do some bit manipulation:

```
data =  (read[1] & 0x03) << 8 |  read[2]
```

The first part of the expression extracts the low three bits from the first byte the slave sent and, as these are the most significant bits, they are shifted up eight places. The rest of the bits are then ORed with them to give the full 10-bit result. To convert to volts we use:

```
volts =  data * 3.3 / 1023.0
```

assuming that VREF is 3.3V.

In a real application you would also need to convert the voltage to some other quantity, like temperature or light level.

If you connect a logic analyzer to the SPI bus you will see something like:

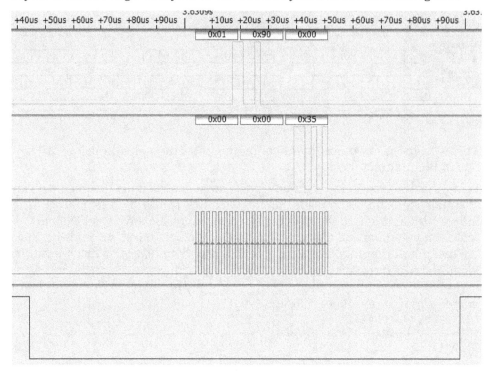

You can see the commands and the response, in this case a reading of 0.17V.

The complete program is:

```
from utime import sleep_ms
from machine import Pin, SPI

spi=SPI(1,sck=Pin(14),miso=Pin(12),mosi=Pin(13))
spi.init(baudrate=500_000, bits=8, polarity=0, phase=0,
                                    firstbit=SPI.MSB)
CS = Pin(4, Pin.OUT)
CS.on()
sleep_ms(1)
CS.off()
write=bytearray([0x01, 0x80, 0x00])
read=bytearray(3)
spi.write_readinto(write,read)
CS.on()
data =  (read[1] & 0x03) << 8 |  read[2]
volts =  data * 3.3 / 1023.0
print(volts)
spi.deinit()
```

SPI ADC Class

This all works, but it would be good to have a class with a method that read the ADC on a specified channel:

```
from utime import sleep_ms
from machine import Pin, SPI
class spiADC:
    def __init__(self,spi,sckNo,misoNo,mosiNo,CSNo):
        self.spi = SPI(spi, sck=Pin(sckNo), miso=Pin(misoNo),
                                          mosi=Pin(mosiNo))
        self.spi.init(baudrate=500_000, bits=8, polarity=0,
                                    phase=0, firstbit=SPI.MSB)
        self.CS = Pin(CSNo, Pin.OUT)
        self.CS.on()
        sleep_ms(1)
    def read(self,chan):
        write=bytearray([0x01, (0x08 | chan) << 4 , 0x00])
        self.CS.off()
        read=bytearray(3)
        self.spi.write_readinto(write,read)
        self.CS.on()
        data =  (read[1] & 0x03) << 8 |  read[2]
        volts =  data * 3.3 / 1023.0
        return volts
```

With this class the main program is very simple:

```
adc=spiADC(1,14,12,13,4)
volts=adc.read(1)
print(volts)
```

How Fast?

Once you have the basic facilities working, the next question is always how fast does something work. In this case we need to know what sort of data rates we can achieve using this ADC. The simplest way of finding this out is to use the fastest read loop for a channel:

```
adc = spiADC(1,14,12,13,15)
while True:
    volts = adc.read(1)
```

With a clock of 500kHz the sampling rate is measured to be 4.15kHz, which is slow compared to the 20kHz achievable with a C program.

Increasing the clock rate has hardly any effect because it is the time to toggle the CS line that slows things down.

Also notice that as the clock rate goes up, you have to ensure that the voltage source is increasingly low-impedance to allow the sample-and-hold to charge in a short time.

Problems

The SPI bus is often a real headache because of the lack of a definitive standard, but in most cases you can make it work. The first problem is in discovering the characteristics of the slave device you want to work with. In general, this is solved by a careful reading of the datasheet or perhaps some trial and error, see the next chapter for an example.

If you are working with a single slave then generally things work once you have the SPI bus configuration set correctly. Things are more difficult when there are multiple devices on the same bus. The ESP32 has enough CS lines to handle eight devices, or more if you only want to use a single SPI interface. Typically you will find SPI devices that don't switch off properly when they are not being addressed. In principle, all SPI devices should present high impedance outputs (i.e. tri-state buffers) when not being addressed, but some don't. If you encounter a problem you need to check that the selected slave is able to control the MISO line properly.

Summary

- The SPI bus is often problematic because there is no SPI standard. Unlike other serial buses, it makes use of unidirectional connections.

- The data lines are MOSI (master output slave input) and MISO (master input slave output). In addition, there is a clock line, output from master, and a number of select lines that you have to drive under program control. Timing for the select lines is a problem as you have to include a delay that makes sure that it remains low until the end of the final clock pulse.

- Data is transferred from the master to the slave and from the slave to the master on each clock pulse, arranged as a circular buffer.

- The ESP32 has two SPI devices which can work with almost any of the GPIO lines but the default lines have the advantage of working faster. MicroPython also provides a software SPI implementation which can be used to convert any GPIO lines into an SPI bus. It isn't as efficient as the hardware implementation.

- You can test the SPI bus using a simple loopback connection.

- Working with a single slave is usually fairly easy, working with multiple slaves can be more of a problem.

- Making SPI work with any particular device has four steps:

    1. Connect the device to the SPI pins by identifying pinouts and discovering what chip selects are supported.
    2. Configure the SPI bus to work with the device - mostly a matter of clock speed and mode.
    3. Identify the commands that you need to send to the device to get it to do something and what data it sends back as a response.
    4. Work out the relationship between the raw reading, the voltage and the quantity the voltage represents.

- The MCP3000 range of A-to-D converters is very easy to use via SPI.

- You can read data at rates as fast as 5kHz.

Chapter 11

Using Analog Sensors

The ESP32 has a wide range of analog capabilities. It has two A-to-D converters (ADCs) and two D-to-A converters (DACs) connected to specific GPIO pins. In addition, it has a set of capacitive input lines which can be used as touch sensors.

ESP32 ADC

The ESP32 has two 12-bit onboard ADCs, ADC1 supports 8 channels in the ESP32 and 10 channels in the ESP S3 and ADC2 supports 10 channels. The only problem is that the WiFi uses one of the two channels, ADC2, and hence its use is best avoided unless you turn WiFi off or use it only when the WiFi is inactive.

The GPIO lines that can be used by the ADC are fixed. In the case of the ESP32 ADC 1 can use GPIO32 to 39 and ADC 2 can use GPIO 0, 2, 4, 12-15 and 25-27. In practice not all of these lines can be used. Of the 8 ADC1 channels only 6 are available on development boards. So even though the hardware seems to offer 18 ADC inputs, this is actually reduced to six that are easy to use. The ESP32 S3 generally offers all of the ADC channels for use. In this case ADC2 occupies GPIO11 to GPIO20.

In most cases it is better to use ADC1:

Channel	ESP GPIO	ESP S3 GPIO	Nano ESP32
ADC1_CH0	GPIO 36	GPIO1	A0
ADC1_CH1		GPIO2	A1
ADC1_CH2		GPIO3	A2
ADC1_CH3	GPIO 39	GPIO4	A3
ADC1_CH4	GPIO 32	GPIO5	D2
ADC1_CH5	GPIO 33	GPIO6	D3
ADC1_CH6	GPIO 34	GPIO7	D4
ADC1_CH7	GPIO 35	GPIO8	D5
ADC1_CH8		GPIO9	D6
ADC1_CH9		GPIO10	D7

ADC2_C0	GPIO4	GPIO11	A4
ADC2_C1	GPIO0	GPIO12	A5
ADC2_C2	GPIO2	GPIO13	A6
ADC2_C3	GPIO15	GPIO14	A7
ADC2_C4	GPIO13	GPIO15	
ADC2_C5	GPIO12	GPIO16	
ADC2_C6	GPIO14	GPIO17	D8
ADC2_C7	GPIO27	GPIO18	D9
ADC2_C8	GPIO25	GPIO19	
ADC2_C9	GPIO26	GPIO20	

In the ESP32 GPIO 36 and 39 were used to read the built-in Hall sensor, but support for this has been removed in the latest version of the SDK and from the ESP32 S3.

The ADC is a successive approximation converter. You don't need to know how it works to use it, but it isn't difficult to understand. The input voltage is compared to a standard voltage, VREF. First a voltage equal to VREF/2 is generated and the input voltage is compared to this. If it is lower then the most significant bit is a 0 and if it is equal or greater then the most significant bit is a 1. At the next step the voltage generated is VREF/2 + VREF/4 and the comparison is repeated to generate the next bit. Successive approximation converters are easy to build, but they are slow.

The ESP32 ADC uses a reference voltage that is generated on-chip and varies between 1000mV and 1200mV. Since 2018 ESP32 chips have the reference voltage burned into the eFuse memory and this makes calibration a matter of reading the value and using it to correct the result. The easiest way to discover if the device you are using has calibration data is to use espefuse.py which is installed along with esptool.py and can be used to read and write the eFuse memory. This is a non-volatile write-once memory that you can use to record small amounts of configuration data, but it is better to avoid using it with MicroPython as there is no easy-to-use interface. It can also damage the ESP32 if you change the wrong bits as once set to 1 a bit cannot be changed back to 0. To discover the calibration data use:

```
python espefuse -p COM6 adc_info
```

replacing COM6 with the serial port that the ESP32 is connected to. If no calibration data is available you will see:

```
ADC VRef calibration: None (1100mV nominal)
```

and the best you can do is assume the middle value for the reference voltage.

If there is calibration data you will see a single point calibration:

```
ADC VRef calibration: 1149mV
```

and you might also see a two-point calibration for each channel:

```
ADC readings stored in efuse BLK3:
    ADC1 Low reading  (150mV): 306
    ADC1 High reading (850mV): 3153
    ADC2 Low reading  (150mV): 389
    ADC2 High reading (850mV): 3206
```

The response is non-linear near zero and the reference voltage:

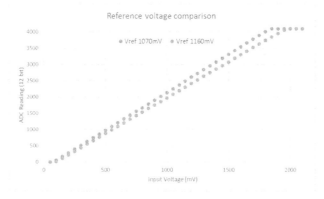

In practice voltages less than 100mV read as zero.

In addition to calibration problems the ADC is also sensitive to noise. You can reduce this by adding a 100nF capacitor across the input line and by averaging multiple readings:

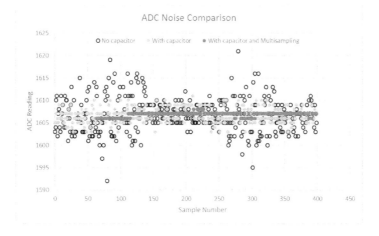

The ADC can be set to do conversions continuously, reading each of the selected inputs and it can work in low-power mode at a lower frequency. Alternatively, you can simply start a conversion on a given input when you need the data – this is the only mode that MicroPython supports.

Reading the ADC

The simplest way of using the ADC is to perform a single read of a single input under software control. Before making use of it, you have to create an ADC object associated with the channel:

```
adc=machine.ADC(pin)
```

Once you have selected the input you are going to read, you can start a conversion and get the result using:

```
adc.read()
```

which returns the raw reading of the ADC. The result is in the range 0 to 4095 for 12-bit resolution supplied by the ESP32 and 8192 for13-bit resolution from the ESP32 S3..

You can also use:

```
ADC.read_u16()
```

which always returns a result in the range 0 to 65535 irrespective of the number of bits actually supplied by the ADC.

Both of these raw readings generally have to be scaled to turn them into physically meaningful values and they are not corrected for any calibration data available.

In most cases you are going to get more accurate and usable results via the method:

```
ADC.read_uv()
```

which returns a result automatically calibrated and converted to µV. The resolution is less than suggested and the result is always a multiple of 1000 µV i.e. millivolts.

The simplest A-to-D program you can write is (use GPIO5 for S3, Nano ESP32 D2:

```
from machine import ADC,Pin
adc = ADC(Pin(32)) #Use GPIO5 for S3
print(adc.read())
print(adc.read_u16())
print(adc.read_uv()/1000000)
```

For example, with an input at around 1V the output is:

```
4095
65535
1.063
```

The actual input voltage may be higher than indicated. If you connect the input to ground you will see:

```
0
0
0.075
```

Indicating that the nonlinear portion of the input between zero and 75mV is measured as 75mV.

To make the ADC more useful it supports changing the input voltage range via attenuators:

- ◆ ADC.ATTN_0DB: No attenuation (100mV - 950mV)
- ◆ ADC.ATTN_2_5DB: 2.5dB attenuation (100mV - 1250mV)
- ◆ ADC.ATTN_6DB: 6dB attenuation (150mV - 1750mV)
- ◆ ADC.ATTN_11DB: 11dB attenuation (150mV - 2450mV)

You can set attenuation in the constructor or in the `atten` method:

```
adc = ADC(Pin(32),atten=ADC.ATTN_11DB)
```

or:

```
adc.atten(ADC.ATTN_11DB)
```

to set the range to approximately 150mV to 2450mV. Notice that the exact range depends on the reference voltage.

The absolute maximum input voltage to the ADC is 3.6V, but using such a high voltage risks damaging the ESP32. In practice keep the input voltage below 3.3V.

You can also set the number of bits to use with the `width` method:

```
adc.width(bits)
```

and `bits` can be any of:

- ◆ `ADC.WIDTH_9BIT`   9-bit data
- ◆ `ADC.WIDTH_10BIT`   10-bit data
- ◆ `ADC.WIDTH_11BIT`   11-bit data
- ◆ `ADC.WIDTH_12BIT`   12-bit data - this is the default configuration

If you want to use any of the more advanced features of the ESP32's ADC you will need either to create the functions that directly access the hardware or move to C.

How Fast?

A rough estimate of how fast each of the read methods are is easy to get:

```
from machine import ADC,Pin
import time
adc = ADC(Pin(32),atten=ADC.ATTN_11DB)#change to 5 for the EPS32 S3

t = time.ticks_us()
for i in range(10000):
    pass
print(time.ticks_diff(time.ticks_us(), t)/10000)

t = time.ticks_us()
for i in range(10000):
    m=adc.read()
print(time.ticks_diff(time.ticks_us(), t)/10000)

t = time.ticks_us()
for i in range(10000):
    m=adc.read_u16()
print(time.ticks_diff(time.ticks_us(), t)/10000)

t = time.ticks_us()
for i in range(10000):
    m=adc.read_uv()
print(time.ticks_diff(time.ticks_us(), t)/10000)
```

The two raw read methods take about 49µs for the ESP32 and 30µs for the ESP32 S3 and the calibrated method read_uv takes about 50µs for the ESP32 and about 32µs for the ESP32 S3 which puts the maximum sampling rate at about 20kHz. Reducing the accuracy to 9-bits reduces the time taken by about 1µs.

Internal Temperature Sensor

The internal temperature sensor which is only available on the ESP32, the ESP32 S3 and Nano ESP32 does not support this in software, is an analog device, but it isn't connected via the ADC. Instead it has its own 8-bit ADC. It is accurate to between 1°C and 3°C depending on the temperature range.

You can read it using:

```
value = esp32.raw_temperature()
```

Although it is referred to as "raw", the actual value returned is the temperature in Fahrenheit.

You can just use this or convert to Centigrade:

```
import esp32
value = esp32.raw_temperature()
value = (value-32.0)/1.8
print(value)
```

The problem with the internal temperature sensor is that it measures the temperature of the processor rather than the outside world. Typically you will get readings of 50°C irrespective of the ambient temperature. If you want to monitor the CPU temperature this is fine, but it isn't if you want to measure the temperature of the outside world.

One possible approach is to put the ESP32 into a deep sleep power-saving mode and then wake it up to read the internal temperature sensor, which is now closer to room temperature. However, this seems to have little effect as, even after being disconnected for some hours, the temperature measured is still as much as 10°C higher than the ambient temperature.

Digital to Analog

The ESP32 S3, and hence the Nano ESP32, doesn't have any DACs and so does not support the DAC object.

The ESP32 and the ESP32 S2 have two 8-bit Digital-to-Analog Converters, DACs. These are connected to GPIO25 (GPIO17 ESP32S2) DAC channel 0 and GPIO26 (GPIO 18 ESP3S2) DAC channel 1 and this cannot be changed. At the time of writing the documentation doesn't mention the DACs, but they are supported.

To enable a DAC use:

```
dac=machine.DAC(pin)
```

where pin is either Pin(25) or Pin(26). To write an 8-bit value to the DAC use:

```
dac.write(data)
```

The output voltage is given by:

output voltage = data * 3.3 / 256 V

For example, to generate a ramp output you can use something like:

```
from machine import Pin, DAC
dac1 = DAC(Pin(26))
while(True):
    for i in range(0,255):
        dac1.write(i)
```

which produces:

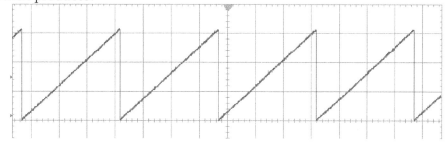

183

The frequency is 380Hz which is surprisingly low, but it is using the full 256 steps of resolution. You can double the frequency by halving the resolution and so on. How high a frequency you can generate depends on how much distortion you can tolerate.

For example, using a step size of 32:

```
from machine import Pin, DAC
dac1 = DAC(Pin(26))
while(True):
    for i in range(0,255,32):
        dac1.write(i)
```

produces:

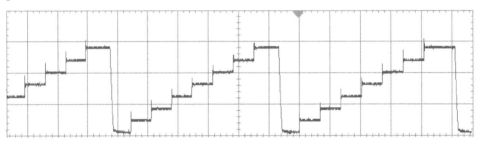

The frequency is roughly 9kHz, but the steps are clearly visible and some filtering would be required to improve the waveform.

If you want other waveforms then the standard technique is to compute a table with 256 values to write to the DAC. For example, to generate a sine wave you could use:

```
from machine import Pin, DAC
import math
dac1 = DAC(Pin(26))

wave = []
for i in range(0,255):
    wave.append(int(127*math.sin(2*math.pi/256*i))+128)
while(True):
    for i in range(0,255):
        dac1.write(wave[i])
```

This creates a reasonable wave form, but at only 230Hz:

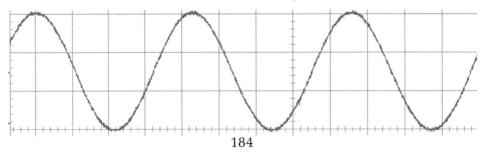

The ESP32's DAC is more sophisticated than MicroPython might suggest. It has a sine wave generator in hardware, but MicroPython doesn't provide access to it. It is, however, fairly easy to configure and enable it by directly working with its registers, see Chapter 18 for more details. There is only one sine wave generator for both DACs, but each one can set its own scale, offset and phase.

We need a set of functions that set the appropriate bits in the control registers:

```
from machine import Pin, DAC, mem32
from time import sleep

def _gpio_get(adr):
    return mem32[adr]
def _gpio_set( adr,value, mask):
    mem32[adr] = mem32[adr] & ~mask | value & mask

def enableSin(chan,f):
    if chan<1 or chan>2:
        return
    setFreq(chan, f)
    setPhase(chan,0x2)
    #enable tone
    _gpio_set(0x3FF48898, 0x10000, 0x10000)
    #select channel
    if chan==1:
        _gpio_set(0x3FF4889c, 1<<24,0x1<<24)
    else:
        _gpio_set(0x3FF4889c, 1<<25, 0x1 <<25)
    #set pad
    pad=0x3FF48484+4*(chan-1)
    _gpio_set(pad, 0x20200, 0x23A00)

def setFreq(chan,f):
    if chan<1 or chan>2:
        return
    step=int(f*65536/8000000) & 0xFFFF
    _gpio_set(0x3FF48898, step, 0x000FF)
def setPhase(chan,p):
    _gpio_set(0x3FF4889c, p << (20 + 2 * (chan − 1)),
                                0x03 << (20 + 2 * (chan - 1)))

def setScale(chan,s):
    _gpio_set(0x3FF4889c, s << (16 + 2 * (chan − 1)),
                                0x03 << (16 + 2 * (chan - 1)))

def setOff(chan,off):
    _gpio_set(0x3FF4889c, off << (8 * (chan − 1)),
                                0xFF << (8 * (chan - 1)))
```

The scale factor s is restricted to two bits and the scaling is given by 2^s. The offset is 7-bits and if the scale factor isn't used clipping will occur. Phase is two bits and only 2 and 3 can be used, corresponding to phase shifts of 0 degrees and 180 degrees. Notice that the phase shift also shifts the offset which is generally undesirable.

Once we have these functions we can make use of the sine wave generator:

```
dac1 = DAC(Pin(26))

enableSin(2,30000)
setScale(2,0x0)
setOff(2,0x0)
while(True):
    sleep(0.001)
    setPhase(2,0x3)
    sleep(.001)
    setPhase(2, 0x2)
```

The standard MicroPython DAC object is used to enable the DAC hardware. After this we can use the functions to modify the control registers. The example sets a frequency of 30KHz and then modulates its phase between 0 and 180 degrees.

Each DAC has to run at the same frequency but you can set scale, offset and phase separately. For example:

```
dac1 = DAC(Pin(26))
dac2 = DAC(Pin(25))
enableSin(1,30000)
enableSin(2,30000)
setPhase(1,0x3)
```

produces two sine waves which are 180 degrees out of phase.

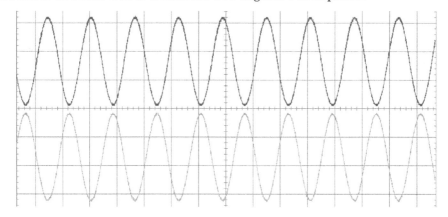

Touch Sensors

The ESP32 has the advantage of providing touch sensors whereas with other devices you usually need to implement your own externally. The number and GPIO assignment of Touch pins varies between the ESP32 and ESP32 S3:

Touch	ESP32	ESP32 S3	Nano ESP32
Touch_0	GPIO4		
Touch_1	GPIO0	GPIO1	A0
Touch_2	GPIO2	GPIO2	A1
Touch_3	GPIO15	GPIO3	A2
Touch_4	GPIO13	GPIO4	A3
Touch_5	GPIO12	GPIO5	D2
Touch_6	GPIO14	GPIO6	D3
Touch_7	GPIO27	GPIO7	D4
Touch_8	GPIO33	GPIO8	D5
Touch_9	GPIO32	GPIO9	D6
Touch_10		GPIO10	D7
Touch_11		GPIO11	A4
Touch_12		GPIO12	A5
Touch_13		GPIO13	A6
Touch_14		GPIO14	A7

Notice that some GPIO lines may be used for other purposes - GPIO0 is used internally and GPIO2 is sometimes used for an on-board LED.

To use a GPIO line as a touch sensor you simply have to construct a touch pad:

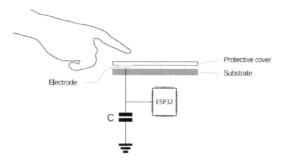

Notice that the user doesn't actually touch the electrode. The protective cover insulates the finger from the GPIO line and hence it is safe and more reliable. The principle is that when a finger, or any part of the body, is placed near the protective cover it forms the second plate of a capacitor and hence the total capacitance changes, usually by increasing. The ESP32 measures the capacitance of the touch pad.

Many projects mistake the touch sensors for resistivity sensors and the metal plate is exposed and the user is expected to actually make a connection with it. This usually works, but it isn't the correct method and it loses many of the advantages of a capacitive touch system. To use touch sensors correctly you don't actually touch the metal part of any wire from the GPIO line.

The capacitance of the sensor is measured by the ESP32 applying a varying voltage. The time to charge and discharge the capacitor depends on the size of the capacitor and a count of pulses in a given time gives an indication if a user is touching the sensor or not. The only real problem in using a touch sensor is knowing what the touch/no touch threshold is. This varies according to the design and implementation of the touch pad. It depends on the size of the electrode and the nature and thickness of the covering.

MicroPython gives limited access to the touch sensor's hardware. You can't configure its operation, but in most cases you don't need to. The TouchPad object supports a single method read which returns the current value of the count which goes down as the capacitance goes up.

To discover the values to use as a threshold for touch/no touch you can use a simple program that displays the current count:

```
from machine import Pin, TouchPad
t = TouchPad(Pin(12))
while(True):
    print(t.read())
```

Construct a touch pad, connect it to the GPIO line and see what readings you get when it is touched and when it is left alone. Hopefully these will be well enough separated for you to pick a threshold that gives reliable operation. If you plan to use a touch pad in a device that you deploy then you should also include a regular check on the value of the touch pad when not touched and use this to set a baseline for the threshold.

The touch sensors can be used to wake the ESP32, see Chapter 18.

Summary

- The ESP32 has two 12-bit ADCs, but only one is available for general use and it provides six easy-to-use channels.

- The calibration voltage is available as a value stored in the eFuse memory. MicroPython makes use of this to correct the measurement.

- The read_uv method is corrected and at around 50µs per sample isn't much slower than the alternatives.

- The ESP32 has an onboard temperature sensor has its own analog input and is really only useful for measuring the processor temperature.

- The ESP32 has two 8-bit ADC channels.

- Using a lookup table you can generate waveforms at 400Hz to 10kHz, depending on resolution.

- The ADC class doesn't support many of the more advanced features of the ADC hardware but you can use the sine wave generator directly.

- There are also touch sensors. These are capacitive sensors and do not require contact with the GPIO line.

The I2C, standing for I-Squared-C or Inter IC, bus is one of the most useful ways of connecting moderately sophisticated sensors and peripherals to any processor. The only problem is that it can seem like a nightmarish confusion of hardware, low-level interaction and high-level software. There are few general introductions to the subject because at first sight every I2C device is different, but there are shared principles that can help you work out how to connect and talk to a new device.

The I2C bus is a serial bus that can be used to connect multiple devices to a controller. It is a simple bus that uses two active wires: one for data and one for a clock. Despite there being lots of problems in using the I2C bus, because it isn't well standardized and devices can conflict and generally do things in their own way, it is still commonly used and too useful to ignore.

The big problem in getting started with the I2C bus is that you will find it described at many different levels of detail, from the physical bus characteristics and protocol to the details of individual devices. It can be difficult to relate all of this together and produce a working project. In fact, you only need to know the general workings of the I2C bus, some general features of the protocol, and know the addresses and commands used by any particular device.

To explain and illustrate these ideas we really do have to work with a particular device to make things concrete. However, the basic stages of getting things to work, the steps, the testing and verification, are more or less the same irrespective of the device.

I2C Hardware Basics

The I2C bus is very simple from the hardware point of view. It has just two signal lines, SDA and SCL, the data and clock lines respectively. Each of these lines is pulled up by a suitable resistor to the supply line at whatever voltage the devices are working - 3.3V and 5V are common choices. The size of the pull-up resistors isn't critical, but 4.7K is typical as shown in the circuit diagram.

You simply connect the SDA and SCL pins of each of the devices to the pull-up resistors. Of course, if any of the devices have built-in pull-up resistors you can omit the external resistors. More of a problem is if multiple devices each have pull-ups. In this case you need to disable all but one.

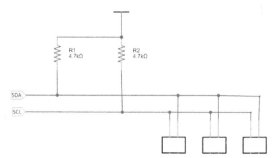

The I2C bus is an open collector bus. This means that it is actively pulled down by a transistor set to on. When the transistor is off, however, the bus returns to the high voltage state via the pull-up resistor. The advantage of this approach is that multiple devices can pull the bus low at the same time. That is, an open collector bus is low when one or more devices pull it low and high when none of the devices is active.

The SCL line provides a clock which is used to set the speed of data transfer, one data bit is presented on the SDA line for each pulse on the SCL line. In all cases, the master drives the clock line to control how fast bits are transferred. The slave can, however, hold the clock line low if it needs to slow down the data transfer. In most cases the I2C bus has a single master device, the ESP32 in our case, which drives the clock and invites the slaves to receive or transmit data. Multiple masters are possible, but this is advanced and usually not necessary.

All you really need to know is that all communication usually occurs in 8-bit packets. The master sends a packet, an address frame, which contains the address of the slave it wants to interact with. Every slave has to have a unique address, which is usually 7 bits, but it can be 10 bits, and the ESP32 does support this in hardware. In the rest of this chapter we will use 7-bit addressing because it is commonly supported.

One of the problems in using the I2C bus is that manufacturers often use the same address, or same set of selectable addresses, and this can make using particular combinations of devices on the same bus difficult or impossible.

The 7-bit address is set as the high-order 7 bits in the byte and this can be confusing as an address that is stated as 0x40 in the datasheet results in 0x80 being sent to the device. The low-order bit of the address signals a write or a read operation depending on whether it is a 0 or a 1 respectively. After sending an address frame it then sends or receives data frames back from the slave. There are also special signals used to mark the start and end of an exchange of packets, but the library functions take care of these.

This is really all you need to know about I2C in general to get started, but it is worth finding out more of the details as you need them. You almost certainly will need them as you debug I2C programs.

The clock (SCL) and data (SDA) lines rest high. The master signals a Start bit, S in the diagram below, by pulling the SDA line down. The clock is then pulled low by the master, during which time the SDA line can change state. The bit is read in the middle of the following high period of the clock pulse, B1, B2 and so on in the diagram. This continues until the last bit has been sent when the data line is allowed to rise while the clock is high, so sending a stoP bit, P in the diagram. Notice that when data is being transmitted the data line doesn't change while the clock is high. Any change in the data line when the clock is high sends a start or a stop bit, i.e. clock high and falling data line is a start bit and clock high and rising data line is a stop bit:

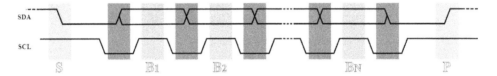

The clock speed was originally set at 100kHz, standard mode, but then increased to 400kHz in fast mode. In practice, devices usually specify a maximum clock speed that they will work with.

The ESP32 I2C

The ESP32 has two I2C controllers, I2C0 and I2C1, that can work as a master or a slave. To use one of the controllers you have to select a pair of GPIO lines to act as SDA and SCL when you create an I2C object.

The machine.I2C object provides access to the hardware-implemented I2C bus, but there is also a software implementation in the form of machine.SoftI2C which is useful if you need an extra I2C controller. The disadvantage is that it places a load on the CPU and so is less efficient. However, the ESP32's I2C hardware as implemented in MicroPython has some serious problems when it comes to reading slow devices. It doesn't support either clock stretching or polling at all well. In practice, it might be better to use the software implementation and accept the lower efficiency. The ESP32 S3 has fewer problems and it is worth using the hardware implementation unless something doesn't work.

The I2C Functions

There are I2C functions for initialization, configuration and for writing and reading to the registers. Let's look at each group in turn.

Initialization

The constructor lets you set up a I2C object ready to use:

```
machine.I2C(id, scl=Pin, sda=Pin, freq=400000,timeout=0x50000)
```

The `id` gives the I2C controller to use and the `scl` and `sda` parameters specify the `Pin` object to use for the I2C lines. The timeout parameter sets the timeout used for the slave to respond in microseconds.

You can also use the `init` method to set things up after the constructor.

The ESP32 doesn't support the most recent high speed modes and the maximum clock rate is 4MHz. MicroPython doesn't support I2C in slave mode, even if the ESP32 does.

There is also a `scan` method that will return a list of addresses that correspond to active I2C devices on the bus. Not all I2C devices respond well to a scan and the method's use is best avoided if possible.

To stop using I2C hardware use the `deinit` method.

Write

There are two similar write methods. The most basic is:

```
I2C.writeto(addr, buf, stop=True)
```

The first parameter is the address of the device and `buf` is a byte array containing the data you want to send.

The final parameter, `stop`, needs some explanation. When you use this method it first sends an address frame, a byte containing the address of the device you specified. Notice that the 7-bit address has to be shifted into the topmost bits and the first bit has to be zeroed for a write operation. So when you write to a device with an address of `0x40`, you will see `0x80` on a logic analyzer, i.e. `0x40<<1`. After the address frame as many data frames are sent as stored in `buf`.

The final parameter controls whether and how the stop bit is sent. The usual write transaction is:

```
START|ADDR|ACK|DATA0|ACK|
            DATA1|ACK|
               ....
            DATAn|ACK|STOP
```

Notice that it is the slave that sends the ACK bit and, if the data is not received correctly, it can send NAK instead. Also notice that there is a single

194

STOP bit at the end of the transaction and this is what you get if you set stop to True. If you set stop to False then the final stop bit isn't sent and the next data transfer can continue as part of the same transaction.

Notice that multibyte transfer is quite different from sending single bytes one at a time:

```
START|  ADDR  |ACK|DATA0|ACK|STOP
START|  ADDR  |ACK|DATA1|ACK|STOP
     ...
START|  ADDR  |ACK|DATAn|ACK|STOP
```

Notice that there are now multiple ADDR frames sent as well as multiple START and STOP bits. What this means in practice is that you have to look at a device's datasheet and send however many bytes it needs as a single operation. You cannot rely on being able to send the same number of bytes broken into chunks.

The other write method works in the same way, but with a slight variation.

```
I2C.writevto(addr, vector, stop=True)
```

This writes vector, which can be a List or a tuple of objects which support the Buffer Protocol. You can create custom objects for this or you can use bytes or a bytearray.

Writing To A Register

A very standard interaction between master and slave is writing data to a register. This isn't anything special and, as far as the I2C bus is concerned, you are simply writing raw data. However, datasheets and users tend to think in terms of reading and writing internal storage locations, i.e. registers in the device. In fact, many devices have lots of internal storage, indeed some I2C devices, for example I2C EPROMS, are nothing but internal storage.

In this case a standard transaction to write to a register is:

1. Send address frame
2. Send a data frame with the command to select the register
3. Send a data frame containing the byte, or word, to be written to the register

So, for example, you might use:

```
buf = bytearray([registerAddress,data])
i2c.writeto(addr,buf,stop = True)
```

Notice the command that has to be sent depends on the device and you have to look it up in its datasheet. Also notice that there is a single start and stop bit at the beginning and end of the transaction.

195

To make working with memory devices easier, MicroPython provides a special method:

```
I2C.writeto_mem(addr, memaddr, buf,  addrsize=8)
```

This writes to a device at `addr` and then accesses its memory location at `memaddr` writing the contents of `buf`. You don't need this method as you can do the same job using more basic methods.

Read

The read functions are similar to the write functions. The most important is:

```
I2C.readfrom_into(addr, buf, stop=True)
```

and the parameters mean the same things as for the corresponding write function. This sends an address frame and then reads as many bytes from the slave as specified by the size of the `buf` bytearray. As in the case of a write operation, the address supplied is shifted up one bit and the lower-order bit is set to 1 to indicate a read operation. So, if the current slave is at address `0x40`, the read sends a read address of `0x81` – this is important to remember if you are viewing the transaction on a logic analyzer.

A simple alternative read method is:

```
buf=I2C.readfrom(addr, nbytes, stop=True)
```

which reads `nbytes` into a byte array.

The read transaction is:

```
START|ADDR|ACK|DATA0|ACK|
            |DATA1|ACK|
            |DATA2|ACK|
       ...
            |DATAn|NAK|STOP
```

The master sends the address frame and the slave sends the `ACK` after the address to acknowledge that it has been received and it is ready to send data. Then, the slave sends bytes, one at a time, and the master sends `ACK` in response to each byte. Finally, the master sends a `NAK` to indicate that the last byte has been read and then a `STOP` bit. That is, the master controls how many bytes are transferred.

As in the case of the write functions, a block transfer of n bytes is different from transferring n bytes one at a time and you can suppress the final stop bit by setting `stop` to `False`.

Reading A Register

As for writing to a register, reading from a register is a very standard operation, but it is slightly more complicated in that you need both a write and a read operation. That is, to read a register you need a write operation to send the address of the register to the device and then a read operation to get the data that the device sends as the contents of the register.

So, for example, you would use something like:

```
buf = bytearray([registerAddress])
i2c.writeto(addr,buf, True)
buf = i2c.readfrom(addr,1,True)
```

If the register sends multiple bytes then you can usually read these one after another as a block transfer without sending an address frame each time. Notice that we don't suppress the stop bit between the read and the write to make it a single transaction.

In theory, and mostly in practice, a register read of this sort can work with a stop-start separating the write and the read operation, which is what you get if you use separate write and read function calls without suppressing the stop bit. That is, the transfer sequence is:

```
START|ADDR|ACK|REGADDR|ACK|STOP|
START|ADDR|ACK|DATA1|ACK|
              |DATA2|ACK|
                 . . .
              |DATAn|NAK|STOP
```

If you look at the end of the write and the start of the read using a logic analyzer, you will see that there is a stop and start bit between them.

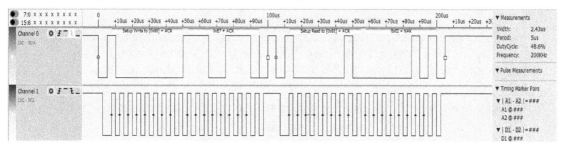

For some devices this is a problem. A stop bit is a signal that another transaction can start and this might allow another master to take over the bus. To avoid this some devices demand a repeated start bit between the write and the read and no stop bit. This is referred to as a "repeated start bit" or a "restart" transaction.

The sequence for a repeated start bit register read is:

```
START|ADDR|ACK|REGADDR|ACK|
START|ADDR|ACK|DATA0|ACK|
              |DATA1|ACK|
        . . .
              |DATAn|NAK|STOP
```

Notice that there is only one STOP.

In theory, either form of transaction should work, but in practice you will find that some slave devices state that they need a repeated start bit and no stop bits in continued transactions. In this case you need to be careful how you send and receive data. For example, to read a register from a device that requires repeated start bits but no stop bit you would use:

```
buf = bytearray([registerAddress])
i2c.writeto(addr,buf, False)
buf = i2c.readfrom(addr,1,True)
```

You can see in the logic analyzer display that there is now just a single start bit between the write and the read.

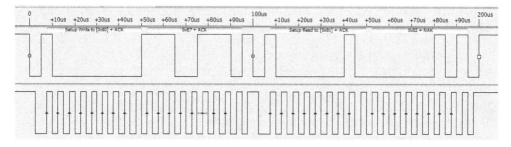

Very few devices need a repeated start transaction. The documentation mentions the MLX90620 IR array, but this is hardly a common peripheral. In practice, it usually doesn't make any difference if you send a stop bit in the middle of a write/read transaction, but you need to know about it just in case.

To make reading from a register easier there are two special methods:

```
I2C.readfrom_mem(addr, memaddr, nbytes, addrsize = 8)
I2C.readfrom_mem_into(addr, memaddr, buf,  addrsize = 8)
```

Both first write the memaddr to the device at addr and then perform a read of that device. They are equivalent to the write/reads given earlier.

Slow Read Protocols

The I2C clock is mostly controlled by the master and this raises the question of how we cope with the speed that a slave can or cannot respond to a request for data.

There are two broad approaches to waiting for data on the I2C bus. The first is simply to request the data and then perform reads in a polling loop. If the device isn't ready with the data, then it sends a data frame with a NAK bit set. In this case the read function throws an exception rather than returns the number of bytes read. So all we have to do is test for an error response with a try/catch. Of course, the polling loop doesn't have to be "tight". The response time is often long enough to do other things and you can use the I2C bus to work with other slave devices while the one you activated gets on with getting the data you requested. All you have to do is to remember to read its data at some later time.

The second way is to allow the slave to hold the clock line low after the master has released it – so called "clock stretching". In most cases the master will simply wait before moving on to the next frame while the clock line is held low. This is very simple and it means you don't have to implement a polling loop, but also notice that your program is frozen until the slave releases the clock line.

Many devices implement both types of slow read protocol and you can use whichever suits your application. The ESP32 has a number of problems with slow reads, however, no matter how you decide to implement it.

A Real Device

Using an I2C device has two problems - the physical connection between master and slave and figuring out what the software has to do to make it work. Here we'll work with the HTU21D/Si7021 and the information in its datasheet to make a working temperature humidity sensor using the I2C functions we've just met.

 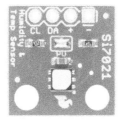

First the hardware. The HTU21D Humidity and Temperature sensor is one of the easiest of I2C devices to use. It's only problem is that it is only available as a surface-mount package. To overcome this you could solder some wires onto the pads or buy a general breakout board. However, it is much simpler to buy the HTU21D breakout board because this has easy connections and built-in pull-up resistors. The HTU21D has been replaced by the Si7021, which is more robust than the original and works in the same way, but the HTU21D is still available from many sources.

If you decide to work with some other I2C device you can still follow the steps given, modifying what you do to suit it. In particular, if you select a device that only works at 5V you might need a level converter.

Given that the HTU21D has pull-up resistors you don't need to enable the onboard pull-ups provided by the ESP32. If you notice any irregularity in the signal at higher frequencies then adding some additional pull-ups might help.

You can use a prototype board to make the connections and this makes it easier to connect other instruments such as a logic analyzer. Given that the pinouts vary according to the exact make of the device, you need to compare the suggested wiring with the breakout board you are actually using.

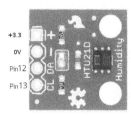

ESP32	HTU21
SDA GPIO12 A5	SDA/DA
SCK GPIO13 A6	SCL/CL
3.3v	VCC/VIN/+
GND	GND/-

A First Program

After wiring up any I2C device, the first question that needs to be answered is, does it work? Unfortunately for most complex devices finding out if it works is a multi-step process. Our first program aims to read some data back from the HTU21D, any data will do. If you look at the datasheet you will find that the device address is 0x40 and that it supports the following commands/registers:

Command	Code	Comment
Trigger Temperature Measurement	0xE3	Hold master
Trigger Humidity Measurement	0xE5	Hold master
Trigger Temperature Measurement	0xF3	No Hold master
Trigger Humidity Measurement	0xF5	No Hold master
Write user register	0xE6	
Read user register	0xE7	
Soft Reset	0xFE	

The easiest of these to get started with is the Read user register command. The user register gives the current setup of the device and can be used to set the resolution of the measurement.

Notice that the codes that you send to the device can be considered as addresses or commands. In this case you can think of sending 0xE7 as a command to read the register or the read address of the register, it makes no difference. In most cases, the term "command" is used when sending the code makes the device do something, and the term "address" is used when it simply makes the device read or write specific data.

To read the user register we have to write a byte containing 0xE7 and then read the byte the device sends back. This involves sending an address frame, a data frame, and then another address frame and reading a data frame. The device seems to be happy if you send a stop bit between each transaction or just a new start bit.

A program to read the user register is fairly easy to put together. The address of the device is 0x40, so its write address is 0x80 and its read address is 0x81. Recall that bus addresses are shifted one bit to the left and the base address is the write address and the read address is base address+1. As the I2C functions adjust the address as needed, we simply use 0x40 as the device's address, but it does affect what you see if you sample the data being exchanged:

```
from machine import Pin,I2C

i2c0 = I2C(0,scl=Pin(13),sda=Pin(12),freq=100000)

buf = bytearray([0xE7])
i2c0.writeto( 0x40, buf, True)
read= i2c0.readfrom(0x40, 1, True)
print("User Register =",read)
```

This sends the address frame 0x80 and then the data byte 0xE7 to select the user register. Next it sends an address frame 0x81 to read the data.

If you run the program you will see:

```
User Register = b'\x02'
```

This is the default value of the register and it corresponds to a resolution of 12 bits and 14 bits for the humidity and temperature respectively and a supply voltage greater than 2.25V.

You can use the special read from a register method to do the same job:

```
read = i2c0.readfrom_mem(0x40,0xE7,1)
```

This does exactly the same as the previous code – it writes 0xE7 to device 0x40 and then reads one byte.

The I2C Protocol In Action

If you have a logic analyzer that can interpret the I2C protocol connected, what you will see is:

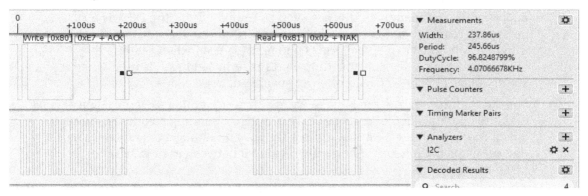

You can see that the write_byte function sends an address packet set to the device's 7-bit address 0x40 as the high-order bits with the low-order bit set to zero to indicate a write, i.e 0x80. After this you get a data packet sent containing 0xE7, the address of the register. After 237 microseconds it sends the address frame again, only this time with the low-order bit set to one to indicate a read. The gap between the operations is rather long and it slows things down. It then receives back a single byte of data from the device, 0x02. Also notice the start and stop bits at the end of each byte. The big gap between the write and the read is due to the time it takes MicroPython to process the method call. It is a limiting factor on how fast I2C can work.

This all demonstrates that the external device is working properly and we can move on to getting some data of interest.

Reading Temperature Data – Clock Stretching

Now we come to reading one of the two quantities that the device measures, temperature. If you look back at the command table you will see that there are two possible commands for reading the temperature:

Command	Code	Comment
Trigger Temperature Measurement	0xE3	Hold master
Trigger Temperature Measurement	0xF3	No Hold master

What is the difference between Hold master and No Hold master? This was discussed earlier in a general context under the section Slow Read Protocols. The device cannot read the temperature instantaneously and the master can either opt to be held waiting for the data, i.e. Hold master, or released to do something else and poll for the data until it is ready, i.e No Hold master.

The Hold master option works by allowing the device to stretch the clock pulse by holding the line low after the master has released it. In this mode the master will wait until the device releases the line. Not all masters support this mode, but the ESP32 does and in theory this makes it the simpler option. To read the temperature using the Hold master mode you simply send 0xE3 and then read three bytes.

The simplest program that might work is:

```
from machine import Pin,I2C
i2c0 = I2C(0,scl=Pin(13),sda=Pin(12),freq=100000)
buf = bytearray([0xE3])
i2c0.writeto( 0x40, buf, True)
read = i2c0.readfrom(0x40, 3, True)
msb = read[0]
lsb = read[1]
check = read[2]
print("msb lsb checksum =", msb, lsb, check)
```

If you try it out on an ESP32 you will see:

Traceback (most recent call last):
  File "<stdin>", line 11, in <module>
OSError: [Errno 116] ETIMEDOUT

The problem is that the ESP32 doesn't wait long enough for the clock stretching to complete. You can try adding timeout=0xFFFFF to set the timeout to its maximum, but this is already the default and so it makes no difference. The reason that the clock stretch times out is that the physical units used for the timeout are very small – number of 80MHz clock pulses set by a 20-bit number. So a maximum timeout of 0xFFFFF is equivalent to about 13ms which is nowhere near the 40ms needed by the device. So the ESP32 does support clock stretching, but only if it is less than around 13ms.

If you try it out on an ESP32 S3 you will find that it works as it has a different way of setting the time out and it can easily cope with 40ms.

To see how clock stretching works on an ESP32, one solution is to switch to the software implementation of I2C:

```
from machine import Pin,SoftI2C
from machine import I2C
i2c0 = SoftI2C(scl=Pin(13),sda=Pin(12),freq=100000)
buf = bytearray([0xE3])
i2c0.writeto( 0x40, buf, False)
read= i2c0.readfrom(0x40, 3, True)
msb = read[0]
lsb = read[1]
check = read[2]
print("msb lsb checksum =", msb, lsb, check)
```

At the time of writing there is a bug that is fixed by starting the program:

```
import time
time.sleep_ms(1)
i2c0 = I2C(0,scl=Pin(13),sda=Pin(12),freq=100000)
```

Now it just works. The read `bytearray` is unpacked into three variables with more meaningful names:

- `msb`   - most significant byte
- `lsb`   - least significant byte
- `check` - checksum

If you try this out you should find that it works and it prints something like:

```
msb lsb checksum = 110 194 29
```

with temperatures in the 20°C range.

You can also use the read register method to do the same job:

```
read=i2c0.readfrom_mem(0x40, 0xE3, 3)
```

The logic analyzer reveals what is happening. First we send the usual address frame and write the `0xE3`. Then, after a short pause, the read address frame is sent and the clock line is held low by the device (lower trace):

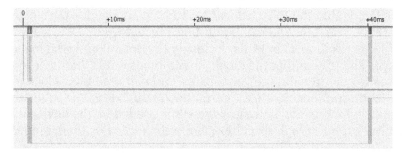

The clock line is held low by the device for about 40ms while it gets the data ready. It is released and the three data frames are sent. This response is a long way down the logic analyzer trace (40ms+) so keep scrolling until you find it.

Notice that we suppress the stop bit between the write and the read to make it a single transaction.

Reading Temperature Data – Polling

As clock stretching doesn't work for everything on the ESP32, let's consider the alternative of polling. Unfortunately there is a problem in using I2C in polling mode as well. The basic idea in polling mode is that the master keeps trying to read the data from the slave but the slave responds with a `NAK` to indicate that data isn't ready.

The problem is that the ESP32 doesn't interpret the NAK to mean "give up this attempt to read" instead it waits for another timeout period to give the slave time to try again. Unfortunately the timeout is set to about one second which severely limits the rate at which you can acquire data.

For example:

```
from machine import Pin,I2C
i2c0=I2C(0,scl=Pin(13),sda=Pin(12),freq=100000)
buf = bytearray([0xF3])
i2c0.writeto( 0x40, buf, True)
while True:
    try:
        read= i2c0.readfrom(0x40, 3, False)
        break
    except:
        continue
msb = read[0]
lsb = read[1]
check = read[2]
print("msb lsb checksum =", msb, lsb, check)
```

You can see that the while loop repeats the attempt to read until it succeeds. The problem is that on an ESP32 the first time through the loop the readfrom ignores the NAK and waits for a few tens milliseconds before throwing an ETIMEDOUT timeout exception.

The next time through the loop the readfrom works and gets the data that has been available since 40ms from the start of the attempt to read.

In other words, this approach works but it is very slow.

The program works perfectly on an ESP32 S3 however.

To see what is supposed to happen on an ESP32, all you have to do is switch to the software I2C:

```
from machine import Pin,SoftI2C
from time import sleep_ms
i2c0 = SoftI2C(scl=Pin(13),sda=Pin(12),freq=100000)
buf = bytearray([0xF3])
i2c0.writeto( 0x40, buf, False)
while True:
    sleep_ms(5)
    try:
        read = i2c0.readfrom(0x40, 3, True)
        break
    except:
        continue
msb = read[0]
lsb = read[1]
check = read[2]
print("msb lsb checksum =", msb, lsb, check)
```

If you run this the `readfrom` throws a `ENODEV` exception each time the slave sends a `NAK`. Eventually the slave is ready with the data and the readfrom reads the three bytes. As the `readfrom` doesn't timeout it returns very quickly and we have to include a sleep in the loop to reduce the number of times the master tries to read the slave. The result on a logic analyzer shows the pattern of polling:

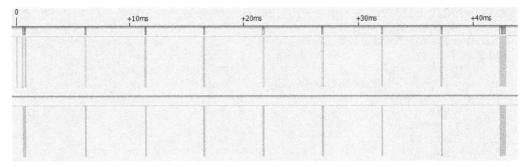

You can see that the master tries to read the data seven times before succeeding:

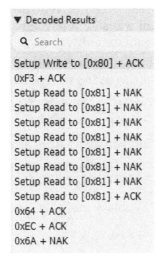

The advantage of this correct procedure is that it only takes 40ms rather than over one second.

One solution to the problem of the hardware not implementing polling correctly is to simply send the commands and then sleep for 50ms before reading the data. If the device is working correctly then the data should be available after this time and can be read without polling or clock stretching.

Processing the Data

Our next task isn't really directly related to the problem of using the I2C bus, but it is a very typical next step. The device returns the data in three bytes, but the way that this data relates to the temperature isn't simple.

If you read the datasheet you will discover that the temperature data is the 14-bit value that results from putting together the most and least significant bytes and zeroing the bottom two bits. The bottom two bits are used as status bits, bit zero currently isn't used and bit one is a 1 if the data is a humidity measurement and a 0 if it is a temperature measurement.

To put the two bytes together we use:

```
data16= (msb << 8) |  (lsb & 0xFC)
```

This zeros the bottom two bits, shifts the `msb` up eight bits and ORs the two together. The result is a 16-bit temperature value with the bottom two bits zeroed. Now we have a raw temperature value but we have still have to convert it to standard units. The datasheet gives the formula:

```
Temperature in °C= -46.85 + 175.72 * data16 / 2¹⁶
```

The only problem in implementing this is working out 2^{16}. You can work out 2^x with the expression `1<<x`, i.e. shift 1 x places to the left.
This gives:

```
temp = (-46.85 +(175.72 * data16 /(1<<16)))
```

Now all we have to do is print the temperature:

```
print("Temperature C ", temp)
```

The full listing is at the end of this chapter.

Reading Humidity

The nice thing about using I2C devices is that it gets easier. Once you have seen how to do it with one device, the skill generalizes and, once you know how to deal with a particular part of a device, other aspects of the device are usually similar. For this reason let's implement the humidity reading using polling which we know works with the hardware and the software I2C. We write the `0xF5` once to the slave and then repeatedly attempt to read the three-byte response. If the slave isn't ready it simply replies with a NAK which the read method interprets as throwing an exception.

Once we have the data, the formula to convert the 16-bit value to percentage humidity is:

```
RH= -6 + 125 * data16 / 2¹⁶
```

Putting all this together, and reusing some variables from the previous parts of the program, we have:

```
buf = bytearray([0xF5])
i2c0.writeto( 0x40, buf, True)
read = bytearray(3)
while True:
    sleep_ms(1)
    try:
        i2c0.readfrom_into(0x40,read, True)
        break
    except:
        continue
msb = read[0]
lsb = read[1]
check = read[2]
print("msb lsb checksum =", msb, lsb, check)
data16 = (msb << 8) | (lsb & 0xFC)
hum = -6 + (125.0 * data16) / 65536
print("Humidity ", hum)
```

Checksum Calculation

Although computing a cyclic redundancy checksum, CRC, isn't specific to I2C, it is another common task. The datasheet explains that the polynomial used is:

$$X^8+X^5+X^4+1$$

Once you have this information you can work out the divisor by writing a binary number with a one in each location corresponding to a power of X in the polynomial, in this case the 8th, 5th, 4th and 1st bit. Hence the divisor is:

```
0x0131
```

What you do next is roughly the same for all CRCs. First you put the data that was used to compute the checksum together with the checksum value as the low-order bits:

```
data32 = (msb << 16)|(lsb <<8)| check
```

Now you have three bytes, i.e 24 bits, in a 32-bit variable. Next you adjust the divisor so that its most significant non-zero bit aligns with the most significant bit of the three bytes. As this divisor has a 1 at bit eight, it needs to be shifted 15 places to the right to move it to be the 24th bit:

```
divisor =  0x0131 <<15
```

or

```
divisor = 0x988000
```

Now that you have both the data and the divisor aligned, you step through the topmost 16 bits, i.e. you don't process the low-order eight bits which hold the received checksum.

For each bit you check to see if it is a 1. If it is, you replace the data with the data XOR divisor. In either case you shift the divisor one place to the right:

```
for i in range(16):
        if data32 & 1<<(23 - i):
            data32 ^= divisor
        divisor>>= 1
```

When the loop ends, if there was no error, the data32 should be zeroed and the received checksum is correct and as computed on the data received.

A complete function to compute the checksum, with some optimization, is:

```
def crcCheck(msb, lsb,check):
    data32 = (msb << 16)|(lsb <<8)| check
    divisor = 0x988000
    for i in range(16):
        if data32 & 1<<(23 - i):
            data32 ^= divisor
        divisor>>= 1
    return data32
```

It is rare to get a CRC error on an I2C bus unless it is overloaded or subject to a lot of noise.

Complete Listing

The complete program for reading temperature and humidity, including checksum, is:

```
from machine import Pin,I2C

def crcCheck(msb, lsb,check):
    data32 = (msb << 16)|(lsb <<8)| check
    divisor = 0x988000
    for i in range(16):
        if data32 & 1<<(23 - i):
            data32 ^= divisor
        divisor>>= 1
    return data32

i2c0=I2C(0,scl=Pin(13),sda=Pin(12),freq=100000)
buf = bytearray([0xF3])
i2c0.writeto( 0x40, buf, False)
while True:
    try:
        read= i2c0.readfrom(0x40, 3, True)
        break
    except:
        continue
msb = read[0]
lsb = read[1]
check = read[2]
print("msb lsb checksum =", msb, lsb, check)
```

```
data16= (msb << 8) |  (lsb & 0xFC)
temp = (-46.85 +(175.72 * data16 /(1<<16))))
print("Temperature C ", temp)
print("Checksum=",crcCheck(msb,lsb,check))

buf = bytearray([0xF5])
i2c0.writeto( 0x40, buf, True)
read=bytearray(3)
while True:
    try:
        i2c0.readfrom_into(0x40,read, True)
        break
    except:
        continue
msb = read[0]
lsb = read[1]
check = read[2]
print("msb lsb checksum =", msb, lsb, check)
data16 = (msb << 8) | (lsb & 0xFC)
hum = -6 + (125.0 * data16) / 65536
print("Humidity ", hum)
print("Checksum=",crcCheck(msb,lsb,check))
```

This works perfectly on an ESP32 S3 but takes more than 400ms to read data that should take 40ms to read on an ESP32. The only solution is to switch to the software I2C implementation. If you do this, include a sleep in each of the while loops to reduce the number of times you attempt to read the data.

If you move to the software implementation then clock stretching is a better approach.

Of course, this is just the start. Once you have the device working and supplying data, it is time to write your code in the form of functions that return the temperature and the humidity and generally make the whole thing more useful and easier to maintain. This is often how this sort of programming goes. First you write a lot of inline code so that it works as fast as it can, then you move blocks of code to functions to make the program more elegant and easy to maintain, checking at each refactoring that it all still works.

Not all devices used standard bus protocols. In Chapter 13 we'll look at a custom serial protocol that we have to implement for ourselves.

Summary

- The I2C bus is simple yet flexible and is one of the most commonly encountered ways of connecting devices.

- The I2C bus uses two wires – a data line and a clock.

- The ESP32 has two I2C interfaces.

- MicroPython provides a software implementation of the I2C bus which can be used with any GPIO lines. It isn't as efficient as the hardware implementation, but it is worth using if the slave device is slow.

- Each I2C interface can be connected to a pair of GPIO lines.

- The I2C protocol isn't standardized and you have to take account of variations in the way devices implement it.

- There are single byte transfer operations and multibyte transfers which differ in when a stop bit is sent.

- The low-level protocol can be made slightly more high-level by thinking of it as a single write/read a register operation.

- Sometimes a device cannot respond immediately and needs to keep the master waiting for data. There are two ways to do this, polling and clock stretching.

- The ESP32 implements clock stretching, but it has a very short timeout, 13ms, that is often too short to work.

- The ESP32 S3 implements clock stretching correctly.

- The ESP32 doesn't implement polling correctly because it doesn't abort the read when it first receives a NAK but only after a one second timeout.

- The HTU21D is a simple I2C device, but getting it working involves using polling with the hardware I2C or clock stretching with the software I2C.

- Computing a checksum is an involved, but common, operation.

Chapter 13

One-Wire Protocols

In this chapter we make use of all the ideas introduced in earlier chapters to create a raw interface with the low-cost DHT11/22 temperature and humidity sensor and the 1-Wire bus device the DS18B20. Both devices have MicroPython drivers and so are easy to use but they make good examples of how to use "bit banging" to create a direct interface with a device.

The DHT22

The DHT22 used in this project is a more accurate version of the DHT11 The software will work with both versions and also with the AM2302, which is equivalent to the DHT22.

Model AM2302/DHT22
Power supply 3.3-5.5V DC
Output signal digital signal via 1-wire bus
Sensing element Polymer humidity capacitor
Operating range
 humidity 0-100%RH;
 temperature -40~80Celsius
Accuracy
 humidity +-2%RH(Max +-5%RH);
 temperature +-0.5Celsius
Resolution or sensitivity
 humidity 0.1%RH;
 temperature 0.1Celsius
Repeatability
 humidity +-1%RH;
 temperature +-0.2Celsius

The device will work at 3.3V and it makes use of a one-wire open collector-style bus, which makes it very easy to make the physical connection to the ESP32, however, the "one-wire bus" used isn't standard and is only used by this family of devices.

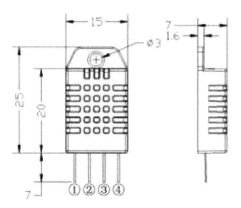

The pinouts are:
1. VDD
2. SDA serial data
3. Not used
4. GND

and the standard way of connecting the device is:

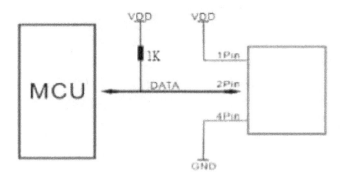

Although the recommended pull-up resistor is 1K, a higher value, typically 4.7K works better and even larger will work.

The Electronics

All you have to do is select a suitable GPIO line – any of those you are not already using will do. In our example GPIO2 is used because it is usable on all three ESP32 versions. Exactly how you build the circuit is a matter of preference. The basic layout can be seen below ESP32 on the left, ESP32 S3 in the middle and Nano ESP32 on the right.

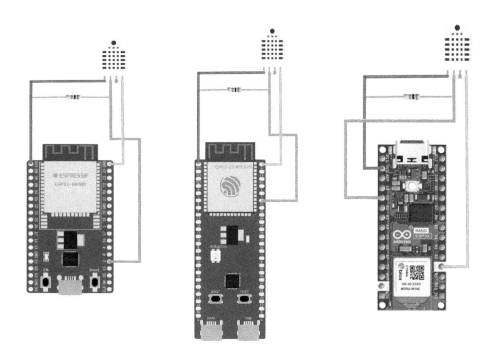

ESP32	DHT22
3.3V OUT	VDD pin 1
GPIO2 A1	SDA serial data pin 2
GND	GND pin 4

It is very easy to create this circuit using a prototyping board and some jumper wires. You can also put the resistor close to the DHT22 to make a sensor package connected to the ESP32 using three cables.

The DHT Driver

There is an under-documented and mostly ignored driver for the DHT11 and DHT22. If you only want to use a temperature and humidity sensor without worrying about how it works then use the driver – it is simple and the only risk is that it fails to be maintained in the future. You use the driver by creating either a DHT11 or DHT22 object connected to a specified pin – any general GPIO line will work. Once you have the object initialized you can use the measure()method to take a reading. This doesn't return any results and to get the temperature and humidity you have to use temperature() to return the temperature in C and humidity() to return the humidity as a percentage.

If you have a DHT22 wired up to GPIO2 then you can display the temperature and humidity readings using:

```
import dht
from machine import Pin
from time import sleep

dht = dht.DHT22(Pin(2))
while True:
    dht.measure()
    temp = dht.temperature()
    print(temp,"C")
    hum = dht.humidity()
    print(hum,"%")
    sleep(1)
```

Using the DHT22 really is this easy, but how does it work? It turns out to be easy and instructive to implement a raw "bit-banging" approach to reading the DHT22 using methods that generalize to situations when you don't have a ready-made driver – which is, of course, based on the same techniques.

The Protocol

The serial protocol used by the DHT22 is fairly simple:

1. The host pulls the line low for between 0.8ms and 29ms, usually around 1ms. This is a request for data from the host to the DHT22.

2. It then releases the bus which is pulled high by the resistor.

3. After between $20\mu s$ and $200\mu s$, usually $30\mu s$, the device starts to send data by pulling the line down for around $80\mu s$ and then lets it float high for another $80\mu s$. This is a "start" bit sent by the DHT22.

4. Next 40 bits of data are sent using a $70\mu s$ high for a 1 and a $26\mu s$ high for a 0 with the high pulses separated by around $50\mu s$ low periods.

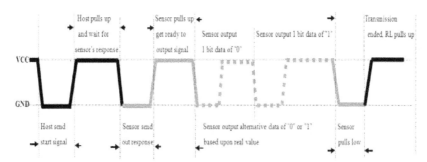

What we have to do is pull the line low for 1ms or so to start the device sending data and this is very easy. Then we have to wait for the device to pull the line down and let it pull up again for about 160μs and then read the time that the line is high or low 40 times.

A 1 corresponds to 70μs and a 0 corresponds to 26 to 28μs. This is within the range of pulse measurements that can be achieved using standard library functions. There is also a 50μs low period between each data bit and this can be used to do some limited processing. The time between falling edge transitions is therefore 120μs for a 1 and 76μs for a 0.

When trying to work out how to decode a new protocol it often helps to try to answer the question, "how can I tell the difference between a 0 and a 1?"

If you have a logic analyzer it can help to look at the waveform and see how you work it out manually. In this case, despite the complex-looking timing diagram, the difference comes down to a short versus a long pulse!

With the hardware shown on the previous page connected to the ESP32, the first thing that we need to do is establish that the system is working. The simplest way to do this is to pull the line down for 1ms and see if the device responds with a stream of pulses. These can be seen on a logic analyzer or an oscilloscope, both are indispensable tools. If you don't have access to either tool then you will just have to skip to the next stage and see if you can read in some data. The simplest code that will do the job is:

```
from machine import Pin
from utime import sleep_ms
DHT = Pin(2,mode=Pin.OUT,value=1)
sleep_ms(1)
DHT.off()
sleep_ms(1)
DHT.init(mode=Pin.IN)
```

Setting the line initially high, to ensure that it is configured as an output, we then set it low, wait for around 1ms and then change its direction to input and so allow the line to be pulled high. There is no need to set the line's pull-up mode because the ESP32 is the only device driving the line until it releases the line by changing its direction to input. When a line is in input mode it is high impedance and this is why we need an external pull-up resistor in the circuit.

As long as the circuit has been correctly assembled and you have a working device, you should see something like:

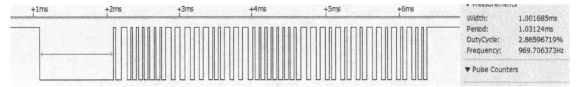

Reading the Data

With preliminary flight checks complete, it is time to read the 40-bit data stream. However, we have a problem in that we can't know how long it takes to convert a GPIO line from output to input. This means that we don't know where we are in the pulse train when the initial pulse is over. The standard solution is to use another GPIO line to signal where we are by toggling the line at the point in the program you want to identify on the logic analyzer plot. For example, we can wait for the low that the device sends before the start bit and then wait for the start bit:

```
DHT.init(mode=Pin.IN)
t = time_pulse_us(DHT, 0, 1000)
t = time_pulse_us(DHT, 1, 1000)
```

The first time_pulse_us measures the duration of the high pause before the device pulls the line low, the second measures the duration of the next high, i.e. the pause before the data is sent. Notice that we don't actually need the time of each of these pulses, but the timeout of $1000\mu s$ can be used to detect if the device is present.

The only question is have we missed the start bit because the initial pause was longer than it took to change the mode of the GPIO line? More directly, where in the pulse train are we after the second time_pulse_us? The answer can be found by toggling another GPIO line and looking at the result:

```
flagPin = Pin(4,mode=Pin.OUT,value=0)
  . . .
DHT.init(mode=Pin.IN)
t=time_pulse_us(DHT, 1, 1000)
t=time_pulse_us(DHT, 0, 1000)
flagPin.on()
flagPin.off()
```

You can see from the logic analyzer trace that for the ESP32 the program is about $12\mu s$ beyond the start bit:

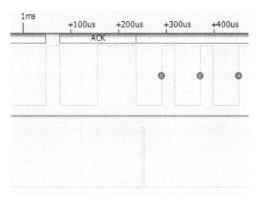

Of course, the extra time needed to generate the pulse throws the timing of the rest of the program. Usually you can only put in one such pulse at a time to verify where the program is in the pulse train.

The timing of the end of the start pulse is reasonable, but investigating the timings using the same technique quickly reveals that this direct approach isn't going to work as it is too slow to keep up with the data bits.

The solution is to move the data acquisition to a function and use the @micropython.native decorator to speed things up. This moves the marker pulse to $9\mu s$ after the end of the start pulse, $8\mu s$ for the S3, which turns out to be accurate enough to read the rest of the data.

A total of 40 bits, i.e. five bytes, is difficult to work with. A good compromise is to read in the first 32 bits into a 32-bit integer and then read the final byte into a separate variable. The reason is that the fifth byte is a checksum, so we have separated out the data and the checksum, but there are many different ways to organize this task.

First we read the 32 data bits:

```
data = 0
for i in range(32):
    t = time_pulse_us(DHT, 1, 1000)
    data = data << 1
    data = data | (t > 50)
```

You can see the general idea is to simply find the time that the line is high and then treat anything bigger then $50\mu s$ as a 1. In practice, the measured times the pulses are measured as high are $25\mu s$ for a 0 and $75\mu s$ for a 1 and $50\mu s$ is a threshold halfway between the two. The bits are shifted into the variable data so that the first byte transmitted is the high-order byte.

Next we need to read the checksum byte:

```
checksum =  0
for i in range(8):
    t = time_pulse_us(DHT, 1, 1000)
    checksum = checksum << 1
    checksum = checksum |(t > 50)
```

This works in the same way. At the end of this we have 32 data bits in `data` and eight checksum bits in `checksum` and all we have to do is process the data to get the temperature and humidity.

All of this should be within a function which returns the raw data:

```
return data,checksum
```

Extracting the Data

You can process the data without unpacking it into individual bytes, but it is easier to see what is happening if we do:

```
byte1 = (data >> 24 & 0xFF)
byte2 = (data >> 16 & 0xFF)
byte3 = (data >> 8 & 0xFF)
byte4 = (data & 0xFF)
```

The first two bytes are the humidity measurement and the second two the temperature.

The checksum is just the sum of the first four bytes reduced to eight bits and we can test it using:

```
print("Checksum",checksum,(byte1+byte2+byte3+byte4)&0xFF)
```

If the two values are different, there has been a transmission error. The addition of the bytes is done as a full integer and then it is reduced back to a single byte by the AND operation. If there is a checksum error, the simplest thing to do is get another reading from the device. Notice, however, that you shouldn't read the device more than once every two seconds.

The humidity and temperature data are also easy to reconstruct as they are transmitted high byte first and 10 times the actual value.

Extracting the humidity data is easy:

```
humidity = ((byte1 <<8)| byte2) / 10.0
print("Humidity= ", humidity)
```

The temperature data is slightly more difficult in that the topmost bit is used to indicate a negative temperature. This means we have to test for the most significant bit and flip the sign of the temperature if it is set:

```
neg = byte3 & 0x80
byte3 = byte3 & 0x7F
temperature =(byte3 << 8 | byte4) / 10.0
if neg > 0:
    temperature = -temperature
print("Temperature=", temperature)
```

This completes the data processing.

A DHT22 Object

The program as presented works, but it would benefit from refactoring into an object with suitable methods. A complete, refactored, listing including a main program can be seen below. This is just one way to break the program down into functions and exactly how best to do it depends on many factors.

```
from machine import Pin,time_pulse_us
from utime import sleep_ms

class DHT22():
    def __init__(self,gpio):
        self.pin = Pin(gpio, mode=Pin.IN)
        self.checksum = 0
        self.temperature = 0
        self.humidity=0
        sleep_ms(1)

    @micropython.native
    def getReading(self):
        data = 0
        checksum = 0
        DHT=self.pin
        DHT.init(mode=Pin.OUT,value=0)
        sleep_ms(1)
        DHT.init(mode=Pin.IN)
        t = time_pulse_us(DHT, 0, 1000)
        t = time_pulse_us(DHT, 1, 1000)

        for i in range(32):
            t = time_pulse_us(DHT, 1, 1000)
            data = data << 1
            data = data | (t > 50)
```

```
for i in range(8):
        t = time_pulse_us(DHT, 1, 1000)
        checksum = checksum << 1
        checksum = checksum |(t > 50)

    byte1 = (data >> 24 & 0xFF)
    byte2 = (data >> 16 & 0xFF)
    byte3 = (data >> 8 & 0xFF)
    byte4 = (data & 0xFF)
    self.checksum =(checksum ==(byte1+byte2+byte3+byte4)&0xFF)
    self.humidity = ((byte1 <<8)| byte2) / 10.0
    neg = byte3 & 0x80
    byte3 = byte3 & 0x7F
    self.temperature = (byte3 << 8 | byte4) / 10.0
    if neg > 0:
        self.temperature = -self.temperature
```

Once you have the class you can write simple programs like:

```
dht = DHT22(2)
dht.getReading()
print("Checksum",dht.checksum)
print("Humidity= ", dht.humidity)
print("Temperature=", dht.temperature)
```

For real use, the program needs to check for a device being present and a check for timeout errors. Notice that you do need the @micropython.native decorator as without it the getReading method is too slow.

The 1-Wire Bus And The DS1820

Unlike the DHT22 which uses a bus that is unique to itself, the 1-Wire bus is more general and there are a range of devices that work with it. It is a proprietary bus, but it has a lot in common with the I2C and SPI buses. That is, it defines a general bus protocol that can be used with a range of different devices. There are many useful devices you can connect to it, including the iButton security devices, memory, data loggers, fuel gauges and more. However, probably the most popular of all 1-Wire devices is the DS18B20 temperature sensor - it is small, very cheap and very easy to use. This chapter shows you how to work with it, but first let's deal with the general techniques needed to work with the 1-Wire bus.

The Hardware

One-wire devices are very simple and only use a single wire to transmit data:

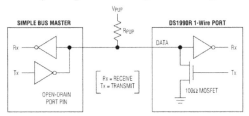

The 1-Wire device can pull the bus low using its Tx line and can read the line using its Rx line. The reason for the pull-up resistor is that both the bus master and the slave can pull the bus low and it will stay low until they both release the bus.

The device can even be powered from the bus line by drawing sufficient current through the pull-up resistor - so called parasitic mode. Low power devices work well in parasitic mode, but some devices have such a heavy current draw that the master has to provide a way to connect them to the power line - so called strong pull-up. In practice, parasitic mode can be difficult to make work reliably for high-power devices.

In normal-powered mode there are just three connections – V, usually 3.3V for the ESP32, Ground and Data. The pull-up resistor varies according to the device, but anything from 2.2K to 4.7kΩ works. The longer the bus, the lower the pull-up resistor has to be to reduce "ringing". There can be multiple devices on the bus and each one has a unique 64-bit lasered ROM code, which can be used as an address to select the active devices.

The OneWire Driver

The 1-Wire bus is general in the sense that you can have multiple slave devices connected to it at the same time. This means that there has to be a way to find out what devices are connected and to select which device you want to talk to. The OneWire class provides a driver that works with any set of 1-Wire devices you care to work with.

You can create an instance of the OneWire class to work with the protocol on any GPIO line:

```
ow = onewire.OneWire(pin)
```

Before you can work with any devices you have to send a reset signal. This causes any connected device to hold the line low and this is used to indicate that there are active devices on the bus:

```
presence = ow.reset(required=False)
```

The returned value is `True` if there are any active devices. If you set `required` to `True` a `OneWireError` exception is thrown if there are no devices connected to the bus.

To discover what devices are connected you can use the `scan` method:

```
roms = onewire.scan()
```

This scans for devices on the bus and returns a list of 64-bit ROM codes. The ROM codes uniquely define both the device and its type:

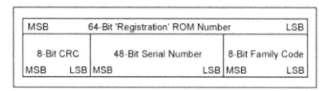

For example, all DS18B20 Temperature Sensors have a serial number that starts with 28-. Variations on the device have different family codes:

```
W1_THERM_DS18S20     0x10
W1_THERM_DS1822      0x22
W1_THERM_DS18B20     0x28
W1_THERM_DS1825      0x3B
W1_THERM_DS28EA00    0x42
```

Once you have a ROM code you can use it to select the device the master is interacting with:

```
ow.select_rom(rom)
```

After this all data transfer occurs between the master and the selected device. All of the other devices ignore what is going on until a reset is sent.

There are some low-level communication functions. For example:

```
ow.writebit(value)
value = ow.readbit()
```

sends and receives a single bit to the currently selected device. You usually don't need to make use of these functions, but there are devices and commands that require that you work with a single bit to signal.

Usually you want to send and receive single bytes:

```
ow.writebyte(value)
value = ow.readbyte()
```

or a set of bytes in a byte array buffer:

```
ow.write(buf)
ow.readinto(buf)
```

Finally we have:

```
ow.crc8(data)
```

which will compute the CRC checksum of the data.

These methods are completely general and will work with any 1-Wire bus device, but we will use the DS18B20 for our example as it is by far the most commonly encountered 1-Wire device. In fact, it is so popular that there is a driver that specifically targets it and makes it very easy to use. We will first look at how to use this driver and then at how to use the OneWire class to use the same device and to access additional features.

The DS18B20 Hardware

The most popular 1-Wire device is the DS18B20. It is available in a number of formats, but the most common makes it look just like a standard BJT (Bipolar Junction Transistor) which can sometimes be a problem when you are trying to find one. You can also get them made up into waterproof sensors complete with cable.

No matter how packaged, they will work at 3.3V or 5V.

The basic specification of the DS18B20 is:

- Measures temperatures from -55°C to +125°C (-67°F to +257°F)
- ±0.5°C accuracy from -10°C to +85°C
- Thermometer resolution is user-selectable from 9 to 12 bits
- Converts temperature to 12-bit digital word in 750ms (max)

It can also be powered from the data line, allowing the bus to operate with only two wires, data and ground. However, this parasitic power mode is difficult to make work reliably and is best avoided in an initial design.

There are also the original DS1820 and the DS18S20, which too are best avoided in new applications.

To supply it with enough power during a conversion, the host has to connect it directly to the data line by providing a "strong pull-up", essentially replicating a transistor. In normal-powered mode there are just three connections:

Ground needs to be connected to the system ground, VDD to 3.3V and DQ to the pull-up resistor of an open collector bus.

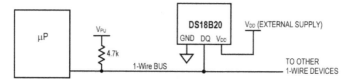

While you can have multiple devices on the same bus, for simplicity it is better to start off with a single device until you know that everything is working.

You can build the circuit in a variety of ways. You can solder the resistor to the temperature sensor and then use some longer wires with clips to connect to the ESP32.

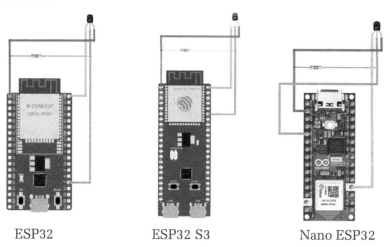

ESP32   ESP32 S3   Nano ESP32

The DS18B20 Driver

The DS18B20 driver builds on the methods provided by the OneWire driver. It makes it easy to read the temperature by supplying all of the commands to select the device, make the DS18B20 take a temperature measurement and retrieve the result. You can, in fact do all of these things with just the OneWire driver as will be explained later, but the DS18B20 driver is easier to use.

To use the ds18x20 driver you have to first create a OneWire driver object which sets the pin and finds out what devices are connected to it. Next you have to create a ds18X20 object which works with any DS18B20 or DS18S20 devices connected to the bus.

You need to find out what devices are connected to the bus and you can use the OneWire object's scan method to do this. The ds18X20 object has its own version of the scan method which only returns devices in the DS family.

You can initiate a temperature reading on all of the connected DS18X20 devices using the convert_temp() method. This causes the temperature to be stored in the device's scratchpad memory. To get the temperature from a specific device you have to use:

```
t = ds.read_temp(rom)
```

where rom is the ROM code of the device you want to read.

So to read a temperature from a single device you can use:

```
from machine import Pin
import onewire,ds18x20

ow = onewire.OneWire(Pin(2))
presence=ow.reset()
if presence:
    print("Device present")
else:
    print("No device")

ds = ds18x20.DS18X20(ow)
roms = ds.scan()
ds.convert_temp()
t = ds.read_temp(roms[0])
print(t)
```

You can see how this program works. After setting up the 1-Wire bus the DS18X20 object is created. The scan of the bus returns a list of DS18X devices and then we initiate a conversion and read the temperature of the first, and often only, device. Notice that you only take a new temperature reading when you use the convert_temp method.

There are some additional methods that provide access to more advanced functions of the DS18B20 and these are discussed at the end of the chapter.

As already said, if you just want to read the temperature the driver is all you need. However, if you want to know how the 1-Wire bus works and how to use other 1-Wire devices, read on.

The 1-Wire Protocol

It is interesting to implement the low-level operation of the 1-Wire bus because it introduces some standard techniques. The DHT22 one wire bus was easy to implement using a single GPIO line because it was slow. We had time to change the GPIO line from output to input mode. The generic 1-Wire bus is too fast to allow for a change in GPIO line direction. The solution is to use two GPIO lines – one for output and one for input. The output line has to be configured as open drain and the two lines are connected together with a single pull-up resistor. This is a fairly standard solution to the problem of implementing a bidirectional line.

Every transaction with a 1-wire device starts with an initialization handshake. This is simply a low pulse that lasts at least 480μs, a pause of 15μs to 60μs follows and then any and all of the devices on the bus pull the line low for 60μs to 240μs. The suggested timings are "set the line low for 480μs and read the line after 70μs followed by a pause of 410μs".

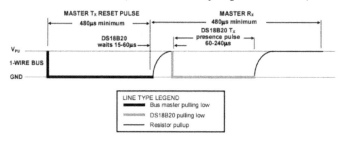

This is fairly easy to implement as a function:

```
OutPin = Pin(4,Pin.OPEN_DRAIN,value=1)
InPin = Pin(2,Pin.IN)

def presence(InPin,OutPin):
    OutPin.on()
    sleep_ms(1)
    OutPin.off()
    sleep_us(480)
    OutPin.on()
    sleep_us(70)
    b = InPin.value()
    sleep_us(410)
    return b
```

The timings in this case are not critical as long as the line is read while it is held low by the slaves, which is never less than $60\mu s$ and is typically as much as $100\mu s$.

If you try this partial program and have a logic analyzer with a 1-wire protocol analyzer you will see something like:

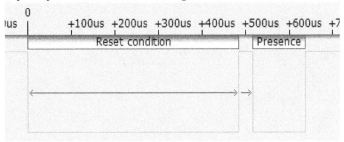

Seeing a presence pulse is the simplest and quickest way to be sure that your hardware is working. Of course, this presence function is equivalent to the driver's reset method.

Our next task is to implement the sending of some data bits to the device. The 1-Wire bus has a very simple data protocol. All bits are sent using a minimum of $60\mu s$ for a read/write slot. Each slot must be separated from the next by a minimum of $1\mu s$.

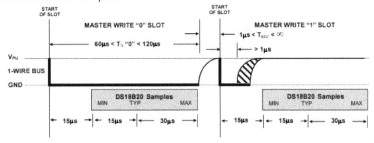

The good news is that timing is only critical within each slot. You can send the first bit in a slot and then take your time before you send the next bit as the device will wait for you. This means you only have to worry about timing within the functions that read and write individual bits.

To send a 0 you have to hold the line low for most of the slot. To send a 1 you have to hold the line low for just between $1\mu s$ and $15\mu s$ and leave the line high for the rest of the slot.

A function to write bits is easy, but to get the necessary speed and accuracy we need to use busy wait `for` loops for the timing and, while the function does just work without, it benefits from using native compilation:

```
@micropython.native
def writeBit(InPin,OutPin,b):
    if b == 1:
        delay1 = 6
        delay2 = 40
    else:
        delay1 = 46
        delay2 = 0
    OutPin.off()
    for i in range(delay1):
        pass
    OutPin.on()
    for i in range(delay2):
        pass
```

The code at the start of the function simply increases the time between slots slightly.

You can see a zero followed by two ones in the following logic analyzer trace:

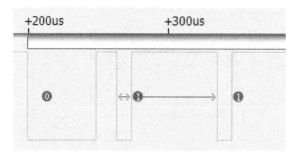

The pulse for a 1 at 10μs is just short enough to work. Each slot is about 70μs.

Of course our `writeBit` function is equivalent, but not as fast, as the OneWire driver's `writebit(value)` method.

Given we know how bits are written to the bus we also know how to read them. The timings are the same and the master still provides the slot's starting pulse. That is, the master starts a slot by pulling the bus down for at least 1μs. Then the slave device either holds the line down for a further 15μs minimum or it simply allows the line to float high for the rest of the slot.

A function to do this is:

```python
@micropython.native
def readBit(InPin,OutPin):
    OutPin.off()
    OutPin.on()
    sleep_us(10)
    b = InPin.value()
    sleep_us(100)
    return b
```

The start of slot pulse is just less than $3\mu s$.

Of course this is the equivalent of the OneWire driver's `readbit()` method.

We could use the bit-banging implementation of the 1-Wire protocol to implement functions that read and write bytes, but at this point it makes more sense to use the methods provided by the OneWire driver.

Match or Skip ROM

After discovering that there is at least one device connected to the bus, the master has to issue a ROM command. In many cases the ROM command used first will be the Search ROM command, which enumerates the 64-bit codes of all of the devices on the bus. After collecting all of these codes, the master can use Match ROM commands with a specific 64-bit code to select the device the master wants to talk to. Having to find and use the ROM codes is often a nuisance and unnecessary if you only have a single device of a known type connected to the bus. If there is only one device then we can use the Skip ROM command, `0xCC`, to tell all the devices, i.e. the only device, on the bus to be active. The only problem is that the DS18X20 driver doesn't support the Skip ROM command and always needs the ROM code to get the temperature. However, it is a good and easy exercise to create another class that will read a single device and this also demonstrates how to read the temperature.

The steps to read the temperature from the only DS18B20 connected to the bus are:

1. Send a reset
2. Send a Skip ROM, `0xCC`, command
3. Send a Convert, `0x44`, command,
4. Wait for the temperature to be read to read
5. Send a Read Scratchpad, `0xBE`, command and then read the nine bytes that the device returns

The Convert command, 0x44, starts the DS18B20 making a temperature measurement. Depending on the resolution selected, this can take as long as 750ms. How the device tells the master that the measurement has completed depends on the mode in which it is operating, but using an external power line, i.e. not using parasitic mode, the device sends a 0 bit in response to a bit read until it is completed, when it sends a 1.

This is how 1-Wire devices that need time to get data ready slow down the master until they are ready. The master can read a single bit as often as it likes and the slave will respond with a 0 bit until it is ready with the data.

As we already have a readBit method this is easy. The software polls for the completion by reading the bus until it gets a 1 bit:

```
def __convert(self):
    self.ow.write([0xCC,0x44])
    for i in range(500):
        sleep_ms(10)
        if self.ow.readbit() == 1:
            j=i
            break
    return j
```

You can, of course, test the return value to check that the result has been obtained. If the convert returns 500 then the loop times out. When the function returns, the new temperature measurement is stored in the device's scratchpad memory and now all we have to do is read it.

The scratchpad memory has nine bytes of storage in total and does things like control the accuracy of conversion and provide status information.

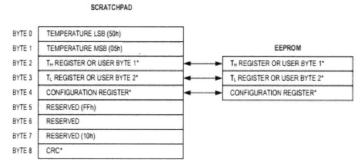

In our simple example the only two bytes of any great interest are the first two, which hold the result of a temperature conversion. However, as we are going to check the CRC for error detection, we need to read all nine bytes.

All we have to do is issue a Read Scratchpad, 0xBE, command and then read the nine bytes that the device returns. To send the new command we have to issue a new initialization pulse and a Skip ROM, 0xCC, command followed by a Read Scratchpad command, 0xBE:

```
self.ow.reset()
self.ow.write([0xCC,0xBE])
```

Now the data is ready to read.

```
Data = bytearray(9)
self.ow.readinto(data)
```

We can read all nine bytes of it or just the first two that we are interested in. The device will keep track of which bytes have been read. If you come back later and read more bytes you will continue the read from where you left off. If you issue another initialization pulse then the device aborts the data transmission.

Now we have all of the data stored in the scratchpad and the CRC byte, we can check for errors:

```
if self.ow.crc8(data)!=0:
    return -2000
```

If there have been no errors the value returned will be 0.

Getting the Temperature

To obtain the temperature measurement we need to work with the first two bytes, namely the least and most significant bytes of the 12-bit temperature reading:

```
t1 = data[0]
t2 = data[1]
```

t1 holds the low-order bits and t2 the high-order bits.

All we now have to do is to put the two bytes together as a 16-bit two's complement integer. We can do this very easily:

```
temp1 = (t2 << 8 | t1)
```

As this is a 32-bit integer, you will have to propagate the sign bit manually into the high order bits to get a negative number:

```
if t2 & 0x80:
    temp1=temp1 | 0xFFFF0000
```

Finally, we have to convert the temperature to a scaled value. As the returned data gives the temperature in centigrade with the low-order four bits giving the fractional part, it has to be scaled by a factor of 1/16:

```
temp = temp1/16
print(temp)
```

A Temperature Class

A complete class to read a DS18B20 using Skip ROM is:

```
from time import sleep_ms
from machine import Pin
import onewire

class DS18B20:
    def __init__(self,pin):
        self.ow = onewire.OneWire(Pin(pin))

    def __convert(self):
        self.ow.write([0xCC,0x44])
        for i in range(500):
            sleep_ms(10)
            if self.ow.readbit() == 1:
                j = i
                break
        return j

    def getTemp(self):
        if not self.ow.reset:
            return -1000
        if self.__convert()==500:
            return -3000
        self.ow.reset()
        self.ow.write([0xCC,0xBE])
        data = bytearray(9)
        self.ow.readinto(data)
        if self.ow.crc8(data)!=0:
            return -2000
        t1 = data[0]
        t2 = data[1]
        temp1 = (t2 << 8 | t1)
        if t2 & 0x80:
            temp1=temp1 | 0xFFFF0000
        return temp1/16

dS18B20=DS18B20(2)
print(dS18B20.getTemp())
```

Notice that the method returns -1000 if there is no device, -2000 if there is a CRC error and -3000 if the device fails to provide data. These values are outside the range of temperatures that can be measured.

Other Commands

As well as the commands that we have used to read the temperature, the DS18B20 supports a range of other commands. There are two commands concerned with when there are more devices on the bus. Search ROM, 0xF0, is used to scan the bus to discover what devices are connected and Match ROM, 0x55, is used to select a particular device.

You can also read the unique 64-bit code of a device using the Read ROM command, 0x33. In this case, the slave transmits eight bytes, comprised of a single-byte device family code, 0x28 for the DS18B20, six bytes of serial number and a single CRC byte.

The OneWire driver supports a scan method which performs a Search ROM and returns a list with a 1-byte array for each ROM found containing its unique id code.

```
ow = onewire.OneWire(Pin(2))
print(ow.scan())
```

Notice that the first byte of the id identifies the type of the device. For example, a DS18B20 starts with 0x10.

There is also a select_rom method which will select a device according to its id. This uses a MatchROM command to select the device and following this all data transfer is between the selected device and the controller until the next reset. For example:

```
ow = onewire.OneWire(Pin(2))
ids=ow.scan()
ow.select_rom(ids[0])
```

selects the first device returned by the scan.

The DS18X20 driver has a specific scan method which only returns the ids of DS18X20 devices.

As well as the Read ScratchPad command that we used to read the temperature, there is also a Write ScratchPad command, 0x4E.

The format of the scratchpad is:

SCRATCHPAD

BYTE 0	TEMPERATURE LSB (50h)
BYTE 1	TEMPERATURE MSB (05h)
BYTE 2	T_H REGISTER OR USER BYTE 1*
BYTE 3	T_L REGISTER OR USER BYTE 2*
BYTE 4	CONFIGURATION REGISTER*
BYTE 5	RESERVED (FFh)
BYTE 6	RESERVED
BYTE 7	RESERVED (10h)
BYTE 8	CRC*

EEPROM

T_H REGISTER OR USER BYTE 1*
T_L REGISTER OR USER BYTE 2*
CONFIGURATION REGISTER*

The first two bytes are the temperature that we have already used. The only writable entries are bytes 2, 3 and 4. The Write ScratchPad command transfers three bytes to these locations. Notice that there is no CRC and no error response if there is a transmission error. The datasheet suggests that you read the scratchpad after writing it to check that you have been successful in setting the three bytes.

The third byte written to the scratchpad is to the configuration register:

BIT 7	BIT 6	BIT 5	BIT 4	BIT 3	BIT 2	BIT 1	BIT 0
0	R1	R0	1	1	1	1	1

Essentially the only thing you can change is the resolution of the temperature measurement.

Configuration Register	Resolution	Time
0x1F	9 bits	93ms
0x3F	10 bits	175ms
0x5F	11 bits	375ms
0x7F	12 bits	750ms

The time quoted is the maximum for a conversion at the given precision. You can see that the only real advantage of decreasing precision is to make conversion faster. The default is 0x7F and 12 bits of precision.

The DS18X20 has a read_scratch method which returns a byte array of the scratchpad data of the specified device. For example:

```
from machine import Pin
import onewire,ds18x20
ow = onewire.OneWire(Pin(2))
presence=ow.reset()
DS=ds18x20.DS18X20(ow)
roms=DS.scan()
print(DS.read_scratch(roms[0]))
```

This prints the scratchpad for the first device returned by the scan. For example:

```
bytearray(b'\xe9\x00\x7f\x80\x7f\xff\x07\x10~')
```

in which the third byte gives the resolution as 12 bits.

You can use write_scratch(id) to write three bytes to the scratchpad.

The first two bytes of the write scratchpad set a high and low temperature alarm. This feature isn't much used, but you can set two temperatures that will trigger the device into alarm mode. Notice you only set the top eight bits of the threshold temperatures. This is easy enough, but the alarm status is set with every read so if the temperature goes outside the set bounds and

236

then back in the alarm is cleared. Notice that you have to use the device's ROM code even if it is the only device on the bus.

The second problem is that, to discover which devices are in alarm mode, you have to use the Alarm Search command, 0xEC. This works like the Search ROM command, but the only devices that respond are the ones with an alarm state. The alarm feature might be useful if you have a lot of devices and simply want to detect an out-of-band temperature. You could set up multiple devices with appropriate temperature limits and then simply repeatedly scan the bus for devices with alarms set.

You may notice that the scratchpad also has an EEPROM memory connected. You can transfer the three bytes of the scratchpad to the EEPROM using Copy Scratchpad, 0x48, and transfer them back using the Recall EEPROM command, 0xB8. You can use this to make the settings non-volatile.

Finally there is the Read Power Supply command, 0xB4. If the master reads the bus after issuing this command, a 0 indicates that there are parasitic powered devices on the bus. If there are such devices the master has to run the bus in such a way that they are powered correctly.

The drivers don't support any of these extended commands, but they are easy enough to implement yourself using the basic read/write methods.

If you want to know how the scan function is implemented, and it is very clever, the description of the algorithm in Chapter 15 of **Raspberry Pi IOT in C, 2nd Ed,** ISBN:978-1871962735 will allow you to implement your own version.

Many one-wire buses can be implemented using a UART. As long as the bit cell is a fixed size it will work. You can see an example of reading a DS18B20 in Chapter 14.

Summary

- The DHT22 is a low-cost temperature and humidity sensor. It uses a custom single wire bus which is not compatible with the well known 1-Wire bus. Its asynchronous protocol is easy to implement directly in MicroPython.

- The 1-Wire bus is a proprietary, but widely-used, bus. It is simple and very capable. As its name suggests it makes use of a single data wire and usually a power supply and ground.

- MicroPython provides a OneWire driver which works with all 1-Wire devices.

- Implementing the 1-Wire protocol is mostly a matter of getting the timing right.

- There are three types of interaction: presence pulse, which simply asks any connected devices to reply and make themselves known, read and write.

- The 1-Wire protocol is easier to implement than you might think because each bit is sent as a "slot" and while timing is critical within the slot, how fast slots are sent isn't and the master is in control of when this happens.

- The DS18B20 temperature sensor is one of the most commonly encountered 1-Wire bus devices. It is small, low-cost and you can use multiple devices on a single bus.

- MicroPython provides a simple DS18X20 driver, but it is also easy to implement your own driver.

- After a convert command is sent to the device, it can take 750ms before a reading is ready. To test for data ready you have to poll on a single bit. Reading a zero means data not ready and reading a one means data ready. When the data is ready, you can read the scratchpad memory where the data is stored.

- The DS18B20 has other commands that can be used to set temperature alarms etc, but these are rarely used.

Chapter 14

The serial port is one of the oldest of ways of connecting devices together, but it is still useful as it provides a reasonably fast communication channel that can be used over a longer distance than most other connections, such as USB. Today, however, its most common and important use is in making connections with small computers and simple peripherals. It can also be used as a custom signal decoder, see later.

Serial Protocol

The serial protocol is very simple. It has to be because it was invented in the days when it was generated using electromechanical components, motors and the like. It was invented to make early teletype machines work and hence you will find abbreviations such as TTY used in connection with it. As the electronic device used for serial communication is called a Universal Asynchronous Receiver/Transmitter, the term UART is also often used to refer to the protocol.

The earliest standards are V24 and RS232. Notice, however, that early serial communications worked between plus and minus 24V and later ones between plus and minus 12V. Today's serial communications work at logic, or TTL, levels of 0V to 5V or 0V to 3.3V. This voltage difference is a problem we will return to later. What matters is that, irrespective of the voltage, the protocol is always the same.

For the moment let's concentrate on the protocol. As already mentioned, it's simple. The line rests high and represents a zero. When the device starts to transmit it first pulls the line low to generate a start bit. The width of this start bit sets the transmission speed as all bits are the same width as the start bit. After the start bit there are a variable number, usually seven or eight, data bits, an optional single parity bit, and finally one or two stop bits.

Originally the purpose of the start bit was to allow the motors etc to get started and allow the receiving end to perform any timing corrections. The stop bits were similarly there to give time for the motors to come back to their rest position. In the early days the protocol was used at very slow speeds; 300 baud, i.e. roughly 300 bits per second, was considered fast enough.

Today the protocol is much the same, but there is little need for multiple stop bits and communication is often so reliable that parity bits are dispensed with. Transmission speeds are also higher, typically 9600 or 115200 baud.

To specify what exact protocol is in use, you will often encounter a short form notation. For example, 9600 baud, 8 data bits, no parity, one stop bit, will be written as 9600 8n1. Here you can see the letter 0 (`01101111` or `0x6F`) transmitted using 8n1:

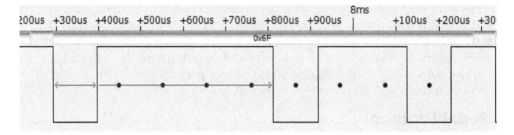

Notice that the signal is sent least significant bit first. The first low is the start bit, then the eight dots show the ideal sampling positions for the receiver. The basic decoding algorithm for receiving serial data is to detect the start of the start bit and then sample the line at the center of each bit time. Notice that the final high on the right is the stop bit. Notice also that the sampling points can be put to use on custom protocols. As long as the data is transmitted in fixed time "cells" indicated by a start bit, you can use a serial port to read individual bits – see later.

For a serial connection to work, it is essential that the transmitter and the receiver are set to the same speed, data bits and parity. Serial interfaces most often fail because they are not working with the same settings. A logic analyzer with a serial decoder option is an essential piece of equipment if you are going to do anything complicated with serial interfacing.

What is a baud? Baud rate refers to the basic bit time. That is, 300 baud has a start bit that is 1/300s wide. This means that for 9600 baud a bit is 1/9600 wide or roughly $104\mu s$ and at 115200 baud a bit is 1/115200 or roughly $8.6\mu s$. Notice that baud rate doesn't equate to the speed of sending data because of the overhead in stop, start and perhaps parity bits to include in the calculation.

UART Hardware

A simple serial interface has a transmit pin, TX, and a receive pin, RX. That is, a full serial interface uses two wires for two-way communications. Typically you connect the TX pin on one device to the RX pin on the other and vice versa. The only problem is that some manufacturers label the pins by what they should be connected to, not what they are and then you have to connect RX to RX and TX to TX. If you are in any doubt you need to check with a meter, logic probe or oscilloscope which pin is which.

In addition to the TX and RX pins, a full serial interface also has a lot of control lines. Most of these were designed to help with old-fashioned teleprinters and they are not often used. For example, RTS - Request To Send is a line that is used to ask permission to send data from the device at the other end of the connection, CTS - Clear To Send is a line that indicates that it is okay to send data and so on. Usually these are set by the hardware automatically when the receive buffer is full or empty.

You can use RTS and CTS as a hardware flow control. There is also a standard software flow control involving sending XON and XOFF characters to start and stop the transmission of data. For most connections between modern devices you can ignore these additional lines and just send and receive data. If you need to interface to something that implements a complex serial interface you are going to have to look up the details and hand-craft a program to interact with it.

The ESP32 has three UARTs which can be used with any GPIO lines that support input and output but there are default assignments:

	UART0	UART1	UART2
TX	1	10	17
RX	3	9	16

On most development boards you cannot use UART1 without changing the default pin allocations as GPIO9 and GPIO10 are generally used to interface flash memory. Also notice that UART0 is mapped to the USB port by default, but if you don't want to use it to implement a REPL while your program is running you can use it as a general UART.

Each UART shares a hardware-implemented 1024-byte buffer which by default is allocated as 128 bytes to a receive and transmit FIFO (first in, first out) for each UART. There is hardware and software flow control, but MicroPython only supports hardware flow control.

There is a problem with making the connection to the ESP32's RX and TX pins in that devices work at different voltages. PC-based serial ports usually use +13V to -13V and all RS232-compliant ports use a + to - voltage swing, which is completely incompatible with most microprocessors which work at 5V or 3.3V.

If you want to connect the ESP32 to a PC or other standard device then you need to use a TTL-to-RS232 level converter. In this case it is easier to use the PC's USB port as a serial interface with a USB-to-TTL level converter. All you have to do is plug the USB port into the PC, install a driver and start to transmit data.

Remember when you connect the ESP32 to another device that TX goes to the other device's RX and RX goes to the other device's TX pin. Also remember that the signaling voltage is 0V to 3.3V.

Setting Up the UART

To create a UART object you use its constructor which at its most basic is:

```
uart = UART(id=, baudrate=, bits=, parity=, stop=,
                                    tx=, rx=, timeout= )
```

There are some more advanced parameters which are described in detail later.

The id has to be 0, 1 or 2 depending on the UART you want to use.

bits specifies the number of bits per character - 7, 8 or 9.

parity can be any of:

```
None    = none
0       = even
1       = odd
```

stop can be 1 or 2 depending on the number of stop bits to be used.
The tx and rx pins are specified as numbers not as Pin objects.

The timeout specifies, in milliseconds, how long read methods will wait for data.

There is also an init method which takes the same parameters as the constructor and can be used to modify how the existing UART instance is configured.

When you have finished with the UART you can release it using

```
UART.deinit()
```

Data Transfer

After you have set up the UART you can start sending and receiving data using methods.

There are three general-purpose read functions:

```
buf = read(nbytes)
readinto(buf,nbytes)
buf = readline()
```

All three return a byte array which you can convert into a string if you need to using encode. If you specify nbytes then only that number of bytes or fewer will be read. If you don't specify nbytes in read then as many bytes as are available are returned. If you don't specify it in readline then at most len(buf) are read. In readline bytes are read in until a newline character is encountered.

There is a single write method:

```
write(buf)
```

this writes the number of bytes in the bytearray or string buf and returns the number of bytes written.

These methods can be more difficult to use than you might expect if you want to send large volumes of data at high speeds. The problems are always about dealing with lots of data at speed. However, if your requirements are more modest things just work.

If you connect GPIO12 (rx) to GPIO13 (tx) (Nano ESP32 A5 and A6) we can use these pins to perform some loopback tests that demonstrate how things work:

```
from machine import UART,Pin
uart = UART(1,baudrate=9600,bits=8,parity=None,rx=12,tx=13)
SendData = bytearray("Hello World \n","utf-8")
uart.write(SendData)
RecData = uart.read()
print(RecData)
```

Notice that we are using UART1 because UART0 is the REPL port for MicroPython. You can use UART2 with no changes and even UART0 if you disable its use as the REPL.

If you try this out you will find that it doesn't work – it displays None rather than the message. The reason is that the write method stores the data in a buffer and returns almost at once and the data is sent by the UART later which at 9600 baud takes around 13.5ms. The problem is that the read tries to read the data even before the first character has arrived.

This is another example of input being harder than output. To send data via a serial port you simply write the data to the buffer and wait while it is sent. To read data from a serial port you need to know when to read.

There are a number of ways around this problem and which one you use depends on the agreed protocol between the transmitter and the receiver. As the UART has buffers it is ready to receive data at any time without the intervention of the MicroPython program and as long as the buffer doesn't fill up you can delay reading until you are ready to process the data. You might think that given the transmitted data only takes 13.5ms, we only need a delay that long to get the data. Adding time.sleep_ms(12) between the write and the read and the program works and you will see the message.

Instead of inserting an estimated delay we can arrange to poll for the data.

Serial Polling

The key method in implementing UART polling is any(), which returns 0 if there are no characters in the RX buffer and the number of characters that are waiting in the buffer otherwise.

It is easy to see that you can use this function to write polling loops which test to see if there is anything to read. For example to create a blocking read:

```
def uart_read(uart):
    while uart.any() == 0:
        pass
    return uart.read()
```

The advantage this offers is that you can do other work within the while loop and check that reading hasn't been waiting too long. That is, you can easily extend it to include a timeout. However, there are still problems with this blocking function. It waits for data to be ready to read but how can you know that all of the data that you are expecting has been read? There are three general solutions to this problem:

1. Work in fixed sized blocks – that is, everything that is exchanged between transmitter and receiver has the same number of bytes. If you want to send something smaller then you need to pad the block with null bytes. Of course, this only works if you can identify a code to use as a null byte.
2. Use a terminator such as a line feed or a carriage return – this is what the readline method is for. Again you have to have a suitable code to use as a terminator.
3. Rely on timing to tell you when a transmission is complete. This is typically how interactions with users take place if they are not line - oriented. The algorithm is – wait till the first character arrives, keep waiting for additional characters until an inter-byte timeout is up. The idea is that a transmission is a continuous flow of bytes separated by a maximum time interval.

244

Buffers

If you read the specifications for the ESP32's UART you will discover that it has a 1-kbyte buffer shared between the three UARTs in 128-byte blocks. The documentation suggests that the buffer size can be varied, but in practice the driver does not implement this and each of the UARTs gets a 128-byte buffer for its RX and TX channels.

What is more difficult to discover is that the UART driver implements a 256-byte ring buffer for both RX and TX channels in addition to the 128-byte FIFO buffer implemented by the hardware. You can change the size of this software buffer and in general this is all you need to do because the 128-byte FIFO buffer is serviced by a regular interrupt and shouldn't fill up unless the ring buffer does so first.

The read and write functions transfer data directly to and from the ring buffer which in turn transfers data to the FIFO buffer as space or data become available. This all works transparently as long as the data doesn't overflow the buffers. If it does then the result might not be what you expect due to the way the two buffers interact.

The write method is only effectively non-blocking if there is space in the ring buffer for it to write its data and return. If the ring buffer is full the write method blocks and waits for space to become free.

Notice that data written to the TX FIFO is transmitted out at a steady rate determined by the baud rate irrespective of whether there is anything receiving that data – i.e. by default there is no flow control. What this means is that the TX ring buffer is filled at the rate that the program can submit data and the TX FIFO buffer empties at the baud rate which is much slower.

For the RX buffers things are the other way round – the FIFO buffer fills at the baud rate and is transferred to the ring buffer at a much higher rate.

Clearly in any given situation the size of the buffers matters. The UART constructor and init method both allow rxbuf= and txbuf= parameters to set the size of the ring buffer. This is often assumed to set the FIFO buffer size, but it doesn't.

This all sounds complicated, but it is easier to understand after a few extreme examples.

First consider what happens when the TX ring buffer is too small for the amount of data being sent, but the RX buffer is more than big enough:

```
from machine import UART,Pin, Timer
from utime import sleep_ms,sleep, time_ns
uart = UART(1,baudrate=9600,bits=8,parity=None,rx=12,tx=13,
                                   txbuf=256,rxbuf=16*1024)
test="A"*252
s = time_ns()
uart.write(test)
print((time_ns()-s)/1000000)
```

If you send only 252 characters then the buffer just copes and the write takes around 0.5 ms or less, if you increase this to 253 characters then the write has to wait for the buffer to be free and takes around 50ms. Notice that the RX buffer is large enough to store all of the data sent and as long as you leave a long enough delay before reading the data or arranging polling then no data is lost. For example, if you send 1000 bytes:

```
test="A"*1000
```

the time to write goes up to 788ms and the time to send the data at 9600 baud is around 1 second – remember the write returns as soon as it has written its last byte to the buffer, but the buffer still has around 250 bytes to send at this point. So if we wait around 300ms all of the data should be in the receive buffer:

```
sleep_ms(300)
RecData = uart.read()
print(RecData)
print(len(RecData))
```

and you will see all of the data printed.

Now consider what happens if the receive buffer is too small. If we arrange to send 1000 bytes with a large enough TX buffer then the write returns in about 0.68 ms and the data then takes just over a second to be transmitted. With an RX buffer of 512 bytes only 613 bytes are ever received:

```
from machine import UART,Pin, Timer
from utime import sleep_ms,sleep, time_ns
uart = UART(1,baudrate=9600,bits=8,parity=None,
                        rx=12,tx=13, txbuf=16*1024,rxbuf=512)
test="A"*1000
s = time_ns()
uart.write(test)
print((time_ns()-s)/1000000)
sleep_ms(4000)
RecData = uart.read()
print(RecData)
print(len(RecData))
```

The extra 100 or so bytes are presumably due to the hardware-provided 128-byte FIFO buffer.

This raises the question of which bytes are missing? A simple minded approach would suggest that the missing bytes should be all of the bytes transmitted after the buffer filled up, but this is not the case. A program to test which bytes are discarded is difficult to implement neatly, but we can create an ad-hoc test by sending an identifiable sequence of bytes:

```
from machine import UART,Pin, Timer
from utime import sleep_ms,sleep, time_ns
uart = UART(1,baudrate=9600,bits=8,parity=None,rx=12,tx=13,
                                    txbuf=4*1024,rxbuf=512)
test = ""
for i in range(280):
    test=test + str(i)+","
print(test)
print(len(test))
s = time_ns()
uart.write(test)
print((time_ns()-s)/1000000)
sleep_ms(4000)
RecData = uart.read()
print(RecData)
print(len(RecData))
```

This writes 1010 characters, but only 623 are received. If you look at the sequence of numbers you will discover that the received data runs from around 0 to 177 and then the sequence jumps to 250 to 279. That is, the end of the transmitted data has overwritten the middle of the sequence. The reason is the way that the ring buffer interacts with the FIFO buffer. When the ring buffer is full it refuses more data but the FIFO buffer continues to receive data and when the transmission is complete the ring buffer has the first part of the transmission and the FIFO buffer has the last part.

To summarize:

- Data is not lost when buffers fill up during writing all that happens is that the write method will take longer to complete.

- Data is lost when buffers fill up while receiving data and the lost data isn't necessarily at the end of the transmission.

- The statement that data isn't lost when writing data has occasional exceptions, but none that are repeatable.

If you want to avoid problems with serial data make sure that the RX buffer is large enough not to fill up, and read data from it often. The size of the TX buffer is less critical, but it can slow your program down.

Timeouts

From the previous section you should be able to see that the usual way that a transmitter and receiver interact is that the transmitter, after perhaps a longish silence, "decides" to send some data. This is usually sent as a block and, as long as the transmitter isn't overloaded, each character follows the next with minimum delay. What this means is that, from the receiver's point of view, there might be a long wait before being able to start reading data, but after that there should be only a short interval between each character. If the receiver finds itself waiting for a long time for the next character then the chances are the transmitter has finished sending a block of data.

Thus there are two sorts of "timeout" we need to specify. An initial timeout, which is how long to wait before the first character is received, and an inter-character timeout, which is the maximum time the receiver should wait between characters before concluding that in all probability the transmitter has finished.

You can specify the two types of timeout in the constructor and the `init` method using the `timeout` and `timeout_char` parameters, both specified in milliseconds. For example:

```
uart = UART(1,baudrate=9600,bits=8,parity=None,rx=12,tx=13,
                            timeout=1,timeout_char=10)
```

waits 1ms for the first character to arrive and then 10ms for each subsequent character to arrive. The time to wait for the first character is usually set by a combination of how much time the receiver can devote to waiting in a polling loop and how often the transmitter sends data. The inter-character time is usually low if the transmitter manages to keep the RX FIFO topped up. It should be set to less than the characteristic time between data blocks from the transmitter.

Polling On Write

Writing data to the UART is much simpler than reading it. Data is written to the TX ring buffer as fast as it can be and the only thing that can go wrong is having to wait because the ring buffer is full. If the ring buffer is full then the call to the write method will block until there is space to accept all of the data. If your program has nothing else to do while the transmission is underway, there is no problem. If, however, your program has to service a polling loop doing a range of other things then it can be a big problem.

There is no MicroPython method to check on the status of the ring buffer. The best you can do is check to see if a transmission is in progress using the `txdone` method. This returns `True` if there is no data to be transmitted and

`False` otherwise. For example, you can use it to block until all of the data has been sent:

```
while(not uart.txdone()):
    pass
```

Notice that this waits for the ring buffer to be emptied after the write method. This isn't ideal as it returns `False` even when there is space in the ring buffer, but it is the best you can do. You can use it to test if the buffer is completely empty before trying to send data.

There is also the `flush` method which simply waits for all of the data to be sent, i.e. it blocks until the ring buffer is empty. This is usually far less useful.

Flow Control

The problem of buffers filling up is usually dealt with by flow control, i.e. signaling whether or not it is okay to send more data. The ESP32 supports both software and hardware flow control, but MicroPython only implements hardware flow control.

Hardware flow control is based on two control lines, Request To Sent (RTS) and Clear To Send (CTS). For the ESP32 RTS is an output and CTS is an input and you can configure any suitable GPIO line to act as either. Exactly how the RTS and CTS lines are actually used depends on what you are connecting to and what control lines it has. A lot of the jargon and procedures involved have their origins back in the days of the mechanical teletype and the non-digital phone system. What matters today is to know that the RTS line is low when there is space in the ESP32's RX FIFO buffer and high when it is full to a specified level – usually 80% or 90% of the buffer capacity. What this means is that the transmitter can use this to determine if it is "clear to send" data to the receiver. That is, if RTS is low, send data, if RTS is high, stop sending data. This is exactly what happens if you connect the RTS line to the CTS line. That is, if the CTS line is low the ESP32 will send any data in its TX FIFO buffer. If the CTS line is high it will hold the data in the TX FIFO buffer.

What this means is if you have two ESP32-like devices, traditionally referred to as DTE (Data Terminal Equipment), then you can connect them together to implement flow control on TX and RX using:

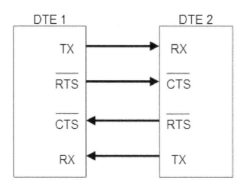

The only complication is that some devices are regarded as DCE, Data Communication Equipment, which are always connected to a DTE and these have their RTS and CTS line labels swapped over. This allows the connections to be specified as "connect RTS to RTS and CTS to CTS". In practice, you need to make sure that RTS is an output connected to CTS, which is an input on the other device, or to RTS, which is an input on the other device.

To test flow control we can simply connect the RTS line on the ESP32 to the CTS line as the ESP32 is acting as DCE1 and DCE2. In the examples given below, it is assumed that GPIO4 is RTS and GPIO5 is CTS and they are connected together in loopback mode.

The biggest complication in using flow control with the ESP32 is that the RTS signal is linked to the RX FIFO buffer and not the RX ring buffer. What this means is that the ESP32 will signal to stop the transmission when its FIFO buffer is full, even though there might be lots of space in the ring buffer.

You can see that this is the case in the following example:

```
from machine import UART,Pin
from utime import sleep_ms, time_ns

uart = UART(1,baudrate=9600,bits=8,parity=None,
            rx=12,tx=13,rts=4,cts=5,
            timeout=0,timeout_char=0,
            txbuf=2000,rxbuf=256,flow=UART.RTS|UART.CTS)

test = "A"*1000
s = time_ns()
uart.write(test)
print((time_ns()-s)/1000000)

RecData = bytes()
while len(RecData)<1000:
    sleep_ms(500)
    if uart.any():
            RecData = RecData + uart.read()
            print(RecData)
            print(len(RecData))
```

This program sets up the UART to use flow control on GPIO4 and GPIO5. It then sends 1000 bytes and attempts to read them back in. The `while` loop reads new data until 1000 bytes have been received. It also contains a delay of 500ms which represents some data processing. Notice that we have set a TX ring buffer large enough to take all of the data to be transmitted. This is important because, in a loopback configuration, if the data could not be sent at once the program would stall at the write method, waiting forever for the ESP32 to read data in after its RX FIFO buffer was full and it had set RTS to low to halt transmission. With all of the data stored in the ring buffer, the program can continue to try to read the data back in. This is not a consideration when the transmitter and receiver are different devices running different programs. In this case the transmitter can just wait till the receiver has read enough to clear its RX FIFO buffer.

Also notice that the way that the FIFO and ring buffers interact complicates the picture. The data from the FIFO buffer is transferred to the ring buffer, which has to fill before the FIFO buffer in turn fills and sets RTS low. The result is that the data is received in blocks of 354 bytes rather than 128 bytes. When the RX FIFO is full, the transmission from the TX FIFO stops emptying, but it too is kept topped up from the TX ring buffer and so, as soon as the RTS line returns high, it starts sending data again. In this way all of the data is sent.

You can see the pattern of start/stop transmission on the logic analyzer:

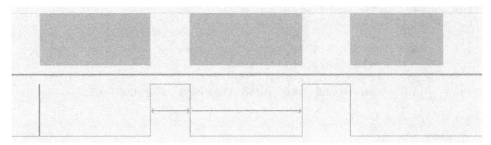

The top trace is the TX line and the bottom trace is the RTS line. The pulse width is 130ms and the period is 501ms.

If you remove the `flow=UART.RTS|UART.CTS` parameter from the constructor and run the program again you will discover that the transmission occurs in one block and you do lose data as the RX ring buffer isn't large enough.

You can discover more about the way flow control works using the loopback configuration, but keep in mind that the fact that the same machine is doing the sending and receiving makes things a little different. For example, as already mentioned, if you drop the size of the TX ring buffer down below the amount of data to be sent the program will hang – this doesn't happen if the data is being transmitted by another device.

Finally, it is worth mentioning that there is a function, `sendbreak()`, that will send a break signal which corresponds to holding the TX line low for more than the time to transmit a single character. It isn't often used today, but there are serial-based protocols that use it to synchronize data transfer often along with flow control.

Using a UART to Decode Data

As an exercise in using a UART to decode a general serial protocol, we can implement the temperature-reading function given in Chapter 13 to read the DS18B20 one-wire device. This is worthwhile as it provides access to the device using hardware.

The first thing we have to do is deal with the electronics. The default configuration of the UART TX pin seems to work reliably with a pull-up. If you are unhappy about this you can use a transistor buffer to act as an open drain output.

The basic idea is that we can use the UART to send an initial stop pulse which pulls the line down. After this we can send data on the line for a write or just allow the DS18B20 to pull the line low. Of course, we have to get the timing right. Let's start with the presence/reset pulse.

If we use a speed of 9600 baud, the start bit pulls the line down for 104.2μs, the next four zero bits holds the line low for 502μs and then the final four 1 bits allow it to be pulled up. If there is a device connected to the line, it will pull the line down for a few microseconds. The serial port will read the line at the same time it is being written as the RX is connected to the TX. The TX sends 0xF0, and you might expect this to be what is received. If there is no device connected then RX will receive 0xF0, but if there is an active device connected the line will be pulled down for some part of the last four bits. As the low-order bits are sent first, this causes the RX to receive something like 0xE0, 0xD0, and so on, i.e. some of the four high order bits are zeroed by the device pulling the line low. You can use this to detect the device.

Assuming that the serial line is set to 9600 baud, the presence/reset pulse can be implemented as a function:

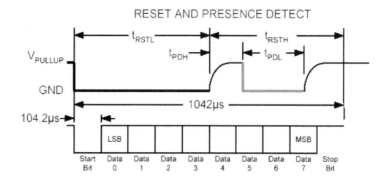

```
def presence(uart):
    uart.init(baudrate=9600)
    uart.write(bytes([0xF0]))
    sleep_ms(20)
    buf = uart.read(1)
    uart.init(baudrate=115200)
    if buf[0] == 0xF0:
        return -1
    return 0
```

To read and write a single bit we need to increase the baud rate to 115200. In this case the start bit lasts 8.7μs, which acts as the initial pulse to read or write a single bit.

To write a zero we simply write 0x00 which holds the line low for eight bits, about 78μs. To write a one we let the line be pulled up after the start bit, which leaves it high for 78μs. To make things slightly faster, we can deal with a single byte at a time:

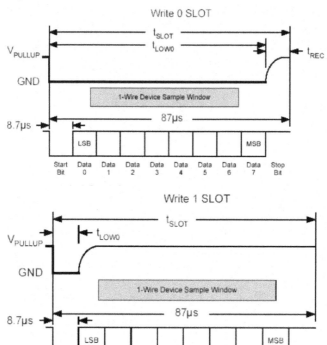

```
def writeByte(uart,byte):
    buf=[]
    for i in range(8):
        if byte & 1 == 1:
            buf.append(0xFF)
        else:
            buf.append(0x00)
        byte = byte >> 1
    uart.write(bytes(buf))
    sleep_ms(10)
    byte=uart.read(8)
```

We have to remember to read the bytes back in otherwise they would still be in the RX buffer. It is also necessary to wait for the data to be sent.

Reading a bit works in the same way. If you write 0xFF then the line is allowed to be pulled high and the remote device can pull it low for a zero or

let it remain high to signal a one. That is, if you write 0xFF and read back
0xFF then you have read a one:

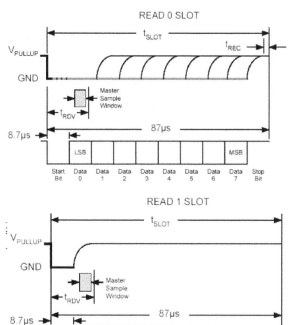

```
def readByte(uart):
    byte = bytes([0xFF]*8)
    uart.write(byte)
    sleep_ms(10)
    byte = uart.read(8)
    result=0
    for b in byte:
        result=result>>1
        if b==0xFF:
            result=result|0x80
    return result
```

Again we can read in a whole byte rather than a bit at a time. With these
modified readByte and writeByte functions we can use the program
developed in Chapter 13 to read the device. The only modifications are to
change the parameter that specifies the GPIO line to be used to one that
specifies the UART being used and the need to open and set the line's baud
rate.

The complete program is:

```
from machine import UART,Pin, mem32
from utime import sleep_ms, time_ns

def presence(uart):
    uart.init(baudrate=9600)
    uart.write(bytes([0xF0]))
    sleep_ms(20)
    buf = uart.read(1)
    uart.init(baudrate=115200)
    if buf[0] == 0xF0:
        return -1
    return 0

def writeByte(uart,byte):
    buf=[]
    for i in range(8):
        if byte & 1 == 1:
            buf.append(0xFF)
        else:
            buf.append(0x00)
        byte = byte >> 1
    uart.write(bytes(buf))
    sleep_ms(10)
    byte=uart.read(8)

def readByte(uart):
    byte = bytes([0xFF]*8)
    uart.write(byte)
    sleep_ms(10)
    byte = uart.read(8)
    result=0
    for b in byte:
        result=result>>1
        if b==0xFF:
            result=result|0x80
    return result
```

```
uart = UART(1,baudrate=115200,bits=8,parity=None,rx=12,tx=13 )
print(presence(uart))

presence(uart)
writeByte(uart, 0xCC)
writeByte(uart, 0x44)
sleep_ms(1000)
presence(uart)
writeByte(uart, 0xCC)
writeByte(uart, 0xBE)

data=[]
for i in range(9):
    data.append(readByte(uart))

t1 = data[0]
t2 = data[1]
temp1 = (t2 << 8 | t1)
if t2 & 0x80:
    temp1=temp1 | 0xFFFF0000
temp=temp1/16
print(temp)
```

Of course, you can use the readByte and writeByte functions within other
one-wire functions with minor modifications.

You can use the UART approach whenever a signaling protocol uses an
initial start bit to signal that the data bits that follow use a fixed size "cell".
However, you cannot use the UART approach with the DHT22 temperature
and humidity sensor because, although it sends each bit with a start bit, the
time to the next start bit varies.

Summary

- The serial port is one of the oldest ways of connecting devices together, but it is still very much in use.

- The serial protocol is asynchronous, but simple. A start bit gives the timing for the entire exchange.

- Many of the control lines once used with telephone equipment are mostly ignored in computer use. Similarly, the original ±12V signaling has been mostly replaced by 5V and even 3.3V signaling.

- The standard hardware that implements a serial connection is usually called a UART.

- The ESP32 contains three UARTs, one of which is used for the USB serial connection.

- MicroPython provides functions for initializing and sending and receiving data.

- Each UART has a 128-element FIFO send and receive buffer and a resizable ring buffer.

- You can use the read and write functions to send and receive byte buffers of data to and from the ring buffer.

- The write method is blocking but as it writes to the ring buffer it returns at once as long as there is free space.

- As the write method waits for space in the ring buffer, data is never lost in transmission.

- As the read method relies on the ring buffer, data can be lost if it fills up.

- If the ring buffer does fill up then the order of the received data might not be what you expect.

- You can specify timeouts for the time the read methods will wait for the first character and for subsequent characters.

- The ESP32 supports simple flow control using the RTS and CTS lines but exactly how these work is complicated by the use of the FIFO and ring buffers.

Chapter 15

Using WiFi

The ESP32 comes complete with a radio capable of 2.4GHz WiFi and Bluetooth. Most of the time you can ignore the technical details as MicroPython provides easy to use objects and methods which enable you to connect to a WiFi network and exchange data. In this chapter we look at the basics and how to create clients and servers. The topic of Bluetooth is omitted as it is so varied it deserves a book to itself.

ESP32 Architecture

You don't really need to know anything about the ESP32's WiFi hardware to make use of it. Indeed there is very little information available apart from how to use the WiFi drivers in the C development kit. The ESP32 usually has two processor cores, which are used to run the WiFi and applications simultaneously. This means that WiFi has little impact on the running of your application. The two cores, Core 0 and Core 1, are named Protocol CPU (PRO_CPU) and Application CPU (APP_CPU). The PRO_CPU processor handles the WiFi, Bluetooth and other internal peripherals like SPI, I2C, ADC etc. The APP_CPU runs the application code, including your MicroPython program.

As well as the radio, the ESP32 also supports four cryptographic accelerators to make the implementation of HTTPS (Hypertext Transfer Protocol Secure) and TLS (Transport Layer Security) in general more efficient.

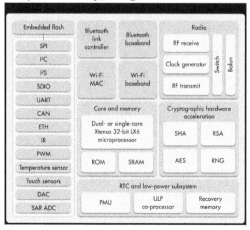

259

The WLAN Class

Networking in MicroPython is taken care of in the network module which contains specific classes to work with different implementations according to the hardware in use. The custom WiFi class for the ESP32 is WLAN. All you have to do is create an instance of the class, set the WiFi to active and then use the connect method. For example:

```
import network
wifi = network.WLAN(network.STA_IF)
wifi.active(True)
wifi.connect("ssid","key")
```

You have to supply the *ssid* and the *key* used to connect to the access point. You can set things up in two modes, STA_IF which makes the ESP32 a client or AP_IF which makes the ESP32 an access point. In most cases you want the ESP32 to be a client of another access point.

It is also a good idea to set the country of operation because different WiFi frequencies are used in different countries and if you don't specify a location not all of the available channels will be used. To set the country you simply call network.country(*"XX"*) with *XX* replaced by the two-character country code specified by ISO 3166-1 alpha-2. For example., to set the country to USA you would use:

```
import network
import rp2
network.country("US")
wifi = network.WLAN(network.STA_IF)
wifi.active(True)
wifi.connect("ssid","key")
```

MicroPython also supports connecting to a specific access point using its bssid, which is the same as the access point's MAC address, but this is really only needed as a security measure.

To disconnect from an access point you can use the disconnect method.

A Practical Connect

In practice, you need to check that the attempted connection has worked. The `connect` method returns at once and usually before the connection has been made. Ideally you would select a connection method that informed you of progress and reported any errors. You can find out the status of the current connection using the `status` method which returns an integer status code:

`network.STAT_IDLE`	1000	No connection and no activity
`network.STAT_CONNECTING`	1001	Connection in progress
`network.STAT_GOT_IP`	1010	Connection successful
`network.STAT_NO_AP_FOUND`	201	Failed because no access point replied
`network.STAT_WRONG_PASSWORD`	202	Failed due to incorrect password
`network.STAT_ASSOC_FAIL`	203	
`network.STAT_HANDSHAKE_TIMEOUT`	204	
`network.STAT_NO_AP_FOUND_W_COMPATIBLE_SECURITY`	210	
`network.STAT_NO_AP_FOUND_IN_AUTHMODE_THRESHOLD`	211	
`network.STAT_NO_AP_FOUND_IN_RSSI_THRESHOLD`	212	

The problem is how to communicate this state to the user? The simplest solution is to flash an LED. For example:

```python
def setup(country, ssid, key):
    network.country(country)
    wifi = network.WLAN(network.STA_IF)
    LED = Pin(2, Pin.OUT)
    LED.on()
    timeout = 20000
    wifi.connect(ssid,key)
    timer = Timer(1)
    timer.init(period=200, mode=Timer.PERIODIC,
                    callback=lambda t:LED.value(not LED.value()))
    s = network.STAT_IDLE
    while timeout>0:
        print("connecting",s)
        s = wifi.status()
        if s != network.STAT_CONNECTING:
            break
        sleep_ms(100)
        timeout = timeout-100
        print("status",s)
    if(s==network.STAT_GOT_IP):
        timer.deinit()
        LED.on()
    else:
        timer.deinit()
        LED.off()
    return wifi
```

This function accepts the country code, SSID (Service Set Identifier), i.e. your network's name and key for the connection. It then creates a WLAN object and activates the hardware. After the attempt to connect, a `While` loop checks the status every 100ms. While the connection is being made, s=1, the LED is flashed every 200ms. If the loop ends with a connection, the LED is switched on, but if there is an error it is turned off.

You can expand the LED feedback to indicate to the user different error conditions using different flashing patterns.

You can get the signal strength of the current connection using:

```
wifi.status('rssi')
```

You can test for a connection using:

```
wifi.isconnected()
```

You can also find out about the current configuration of the connection using:

```
wifi.ifconfig()
```

which returns a tuple of:

(*ip address*, *subnet mask*, *gateway ip*, *dns ip*)

You can also set these parameters by calling `ifconfig` with an appropriate tuple. For example:

```
wifi.ifconfig(("192.168.253.120","255.255.255.0",
                      "192.168.253.1","8.8.8.8"))
```

You can also read and set some general configuration parameters using `wifi.config("`*parameter*`")` which returns the value of the named parameter. In theory you can request any of the following:

`mac`	MAC address (bytes)
`ssid/essid`	WiFi access point name (string)
`channel`	WiFi channel (integer)
`hidden`	Whether SSID is hidden (boolean), AP mode only
`security/authmode`	Security protocol supported, AP mode only
`hostname/` `dhcphostname`	The name that will be sent to DHCP (STA interfaces) and mDNS (if supported, both STA and AP)
`reconnects`	Number of reconnect attempts to make (0=none, -1=unlimited)
`txpower`	Maximum transmit power in dBm (integer or float)

You can also use the parameter names as named parameters in a call to `config` to set the corresponding parameter. For example, to set the most important, hostname:

```
wifi.config(hostname = "myESP")
```

WiFi Scan

The scan method can be used to survey what access points are available. It returns a list of tuples, each tuple of which has the format:

(*ssid*, *bssid*, *channel*, *RSSI*, *security*, *hidden*)

where *ssid* is the usual name of the network, *bssid* is the MAC address of the access point, *channel* is the channel number of the access point and *RSSI* is a relative measure of the strength of the received signal. If your app needs to choose an access point, then picking the one with the highest RSSI is reasonable. The *security* item is one of:

0 – open

1 – WEP

2 – WPA-PSK

3 – WPA2-PSK

4 – WPA/WPA2-PSK

Finally *hidden* is False if the access point is broadcasting its SSID and True if not.

To display the WiFi access points in range you could use:

```
import network
wifi = network.WLAN(network.STA_IF)
wifi.active(True)
wifi.disconnect()
aps = wifi.scan()
for ap in aps:
    print(ap)
```

A Simple HTTP Client

The simplest way to make use of a WiFi connection is to work with an HTTP server. This approach means the difficult parts of the transaction are handled by the server, making the client much easier to implement. MicroPython makes this even easier by providing urequests which is a port of the Python requests module. This has methods that implement the standard HTTP transactions and a request object which wraps the data involved in the transaction.

The urequests module should work on any MicroPython implementation and it is built on top of the sockets module which is discussed later. The sockets module provides a lower-level interface to the network and urequests uses this to implement the HTTP protocol. While HTTP was invented to allow the transport of HTML pages, it can be used to transfer any data between the client and the server.

It is important to understand the distinction between the client and the server. In this case the client initiates the connection and the server accepts the connection. The connection once established is two-way – the client can send data to the server and vice versa. This said, HTTP is most commonly used to send data from the server to the client in the form of web pages.

Request Methods

HTTP supports a number of request methods which transfer data. Usually these are described in terms of what they do to resources hosted by a web server, but from our point of view what matters is what happens to the data.

The HTTP request methods available are:

GET	Transfers data from server to client
HEAD	Transfers HTTP headers for the equivalent GET request
PUT	Transfers data from the client to the server
POST	Transfers data from the client to the server
PATCH	Transfers data from the client to the server
DELETE	Specifies that the data on the server should be deleted
OPTIONS	Transfers data from the client to the server

If you know about HTTP request methods you will find the above list disconcerting. If you don't know about HTTP requests then you will be wondering why there are so many requests that transfer data from the client to the server? The answer is that in the HTTP model the server stores the master copy of the resource – usually a file or a database entry. The client can request a copy of the resource using GET and then ask the server to modify the resource using the other requests. For example, the PUT request sends a new copy of the resource for the server to use, i.e. it replaces the old copy. POST does the same thing, but PUT should be idempotent which means if you repeat it the result is as if you had done it just once. With POST you are allowed side effects. For example, PUT 1 might just store 1 but POST 1 might increment a count.

Another example is where you send some text to the server to save under a supplied file name. For this you should use a PUT as repeating the request with the same text changes nothing. If, on the other hand, you supply text to the server and allow it to assign a name and store it then you should use a POST as you get a new file each time you send the data, even if it is the same.

Similarly the PATCH request should be used by the client to request that that server makes a change to part of an existing resource. Exactly how the change is specified depends on the server. Usually a key value scheme is used, but this isn't part of the specification.

Notice that all of these interpretations of the HTTP request methods are "optional" in the sense that it is up to you and the server you are using to interpret them and implement them. If you write your own server, or server application, then you can treat POST as if it was PUT and vice versa.

A Custom Server

The problem with writing HTTP examples is that how they are handled depends on the server in use. Not all HTTP servers implement the same range of requests. A simple solution to this problem is to write a custom server and Python makes this very easy. Before you try any of the following examples, create the following Python program on a suitable machine on your local network. Notice that this code is in Python, not MicroPython:

```python
from http.server import HTTPServer, BaseHTTPRequestHandler
from io import BytesIO


class SimpleHTTPRequestHandler(BaseHTTPRequestHandler):

    def sendResponse(self, cmd):
        content_length = int(self.headers['Content-Length'])
        body = self.rfile.read(content_length)
        self.send_response(200)
        self.end_headers()
        response = BytesIO()
        response.write(b'This is a '+bytes(cmd, 'utf-8')+
                                                b' request. ')
        response.write(b'Received: ')
        response.write(body)
        self.wfile.write(response.getvalue())

    def do_GET(self):
        self.send_response(200)
        self.end_headers()
        self.wfile.write(b'Hello, world!')


    def do_HEAD(self):
        self.send_response(200)
        self.end_headers()
```

```
def do_POST(self):
    self.sendResponse("POST")

def do_PUT(self):
    self.sendResponse("PUT")

def do_DELETE(self):
    self.sendResponse("DELETE")

def do_PATCH(self):
    self.sendResponse("PATCH")


httpd = HTTPServer(('', 8080), SimpleHTTPRequestHandler)
httpd.serve_forever()
```

This server implements simple methods to respond to GET, HEAD, PUT, POST, DELETE and PATCH requests. If you want to support a custom request simply include a method that is called do_*request* where *request* is the command you want to use. Notice that this custom request is unlikely to be serviced by a standard server, but there is nothing stopping you from implementing your own. In the case of GET, the server sends fixed data – "Hello World" - and for the others it sends back whatever was sent to it by the client, with the exception of HEAD that sends nothing at all except for the headers.

If you install this program on a remote machine on the same network as the ESP32 then you can use it to test HTTP request programs. With a little work you can also turn it into a server that supports your app in the real world. You can even convert it into an SSL server for HTTPS connections using the Python SSL module.

The urequests Module

The urequests module implements the GET, PUT, POST, PATCH, HEAD and DELETE requests. The most commonly used is GET to retrieve data from a server. All of the methods return a Response object which contains details of the server's response.

This supports a subset of the Python `Response` object's properties/methods:

status_code	Integer HTTP status code
reason	Text from of HTTP status code
headers	Dictionary of headers sent by server
content	Data returned by server as bytes
text	Data returned by server as a string
raw	Data returned by server as a file-like object
json	Data returned by server as a JSON object
encoding	Encoding to be used to convert raw to text utf-8 by default
close	Release Response object

It also has a set of methods – one for each type of request:

```
head(url)
get(url)
post(url,data = data to send)
put(url,data = data to send)
patch(url,data = data to send)
delete(url)
```

There is also a single general-purpose `request` method which implements any type of request, including custom requests. It is used by the earlier request methods:

```
request(
    method,
    url,
    data = None,
    json = None,
    headers = {},
    stream = None,
    auth = None,
    timeout = None,
    parse_headers = True,
)
```

So for example, a call to `get(url)` is translated into:

```
request(url,"GET")
```

The `request` method will supply the basic HTTP/HTTPS header and the host header if these are not provided in the headers dictionary. You can include a user name and password as a tuple for the `auth` parameter and these are passed to the server in an authorization header. You can also set `json=object` as an alternative to using data and have the `urequests` module send a JSON encoded string, see later. All of the specific request methods will pass on any keyword parameters you include in the general request method.

267

Notice that the `urequests` module works with both HTTP and HTTPS and you don't have to do anything to make HTTPS work. However, at the time of writing, the support only extends to encrypting the data transfer and the server's certificate is not checked for validity.

For example, to download a web page using HTTPS you might use:

```
import network
from machine import Pin, Timer
from time import sleep_ms
import urequests

def setup(country, ssid, key):
    .    .    .

wifi=setup(country, ssid, key)
print("Connected")
r = urequests.get("https://www.example.com")
print(r.content)
r.close()
```

This assumes that you have the setup function given earlier. The site `www.example.com` provides a test server which works with HTTP and HTTPS. If you run this program you will see the HTML that makes up its standard web page.

If you target the Python custom server then you can see all of the request methods in action:

```
import network
from machine import Pin, Timer
from time import sleep_ms
import urequests

def setup(country, ssid, key):
    .    .    .
wifi=setup(country, ssid, key)
print("Connected")

url="http://192.168.253.72:8080"
r = urequests.get(url)
print(r.content)
r.close()

buf= b'Hello World'
r=urequests.post(url,data=buf)
print(r.content)
r.close()

r=urequests.put(url,data=buf)
print(r.content)
r.close()
```

```
r=urequests.patch(url,data=buf)
print(r.content)
r.close()

r=urequests.head(url)
print(r.content)
print(r.headers)
r.close()

r=urequests.delete(url,data=buf)
print(r.content)
r.close()
```

Of course, to make this work you have to substitute the IP address of the machine running the Python custom server. Notice that the custom server only supports HTTP, but it is relatively easy to convert it to HTTPS.

If you run this program you will see something like:

```
b'Hello, world!'
b'This is a POST request. Received: Hello World'
b'This is a PUT request. Received: Hello World'
b'This is a PATCH request. Received: Hello World'
b''
{'Server': 'BaseHTTP/0.6 Python/3.9.2',
                    'Date': 'Thu, 17 Nov 2022 18:20:42 GMT'}
b'This is a DELETE request. Received: Hello World'
```

If you run this with a standard web server it is unlikely you will see anything other than error messages. The response of a standard web server has to be configured to respond to anything but a simple GET. Usually you have to install a CGI script to deal with anything that sends data to the server.

You should be able to see now that the only difference between an HTTP client and server is that the client initiates the connection and the request. The server simply responds to the client, but it can send data to and receive data from the client. Using this it is possible to implement a simple sensor feeding data to a central server.

A Temperature Sensor Client

The standard approach to implementing a sensor device that makes its readings available to other devices is to implement a web server or a custom protocol that allows other devices to connect. A simpler solution is to implement an HTTP client and allow the sensor device to send data to a server which other devices can then connect to as required.

As we have already seen in Chapter 13, it is very easy to use the DS18B20 to collect data about ambient temperature. All we have to do is take a reading every so often, convert the floating-point value to a byte object and send it to the server using a PUT:

```
import network
from machine import Pin, Timer
from time import sleep_ms
import urequests
import onewire
import ds18x20

def setup(country, ssid, key):
    .   .   .

wifi=setup(country, ssid, key)
print("Connected")
url = "http://192.168.253.72:8080"
ow = onewire.OneWire(Pin(22))
presence = ow.reset()
if presence:
    print("Device present")
else:
    print("No device")

DS = ds18x20.DS18X20(ow)
roms = DS.scan()

while True:
    DS.convert_temp()
    temp = DS.read_temp(roms[0])
    buf = str(temp).encode("utf-8")
    try:
        r = urequests.put(url, data=buf)
        r.close()
    except:
        print("Server Not Online")
    sleep_ms(500)
```

The setup function given earlier, which makes the WiFi connection, has been omitted.

The server simply has to respond to the PUT request and convert the bytes to a string and then a float:

```
from http.server import HTTPServer, BaseHTTPRequestHandler
from io import BytesIO

class SimpleHTTPRequestHandler(BaseHTTPRequestHandler):

    def log_message(self,*args, **kwargs):
        pass

    def do_PUT(self):
        content_length = int(self.headers['Content-Length'])
        body = self.rfile.read(content_length)
        bodyString= body.decode(encoding="utf-8")
        temp=float(bodyString)
        print(temp)
        self.send_response(200)
        self.end_headers()

httpd = HTTPServer(('', 8080), SimpleHTTPRequestHandler)
httpd.serve_forever()
```

As before, it is simple enough to convert the server to HTTPS. The overriding of the log_message method is to suppress the regular printing of status messages. The do_PUT handler method simply prints the temperature. It could, of course, do much more.

You can appreciate that this architecture works well if you can allocate a simple device to act as a server. If the sensor supplies more data than a single measurement then using a JSON encoding makes things easier. For example, if you want to send a timestamp along with the temperature you could change the while loop to read:

```
while True:
    DS.convert_temp()
    temp = DS.read_temp(roms[0])
    jsonData = {"temp":temp,"time":time()}

    try:
        r = urequests.put(url,json-=-jsonData)
        r.close()
    except:
        print("Server Not Online")
    sleep_ms(500)
```

You can see that the only difference is that now we make up a dictionary with key/value pairs corresponding to the data we want to send to the server. The only other difference is that we now set json-=-jsonData rather than setting it to data and the urequests module converts the dictionary into a JSON string.

271

To process the JSON string the server's do_PUT method now has to use the json module to convert the received JSON string back into a dictionary object:

```
def do_PUT(self):
    content_length = int(self.headers['Content-Length'])
    body = self.rfile.read(content_length)
    bodyString= body.decode(encoding="utf-8")
    jsonData=json.loads(bodyString)
    print(jsonData)
    self.send_response(200)
    self.end_headers()
```

If you run the client and the server with these changes you will see something like:

```
{'time': 1609459985, 'temp': 14.4375}
{'time': 1609459986, 'temp': 14.5}
{'time': 1609459987, 'temp': 14.4375}
```

You can unpack the data from the dictionary and use it as you would any other data.

Summary

- Connecting to a WiFi network is a matter of using the WLAN class.

- Implementing error handling for a WiFi connection can be challenging.

- The simplest way of implementing an HTTP client is to use urequests.

- An HTTP client can both send and receive data to the server depending on the request it makes.

- The most common request is GET which accepts data from the server.

- Both POST and PUT can be used to send data to the server.

- The only difference between a client and server is that a client can only make a connection, a server can accept a connection.

- It is possible to avoid having to implement a server on the ESP32 by allowing a client to connect to a server running on another machine and send its data using a PUT or POST request.

If you want to go beyond a simple client you need to make use of a more general network connection method. The usual way of doing this is to make use of "sockets". This is a widely supported internet standard and most servers support socket connections.

MicroPython supports a limited version of the full Python Sockets module. The parts of the module that are not supported are mostly those concerned with making connections using non-IP networks and hence are generally minor.

The most important thing to understand about sockets is that they are a very general way of making a two-way connection between a client and a server. A client can create a socket to transfer data between itself and a server and a server can use a socket to accept a connection from a client. The only difference between the two situations is that the server has to either poll or use interrupts to detect a new connection attempt.

Socket Objects

Before you can start to send and receive data you have to create a socket object:

```
import socket
s = socket.socket()
```

This default constructor creates a socket suitable for IPv4 connections.

If you want to specify the type of socket being created you have to use:

```
socket(af=AF_INET, type=SOCK_STREAM, proto=IPPROTO_TCP)
```

The af parameter gives the address family and it is either AF_INET for IPv4 or AF_INET6 for IPv6 – at the time of writing only IPv4 is supported. The type parameter indicates either SOCK_STREAM or SOCK_DGRAM, the stream option. The default, SOCK_STREAM, corresponds to the usual TCP/IP connection used to transfer web pages and files in general. It is a persisted and error-corrected connection whereas SOCK_DGRAM sends individual packets without error checking or confirmation that the data was received.

The final parameter, proto, sets the exact type of protocol, but as the only two supported are IPPROTO_TCP and IPPROTO_UDP this is set according to the type parameter:

type	proto
SOCK_STREAM	IPPROTO_TCP
SOCK_DGRAM	IPPROTO_UDP

In a more general setting there could be more types of proto supported for each type.

Socket Addresses

After defining the type of connection, you need to specify the addresses involved in the connection. As sockets can be used to connect to a wide range of different types of network, the address format can vary a lot and not just be a simple URL or an IP address. For this reason sockets are used with their own internal address representation and you have to use the getaddrinfo method:

socket.getaddrinfo(*host*, *port*, af=0, type=0, proto=0, flags=0)

The first two parameters are familiar and simple. The *host* has to be specified using a URL or an IP address. The second is the numeric port to use with the socket. The next three parameters are the same as used in creating the socket. In general you use the same parameter values for an address intended to be used with a socket as used to create the socket. If you don't specify a parameter then getaddrinfo will return a list of tuples for each possible address type. Each tuple has the following format:

(*af*, *type*, *proto*, *canonname*, *sockaddr*)

where *af*, *type* and *proto* are as before and *canonname* is the canonical name for the address type and *sockaddr* is the actual address, which may also be a tuple. In the case of an IP address, the *sockaddr* is a tuple with the format:

(*IP*, *port*)

At the time of writing ESP32 only supports IPv4 and it only returns a list with a single tuple. The only really useful part of this tuple is the final element which is an IP tuple used by most of the socket methods. You could short circuit everything by simply creating the IP tuple and not use getaddrinfo. However, you should use getaddrinfo to allow for compatibility with the full sockets module and for future development.

For example:
```
ai = socket.getaddrinfo("www.example.com",
                        80,socket.AF_INET,socket.SOCK_DGRAM)
```
returns the list:
```
[(2, 1, 0, '', ('93.184.216.34', 80))]
```
and is it the final tuple:
```
('93.184.216.34', 80)
```
which we actually use in calls to socket methods. To extract this final tuple we use:
```
addr = ai[0][-1]
```
While on the subject of addresses, there are two functions which can be used to convert an IP address in "dotted" form to a byte value and vice versa:
```
socket.inet_ntop(socket.AF_INET,bytes)
```
gives the dotted text form and:
```
socket.inet_pton(socket.AF_INET,string)
```
gives the binary form of the IP address.

Client Sockets

Once we have a socket object and the ability to specify an address, we have to connect it to another socket to make a two-way communication channel. Data can be written and read at both sockets that form the connection. Exactly how sockets are connected depends on which is the client and which the server. In this section we look at how to connect to a server. By default all socket methods are blocking. See later for non-blocking operation.

If you want to connect a socket to a server socket than all you have to do is use:
```
socket.connect(address)
```
where *address* is the address of the server socket you are trying to connect to and has to be specified as an IP tuple:
```
(ip,port)
```
For example:
```
socket.connect(('93.184.216.34',80))
```
While you can use an IP tuple, it is more usual to use `socket.getaddrinfo` to generate it.

You should always close a socket when you are finished using it with a call to the `close` method.

Once you have a connected socket you can send and receive data using a range of methods.

The methods used to send data are:

send(bytes)	Returns the number of bytes actually sent.
sendall(bytes)	Sends all the data even if it takes multiple chunks of data. Doesn't work well with non-blocking sockets and write is preferred.
write(buf)	Tries to write all of the buffer. This may not be possible with a non-blocking socket. It returns the number of bytes actually sent.

The receive methods are:

recv(len)	Returns no more than len bytes as a Bytes object.
recvfrom(len)	Returns no more than len bytes as a tuple *(bytes,address)* where *address* is the address of the device sending the database.
read(len)	Returns no more than len bytes as a bytes object. If len is not specified it reads as much data as is sent until the socket is closed.
readinto(buf, len)	Reads no more than len bytes into the buf. If len is not specified len(buf) is used. Returns the number of bytes actually read.
readline()	Reads a line, ending in a newline character.

There are also:

sendto(bytes, *address*)	Sends data to the address specified – the socket used has to be unconnected for this to work.
makefile(mode = 'rb', buffering = 0)	Available for compatibility with Python which needs the socket to be converted to a file before reading or writing. In MicroPython this can be used but it does nothing.

A Socket Web Client

Using what we know so far about sockets, we can easily connect to a server and send and receive data. What data we actually send and receive depends on the protocol in use. Web servers use HTTP, which is a very simple text-based protocol. Using the urequests module we could ignore the nature of the protocol as it implemented most of it for us. When it comes to using sockets we have to work out what to send in detail.

The HTTP protocol is essentially a set of text headers of the form:

`headername: headerdata \r\n`

that tell the server what to do, and a set of headers that the server sends back to tell you what it has done. You can look up the details of HTTP headers in the documentation – there are a lot of them.

The most basic transaction the client can have with the server is to send a `GET` request for the server to send back a particular file. Thus the simplest header is:

`"GET /index.html HTTP/1.1\r\n\r\n"`

which is a request for the server to send `index.html`. In most cases we need one more header, `HOST`, which gives the domain name of the server. Why do we need it? Simply because HTTP says you should, and many websites are hosted by a single server at the same IP address. Which website the server retrieves the file from is governed by the domain name you specify in the `HOST` header.

This means that the simplest set of headers we can send the server is:
`"GET /index.htm HTTP/1.1\r\nHOST:example.org\r\n\r\n";`
which corresponds to the headers:

`GET /index.html HTTP/1.1`
`HOST:example.org`

An HTTP request always ends with a blank line. If you don't send the blank line then you will get no response from most servers. In addition, the `HOST` header has to have the domain name with no additional syntax - no slashes and no `http:` or similar.

`request = b"GET /index.html HTTP/1.1\r\nHost:example.org\r\n\r\n"`

Now we are ready to send our request to the server, but first we need its address and we need to connect the socket:

```
ai = socket.getaddrinfo("www.example.com", 80,socket.AF_INET)
addr = ai[0][-1]
s = socket.socket(socket.AF_INET)
s.connect(addr)
```

Now we can send the headers which constitute the GET request:

```
request = b"GET /index.html HTTP/1.1\r\nHost:example.org\r\n\r\n"
s.send(request)
```

Finally, we can wait for the response from the server and display it:

`print(s.recv(512))`

Notice that all of the methods are blocking in the sense that they don't return until the operation is complete.

The complete program, with the setup function given earlier omitted is:

```
import network
import socket
from machine import Pin, Timer
from time import sleep_ms

def setup(country, ssid, key):
    .  .  .

wifi=setup(country, ssid, key)
print("Connected")
url = "http://192.168.253.72:8080"
ai = socket.getaddrinfo("www.example.com", 80,socket.AF_INET)
addr = ai[0][-1]
s = socket.socket(socket.AF_INET)
s.connect(addr)

request = b"GET /index.html HTTP/1.1\r\nHost:example.org\r\n\r\n"
s.send(request)
print(s.recv(512))
```

You can see that the urequests module is much easier to use. Of course, it makes use of sockets to do its job.

SSL Socket-Based HTTPS Client

Many websites now refuse to serve unencrypted data and insist on HTTPS. Fortunately it is very easy to create an HTTPS client as you don't need to create a digital certificate. If you need to prove to a server that it is indeed you trying to connect then you should install a new certificate and use it. This is exactly the same procedure as installing a new server certificate, see later.

MicroPython has a very minimal implementation of the Python ssl module, but it is enough to do what you need to make an HTTPS client or server. It only has a single function wrap_socket which adds encryption, and in some cases authentication, to an existing socket. At the time of writing, MicroPython for the ESP32 doesn't support authentication.

The wrap_socket function is:

```
ssl.wrap_socket(sock, keyfile=None, certfile=None,
                server_side=False, cert_reqs=CERT_NONE,
                ca_certs=None,
                do_handshake_on_connect=True,
                )
```

This takes an existing socket specified by sock and turns it into an encrypted SSL socket. Apart from sock, all its parameters, including keyfile and certfile which specify files containing the certificate and/or key, are optional.

All certificates have to be in PEM (Privacy-Enhanced Mail) format. If the key is stored in the certificate then you only need to use certfile. If the key is stored separately from the certificate you need both certfile and keyfile. When True, the server_side parameter sets the behavior appropriate to a server and when False to a client and cert_reqs determines the level of certificate checking, from CERT_NONE, CERT_OPTIONAL to CERT_REQUIRED. The validity of the certificate is only checked if you select CERT_REQUIRED and currently the ESP32 never checks the certificate for validity. ca_certs is a bytes object containing the certificate change to be used to validate the client's certificate. server_hostname is used to set the server's hostname so that the certificate can be checked to ascertain that it does belong to the website and to allow the server to present the appropriate certificate if it is hosting multiple sites. do_handshake should be used with non-blocking sockets and when True defers the handshake whereas when False, the function doesn't return until the handshake is complete.

Notice that not all of the full Python wrap_socket parameters are supported and not all TLS and encryption levels work. This means that you will discover that, at the moment, connecting to some websites is difficult, if not impossible. However, in many cases it should simply work, as long as the website concerned is not using a cutting edge implementation.

The only modification that the previous HTTP client needs to work with an HTTPS website is:

```python
import network
import socket
import ssl
from machine import Pin, Timer
from time import sleep_ms

def setup(country, ssid, key):
    .   .   .

wifi=setup(country, ssid, key)
print("Connected")

ai = socket.getaddrinfo("example.com", 443,socket.AF_INET)
addr = ai[0][-1]
s = socket.socket(socket.AF_INET)
s.connect(addr)
sslSock=ssl.wrap_socket(s)
request = b"GET / HTTP/1.1\r\nHost:example.com\r\n\r\n"
sslSock.write(request)
print(sslSock.read(1024))
```

where the setup function has been omitted.

Notice that all we need to do is perform a default `wrap_socket` after making the connection. The downloaded HTML is now fetched using HTTPS. The `sslSock` returned by the `wrap_socket` function only has stream `read` and `write` methods.

Socket Server

The problem of connecting a socket when you are the server is more complicated than when you are a client. In this case the socket has to be ready and listening for a client to make a connection. It then sets up a completely new socket which is used to communicate with the client. This new socket is destroyed when the communication with the client is over. The original socket continues listening for new client connections.

In principle, the listening socket can create multiple new sockets, one for each client that wants to connect to the server. In this way, in theory, the server is capable of handling multiple clients at the same time. The problem is that to handle more than one client implies that the program is organized to process multiple clients and, as always, there are various ways of doing this. You can simply implement a polling loop that cycles round the set of active clients, you can implement a multithreaded program, one thread per client, or you can adopt an asynchronous task approach where a single thread services all of the clients using an event queue. If you would like to know more about asynchronous programming in Python, see **Programmer's Python: Async**, ISBN:9781871962765.

The problem with implementing a server for the ESP32 and in MicroPython is that neither makes use of an operating system that manages threads and processes. As a result we can either opt to handle clients using polling or using a single-threaded asynchronous event queue. If you want to use an event queue then you can use the MicroPython implementation of the `asyncio` module, which is the topic of Chapter 17.

To use a socket as a server you first have to bind it to the external network ports that you want it to respond to. A machine might well have more than one internet adapter and hence more than one IP address. In the case of the ESP32 the only thing that might vary is the port in use. For example:

```
addr = socket.getaddrinfo('0.0.0.0', 8080)[0][-1]
```

creates an IP tuple with the current IP address and port 8080. The IP address '0.0.0.0' means any IP address you have available. Once you have the address, the socket can be made to use it with the `bind` method:

```
s = socket.socket(socket.AF_INET)
s.bind(addr)
```

Now the socket will use the specified address, but to make it listen out for connecting clients you have to use the `listen` method:

```
s.listen(backlog)
```

The `backlog` parameter specifies the number of unaccepted clients allowed before the socket responds by refusing the connection. To actually work with the client you have to accept the connection using the `accept` method.

```
s.accept()
```

This blocks until a client tries to connect and then returns a tuple of the form:

```
(socket, address)
```

The socket can be used to communicate with the client at the specified address. You can use all of the standard socket methods with this new socket and you should close it when you have finished communicating with the client.

A Socket Temperature Server

With all of this in place we can now use sockets to build a server.

First we need to create a socket and bind it to the local IP address:

```
addr = socket.getaddrinfo('192.168.253.58', 8080)[0][-1]
s = socket.socket()
s.setsockopt(socket.SOL_SOCKET, socket.SO_REUSEADDR, 1)
s.bind(addr)
s.listen(0)
```

Of course, you need to change the IP address to that of the ESP32 that the program is running on. The only new element is that we have used the `setsockopt` method to allow the socket to reuse the address – without this you would get an error that the address was in use after each restart.

Now we have a socket listening on port 8080 and we can wait until a client attempts to connect:

```
cl, addr = s.accept()
```

This waits until a client connects and returns the socket `cl` and its IP address. We can now use the socket to read the request from the client:

```
print('client connected from', addr)
print(cl.recv(512))
```

In this case we aren't particularly interested in the content of the request because we are going to serve the same content no matter what. However, this does mean that we will probably serve the same content twice to any client as even the simplest web page request generates an additional file download request for the site's icon which is used in the browser's tab.

If the client used the url:

```
http://192.168.253.58:8080/temperature
```

the request would start with:

```
b'GET /temperature HTTP/1.1\r\n
Host: 192.168.253.58\r\n
Connection: keep-alive\r\n
```

and so on.

You can use the string following GET to determine what the client wants in return. In this case you would test for temperature before returning a value.

Now all we have to do is send a web page with the current temperature in it. Logically we first need to create the headers, but one of the headers, Content-Length, needs to contain the number of bytes in the content. This means we first have to create the content so we can obtain its size.

A simple HTML page is:

```
template = """<!DOCTYPE html>
<html>
<head> <title>Temperature</title> </head>
<body> <h1>Current Temperature</h1>
Hello ESP32 Server World <br/>
The Temperature is: <!--#temp--><br/>
</body>
</html>
"""
```

The idea is that we will use this as a template and replace <!--#temp-> by the measured temperature each time the page is served:

```
html = template.replace("<!--#temp->",str(temp))
```

assuming temp has the current temperature. Now we can create the headers:

```
headers = ("HTTP/1.1 200 OK\r\n"
          "Content-Type: text/html; charset=UTF-8\r\n"
          "Server:ESP32\r\n"
          f"Content-Length:{len(html)}\r\n\r\n"
          )
```

Notice the way that we use a formatted string, an f string, to add the length of the html into the Content-Length header.

Now we can send the response to the client:

```
buf = headers.encode("utf-8")+html.encode("utf-8")
cl.send(buf)
cl.close()
```

The client now has the web page that displays the current temperature and so we can close the client socket.

Of course, this only serves a single request from a single client. To keep on serving as clients try to connect, we need to put the accept and what we do to send the data into an infinite loop.

The complete program minus the setup function given earlier, but including reading a DS18B20 temperature connected on GPIO4 sensor, is:

```python
import network
import socket
from time import sleep_ms
from machine import Pin, Timer
import onewire
import ds18x20
def setup(country, ssid, key):
    ...
wifi = setup("country", "ssid", "key")
ow = onewire.OneWire(Pin(4))
presence = ow.reset()
if presence:
    print("Device present")
else:
    print("No device")
DS = ds18x20.DS18X20(ow)
roms = DS.scan()
template = """<!DOCTYPE html>
<html>
<head> <title>Temperature</title> </head>
<body> <h1>Current Temperature</h1>
Hello ESP32 Server World <br/>
The Temperature is: <!--#temp--><br/>
</body>
</html>
"""
addr = socket.getaddrinfo('192.168.253.24', 8080)[0][-1]
print(addr)
s = socket.socket()
s.setsockopt(socket.SOL_SOCKET, socket.SO_REUSEADDR, 1)
s.bind(addr)
s.listen(0)
while True:
    cl, addr = s.accept()
    print('client connected from', addr)
    print(cl.recv(512))
    DS.convert_temp()
    temp = DS.read_temp(roms[0])
    html=template.replace("<!--#temp-->",str(temp))
    headers = ("HTTP/1.1 200 OK\r\n"
            "Content-Type: text/html; charset=UTF-8\r\n"
            "Server:ESP32\r\n"
            f"Content-Length:{len(html)}\r\n\r\n"
            )
    buf = headers.encode("utf-8")+html.encode("utf-8")
    cl.send(buf)
    cl.close()
s.close()
```

If you try this out and connect a browser you will see:

Current Temperature

Hello ESP32 Server World
The Temperature is: 19.375

You can modify this program to send as much data as you like and you can
make it machine readable by using JSON or another similar format.

An SSL HTTPS Server

If you want to implement an SSL server then things are slightly more
complicated because you need to provide a certificate. Getting a certificate
can be an involved process. Even popular free certificate-issuing sites like
Let's Encrypt require proof that you own the domain that the certificate
applies to. To do this you have to write code which generates a new key pair
and then either create a specific DNS record or store a file on the website.
This is easy enough for production purposes, but not so easy when you are
in the process of creating a program.

The usual solution is to create a self-signed certificate. If the operating
system has OpenSSL installed, and Windows and most versions of Linux do,
then you can create a key and certificate pair using:

```
openssl req -newkey rsa:2048 -nodes -keyout iopress.key -x509
                -days 365 -out iopress.crt
```

changing *iopress* to the name of your server. You will be asked a set of
questions for information that is included in the certificate. How you answer
these questions only modifies what the user sees if they ask to inspect the
certificate so you can simply accept the defaults.

The openssl command creates two files, a .key file and a .crt file, which
need to be processed to create strings that can be used in the MicroPython
program. Normally the files would be loaded into the server, but
MicroPython doesn't support a standard filing system and so the binary in
the files needs to be loaded into a pair of strings. The certificate and key are
saved on disk using an encoding called Base64 with a line of unencoded
ASCII text at the start and end. To make use of this data we have to remove
the first and last line of the file and unencode the Base64 to a standard byte
or ASCII string. This can be done using standard operating system command

line programs, but it is also very easy to write a standard Python program to do the job:

```
import binascii

with open("iopress.key", 'rb') as f:
    lines = f.readlines()
lines = b"".join(lines[1:-1])
key = binascii.a2b_base64(lines)
print("key=", key)

with open("iopress.crt", 'rb') as f:
    lines = f.readlines()
lines = b"".join(lines[1:-1])
cert = binascii.a2b_base64(lines)
print()
print("cert=", cert)
```

If you run this program, with the names of the .key and .crt files corrected to apply to the certificate you have generated, then it will read in each file, remove the first and last line, remove the Base64 encoding and print the MicroPython line needed to load the file's contents into a string:

```
key= b'0\x82\x04\xbf\x02\x01\x000\r\x06\t*\x86H\ ...
cert= b'0\x82\x03k0\x82\x02S\xa0\x03\x02\x01\x02\...
```

where the long list of hex codes has been truncated to save space.

You can simply copy and paste these two lines to get the certificate you have generated into the program. Once we have the certificates in the program the rest is fairly straightforward. The listening socket is the same as before, but it now listens on 443 which is the standard HTTPS port:

```
addr = socket.getaddrinfo('0.0.0.0', 443)[0][-1]
s = socket.socket()
s.setsockopt(socket.SOL_SOCKET, socket.SO_REUSEADDR, 1)
s.bind(addr)
s.listen(5)
```

The socket that you accept from the client has to be wrapped in an SSL socket before you try to transfer any data:

```
    cl, addr = s.accept()
    print('client connected from', addr)
    client_s = None
    try:
        client_s = ssl.wrap_socket(cl, server_side=True,
                                   key=key, cert=cert)
```

The wrap_socket function has to be in a try clause because with a self-signed certificate the client will abort the connection unless the site is added as a security exception. Notice that the key and the certificate are specified as the strings that we created earlier.

Once the client socket is wrapped we can start reading data, but the SSL handshaking procedure is messy and we need to allow the client to send some null packets and some packets containing a blank line when it encounters a problem with the connection. When you detect that a connection has gone wrong, the correct thing to do is abandon the transaction and wait for a new one. The client generally gets it right eventually. If we don't handle broken connections correctly then the server will block, waiting for more headers to be sent:

```
while True:
    h = client_s.readline()
    if h == b"" or h == b"\r\n":
        break
    print(h.decode(), end="")
```

In a more complicated program you might well have to gather and process the headers that the client sends. In this case we simply display them.

With these changes everything should work and the complete listing of the DS18x20 temperature sensor program given earlier converted to SSL is:

```
import network
import socket
from time import sleep_ms
from machine import Pin, Timer
import onewire
import ds18x20
import ssl


def setup(country, ssid, key):
    .   .   .

wifi=setup(country, ssid, key)
print("Connected")
print(wifi.ifconfig())

key=b'0\x82\x04\xbf\ . . .xabp\xd1'

cert=b'0\x82\x03k0\ . . .\x98\x8a'

ow = onewire.OneWire(Pin(4))
presence = ow.reset()
if presence:
 print("Device present")
else:
 print("No device")
```

```python
DS = ds18x20.DS18X20(ow)
roms = DS.scan()

template = """"""<!DOCTYPE html>
<html>
<head> <title>Temperature</title> </head>
<body> <h1>Current Temperature</h1>
Hello ESP32 Server World <br/>
The Temperature is: <!--#temp--><br/>
</body>
</html>
"""

addr = socket.getaddrinfo('0.0.0.0', 443)[0][-1]

s = socket.socket()
s.setsockopt(socket.SOL_SOCKET, socket.SO_REUSEADDR, 1)
s.bind(addr)
s.listen(5)

while True:
    cl, addr = s.accept()
    print('client connected from', addr)
    client_s =None

    try:
        client_s = ssl.wrap_socket(cl, server_side=True,
                                        key=key, cert=cert)

        while True:
            h = client_s.readline()
            if h == b"" or h == b"\r\n":
                    break
            print(h.decode(), end="")

        DS.convert_temp()
        temp = DS.read_temp(roms[0])
        html=template.replace("<!--#temp-->",str(temp))
        headers = ("HTTP/1.1 200 OK\r\n"
                "Content-Type: text/html; charset=UTF-8\r\n"
                "Server:ESP32\r\n"
                f"Content-Length:{len(html)}\r\n\r\n"
                )
        buf = headers.encode("utf-8")+html.encode("utf-8")

        client_s.write(buf)
        client_s.close()
    except Exception as e:
        print("exception ",e)
s.close()
```

As usual, the `setup` function has been omitted from the listing and the certificate strings have been truncated to save space. If you want to see what the full program looks like, the listing is on this book's page at www.iopress.info, along with all the other substantial programs.

If you try this out you will find that connecting with a browser using

`https:// ip of server`

causes a security warning to pop-up due to the use of a self-signed certificate.

The following is what you will see if you use Chrome.

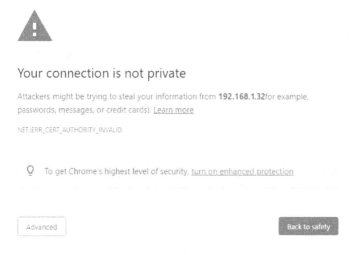

Messages like this are because browsers don't trust self-signed certificates. However, if you allow the page to download it will use SSL encryption. To do this click on Advanced and then confirm that you want to proceed. You can force a browser to accept the certificate by adding it to its trusted root certification authorities tab. However, for most testing purposes this isn't necessary. If you have a valid certificate and key for a particular web server you can substitute it for the self-signed certificates.

It is worth saying that making an SSL connection is not fast. The ESP32 is being asked to do significant computation to implement the cryptography and the handshake process is involved and hence time-consuming. You will also see a number of exceptions caused by the client aborting the connection due to the self-signed certificate, which is perfectly normal. Firefox is a much more friendly browser to use when testing SSL connections. Chrome tends to want to lock things down as soon as it detects a problem with the certificate.

Non-Blocking Sockets

The problem with the approach we have been using is that it is synchronous and you have to poll to see if there is a client wanting data. This has the unfortunate effect of stalling the polling loop while it waits for accept to return. This is fine if you only have to do something when a request from a client comes in, but if you need to do other things like flash an LED or adjust a heater then stalling the polling loop isn't a good idea. There are a number of solutions to this, but the simplest is to make the socket non-blocking.

The MicroPython implementation of sockets allows you to set a timeout in milliseconds for all socket operations:

```
s.settimeout(time)
```

After you have set a non-zero timeout any operation will raise an OSError if it isn't complete in the specified time. If you set it to None, which is the default, all operations are blocking and will wait until the operation is complete or a timeout occurs due to the client or the server. Setting a timeout of zero makes the socket non-blocking and setting a positive value provides a behavior that is somewhere between blocking and non-blocking.

You can use:

```
s.setblocking(True or False)
```

as a shorthand for:

```
True = s.settimeout(None)
False = s.settimeout(0)
```

In the first case operations are blocking; in the second they are non-blocking in the sense that they return with a result immediately or raise an OSError.

To see how to make use of this we can change the polling loop to:

```
s = socket.socket()
s.setsockopt(socket.SOL_SOCKET, socket.SO_REUSEADDR, 1)
s.setblocking(False)
s.bind(addr)
s.listen(0)
while True:
    print("doing something")
    try:
        cl, addr = s.accept()
    except(OSError):
        continue
    cl.setblocking(True)

    print('client connected from', addr)
    print(cl.recv(512))
    DS.convert_temp()
    temp = DS.read_temp(roms[0])
```

```
html=template.replace("<!--#temp-->",str(temp))
headers = ("HTTP/1.1 200 OK\r\n"
          "Content-Type: text/html; charset=UTF-8\r\n"
          "Server:ESP32\r\n"
          f"Content-Length:{len(html)}\r\n\r\n"
          )
buf = headers.encode("utf-8")+html.encode("utf-8")

cl.send(buf)

cl.close()
```

Notice that now the listening socket is set to non-blocking, which means that the `accept` returns at once. If there is no client waiting it raises an `OSError` and the loop continues skipping the processing of the client's request. If there is a client waiting then its request is processed as before. Notice that the client's socket inherits the timeout value of the listening socket and in this case we change it to blocking to make processing the request simpler. If the request takes too long to process, it too can be converted to non-blocking.

If you run this modified server you will see "doing something" repeatedly displayed as the polling loop waits for a client. If you remove the `setblocking` call then you will see `doing something` displayed twice per client connect – once for the temperature request and once for the web page's icon request.

The Connection Queue

Using non-blocking sockets usually provides the responsiveness you need to serve clients and get other jobs done at the same time. There are generally sufficient timeouts and retries built into browsers to allow clients to connect even if the server is busy. If, however, the clients are not browsers but applications making direct use of sockets then they might not be so forgiving. In this case you can use the connection queue to avoid losing clients.

When you start a socket listening you can specify the size of the connection queue with:

`s.listen(n)`

which starts the socket listening with a queue of size *n*. When the first client connects it is processed. When subsequent clients try to connect while the first one is still being processed they are added to the queue until it is full, at which point the client connection is reset.

If you try this out, with a long delay in processing a client, what you see will be complicated by the way the client tries to connect. For example, if you try to connect using Chrome it uses a long timeout with a retry algorithm that effectively makes the connect queue irrelevant. It you try the same thing with Firefox you will see that, with a queue of zero, two requests succeed and the rest return a "The connection was reset" error. Why two and not one isn't clear, but you also have to remember that each web page request generates at least two requests – one for the page and one for the page icon. If you set the queue size to one you will still see two requests succeed. Setting the queue to two and you will see three pages or more succeed in loading. The reason for more than three pages is that the page requested will be cached. Things get confusing after this because of additional requests for the page icon and the effect of caching it.

What all this means is that the connect queue's effect on a client trying to connect is real, but complicated. It all depends on the connection algorithm the client uses. In most cases a browser will manage to connect unless the server is extremely overloaded.

Summary

- If you want to do anything beyond HTTP, or you want to implement an HTTP server, then you need to make use of sockets.

- Sockets are completely general and you can use them to implement an HTTP client or a server.

- To allow for different types of connection, sockets can be used with a range of different types of addresses. In the case of the ESP32, however, we only need to use IP addresses.

- A socket client has to handle the details of the data transferred. In particular, you have to handle the details of HTTP headers.

- Implementing a socket server is easy, but it can be difficult to ensure that both clients and internal services are both attended to.

- The simplest solution to the server problem is to implement a polling loop and to do this you need to make use of non-blocking sockets.

- Simple sockets work with unencrypted data. If you want to use encryption you have to "wrap" the socket using the ssl module.

- HTTPS clients don't need a certificate to implement encryption, but servers do.

- For testing you can generate your own "self-signed" certificates although most browsers will complain that this isn't secure.

- The connection queue allows you to handle more than one client connection at a time.

Chapter 17

Asyncio And Servers

MicroPython has a basic implementation of the Python `asyncio` module. The `asyncio` module is very useful in providing asynchronous programming in Python and you might think that it would be exceptionally useful in low-level hardware applications as an alternative to polling or event driven approaches. In fact it isn't quite as useful as you might expect as there are few existing asynchronous subsystems. In full Python we have a complete filing system and network connections and this means that asynchronous programming can improve efficiency by putting the processor to work while waiting for I/O operations to complete. In general the only I/O operations that are lengthy enough to involve waiting for sufficient time to get other tasks completed are WiFi related and this makes WiFi an ideal use case for the `asyncio` module.

In this chapter we first look at the basic idea of asynchronous programming as implemented by `uasyncio`, the MicroPython version of `asyncio`, and then at how to use it to implement a server asynchronously. If you want to know more about asynchronous programming in general and `asyncio` in particular see ***Programmer's Python: Async***, ISBN:9781871962765.

Coroutines and Tasks

Asyncio is all about sharing a single thread of execution between different tasks. A key ability of a task is that it can be suspended and resumed and this is what a coroutine is all about. In a single-threaded environment the thread has to save its current state, start or resume work on another function and restore the state when it returns to the previous function. A function that can be suspended and restarted in this way is generally called a "coroutine".

A modern MicroPython coroutine is created using the `async` keyword:

```
async def myCo():
    print("Hello Coroutine World")
    return 42
```

When you call `myCo` it doesn't execute its code, instead it returns a coroutine object which can execute the code. The only problem is that a coroutine isn't a runnable. You have to use features provided by `uasyncio` to run a coroutine. The simplest is the `uasyncio.run` method which creates and manages the task loop without you having to know anything about it:

```
import uasyncio
async def myCo():
    print("Hello Coroutine World")
    return 42

myCoObject=myCo()
result= uasyncio.run(myCoObject)
print(result)
```

This runs the coroutine object and displays:

```
Hello Coroutine World
42
```

Instead of passing the coroutine object, the `uasyncio.run` call is usually written as a single action:

```
result= uasyncio.run(myCo())
```

It is also important to realize that `uasyncio.run` runs `myCo` at once and the thread doesn't return until `myCo` is completed. While running `myCo` a task loop is started and if the thread is freed it starts running any tasks queued before returning to `myCo`. In this sense the call to `uasyncio.run` is where the asynchronous part of your program starts and you can think of it as starting the asynchronous main program.

Await

As it stands our coroutine might as well be a standard function as it doesn't suspend and resume its operation. To suspend a coroutine you have to use the `await` keyword to pause the coroutine while an awaitable completes.

An `await` suspends the awaiting program and this means it can only be used within a coroutine, i.e. the only code in Python that can be suspended and resumed. Once you have a coroutine running you can use `await` within it and within any coroutines it awaits.

What this means is that you have to use `uasyncio.run` to get a first coroutine running, but after this you can use `await` to run other coroutines as `Tasks`.

Most asyncio programs are organized so that there is a single `uasyncio.run` instruction at the top level of the program and this starts a coroutine, often called `main`, which then runs the rest of the asynchronous program by awaiting other coroutines. That is, a typical `uasyncio` program is:

```
async def main():
    call other coroutines using await

uasyncio.run(main())
```

The call to `uasyncio.run` sets up the event loop as well as starting `main` running. You can call ordinary, i.e. non-coroutine, functions from within coroutines, but these cannot use `await`. Only a coroutine can use `await`, for example:

```
import uasyncio

async def test1(msg):
    print(msg)

async def main():
    await test1("Hello Coroutine World")

uasyncio.run(main())
```

Notice that even though `main` now awaits the `test1` coroutine there is no new behavior. The program would work in exactly the same way with functions replacing coroutines. The reason is that none of our coroutines actually release the main thread, they simply keep running.

There are two distinct things that can occur when you `await` another coroutine. Some coroutines hold onto the main thread and continue to execute instructions until they finish – they are essentially synchronous coroutines. Some release the main thread while they wait for some operation to complete and only these are truly asynchronous coroutines. At the moment we only know about synchronous coroutines.

Awaiting Sleep

The simplest asynchronous coroutine is `uasyncio.sleep`:

`uasyncio.sleep(`*delay*`)`

which returns after *delay* seconds.

There is also a MicroPython extension:

`uasyncio.sleep_ms(`*delay*`)`

which returns after *delay* milliseconds.

Notice that these are not the same as the corresponding sleep function in the `time` module and it is important to understand the difference. The `time.sleep` function suspends the current thread for the specified amount of time. That is, the one thread that you were depending on to do the work would be frozen and if used in an asynchronous program so would the task loop. In fact `time.sleep` is a very good way to keep the thread busy and so simulate a coroutine that doesn't give up the thread.

Compare this to `uasyncio.sleep` which doesn't suspend the thread at all - it suspends the coroutine. The main thread stops running the coroutine and returns to the event loop to find another coroutine to run. When the time delay is up and the main thread next visits the task loop for more work, the suspended coroutine is restarted. Of course, this means that the coroutine might be suspended for longer than the specified time and this is usually the case. The coroutine is restarted when the main thread is free to run it and the time delay is up.

The `uasyncio.sleep` function suspends the current coroutine and not the thread.

A standard idiom is to call `sleep` with a value of zero seconds:

```
await uasyncio.sleep(0)
```

or

```
await usasyncio.sleep_ms(0)
```

This gives up the thread to the task loop with the minimum delay if there is nothing to be done in the event loop queue. That is, all that happens is that the main thread is freed and, if there is nothing waiting to be executed in the task loop, it returns at once to running the coroutine. This gives the event loop a chance to run other coroutines and it is a good idea to include any coroutine that runs for a long time. The call `sleep(0)` is equivalent to DoEvents in other languages, i.e. an instruction to process the event loop's queue.

We can easily add an `await` for 10 seconds to our example:

```
import uasyncio

async def main(myValue):
    print("Hello Coroutine World")
    await uasyncio.sleep(10)
    return myValue

result= uasyncio.run(main(42))
print(result)
```

There is now a ten-second delay between displaying `Hello Coroutine World` and the result, i.e. `42`. In this case the main thread is freed when the `await` starts and has `10` seconds in which to run any other coroutines waiting in the task loop. In this case there aren't any and so it just waits for the time to be up. We next need to know how to add coroutines to the task loop so that they can be run when the main thread is free.

Tasks

A Task is a coroutine that you have added to the task loop for execution by the thread when the opportunity arises. A Task has some additional methods added to the basic coroutine and in Python it inherits from a Future, but in MicroPython things are simpler.

To add a Task to the task loop you need to use:

```
uasyncio.create_task(coroutine)
```

This adds *coroutine* to the task loop as a Task. It adds the coroutine to the task loop queue ready to be executed. It doesn't actually get to run until the main thread is free to return to the task loop and run the tasks that it finds there. This only happens when the currently executing coroutine awaits an asynchronous coroutine or terminates.

The uasyncio.create_task function returns a Task which behaves like a Future in Python. The only important point for MicroPython is that any result that the task returns is only available after the task has completed, or "resolved" in the terminology. To get the result we need to use an await to retrieve a result. For example, if we create a coroutine that prints a range of numbers then this can be added to the event loop within main:

```
import uasyncio

async def count(n):
    for i in range(n):
        print(i)
    return n

async def main(myValue):
    t1 = uasyncio.create_task(count(10))
    print("Hello Coroutine World")
    await uasyncio.sleep(5)
    result = await t1
    print("The result of the task =",result)
    return myValue

result= uasyncio.run(main(42))
print(result)
```

The count coroutine is added to the task loop before the print, but it doesn't get to run until main awaits sleep for 5 seconds and so frees the thread. This allows the count function to display 0 to 9 but then the thread continues to wait till the full five seconds are up. At this point it awaits the task so as to get its result. If t1 hadn't completed then the thread would execute it until it was complete. As it is, t1 is complete and so returns its result at once and there is no delay before it is printed.

What you see displayed is:

```
Hello Coroutine World
0
1
2
3
4
5
6
7
8
9
The result of the task = 10
42
```

Make sure that this example makes sense before you move on to more complex things.

At this point you should be wondering why we bothered creating a Task and adding it to the event loops's queue? Why not just use await count? This produces the same result, but for different reasons. In this case the Task isn't added to the task queue until the await and then the Task is run to completion. This means that it isn't in the queue earlier and cannot benefit from any time that the thread might be free.

You will sometimes see instructions like:

```
value = await asyncio.create_task(count(10))
```

This adds the coroutine to the queue as a Task and then immediately awaits it, which of course, starts it running. There is no point in doing this and it is entirely equivalent to:

```
value = await count(10)
```

To summarize:

- create_task(*coroutine*) runs the *coroutine* at a later time. It adds it as a Task to the task loop's queue for execution when the thread is free
- await *coroutine* runs the *coroutine* immediately
- await *Task* runs the Task to completion taking into account any process it might have already made by being on the task queue.

Another way of thinking about this is to use create_task when you want the coroutine to run when the thread is free and use await when you need the coroutine to run immediately.

There is also a way to `await` a coroutine with a timeout:

```
uasyncio.wait_for(aw, timeout)
```

which waits for *aw*, an awaitable, to complete or until the *timeout* in seconds is up.
MicroPython also adds:

```
uasyncio.wait_for_ms(aw, timeout)
```

which, of course, specifies the timeout in milliseconds. If the timeout happens the task raises a `uasyncio.TimeoutError` in the waiting code and a `uasyncio.CancelledError` in the task. Each of these methods is a coroutine so to use them you write:

```
await uasyncio.wait_for(t1,1)
```

Sequential and Concurrent

The `gather` function is usually described as being a way of running `task` coroutines concurrently, but it is better thought of as a way of running and waiting for a set of them to complete:

```
uasyncio.gather(tasks, return_exceptions = False)
```

Any coroutine in the `task`'s comma-separated list of tasks is added to the task queue as a `Task`. All of the tasks are then executed as the queue schedules them with the calling coroutine suspended until all of them complete. The function returns a list of results in the same order as the awaitables were originally listed in `tasks`. If `return_exceptions` is `False` then any exception is propagated to the calling coroutine, but the other coroutines in the `tasks` list are left to complete. If it is `True` then the exceptions are returned as valid results in the list.

If the `gather` is canceled all of the items in `aws` are canceled. If any of the items in `aws` are canceled then it raises a `CancelledError`, which is either passed to the calling coroutine or added to the result list and the `gather` itself is not canceled. Using `gather` is almost the same as adding coroutines to the event loop using `asyncio.create_task` and then waiting for them to complete. For example:

```
import uasyncio
async def test1(msg):
    print(msg)
    return msg

async def main():
    result = await uasyncio.gather(test1("one"),test1("two"))
    print(result)
    print("Hello Coroutine World")

uasyncio.run(main())
```

301

This starts two copies of the `test1` coroutine running as tasks on the task loop. As we await them immediately the `main` coroutine pauses until both are complete and then prints the results as a list. As `test1` doesn't release the main thread the first task runs to completion and then the second is run. This isn't necessarily the case if either of the tasks releases the thread. The order in which they execute in isn't determined by the order in which they occur in the `gather`.

It should be obvious by this point, but is worth making clear, that if you want to run coroutines one after another, i.e. sequentially, then you should use:

```
await coroutine1()
await coroutine2()
await coroutine3()
```

and so on. This adds each coroutine to the task loop queue one at a time and the calling coroutine waits for each one to end in turn. If the called coroutine releases the main thread other coroutines, if any, already on the task loop get a chance to run. You can be sure, however, that `coroutine1` completes before `coroutine2` starts and `coroutine2` completes before `coroutine3` starts.

Compare this to:

```
await gather(coroutine1(), coroutine2(), coroutine3(), …)
```

which adds all of the coroutines to the event loop and then runs each one in turn. If any of the coroutines releases the main thread the other coroutines listed get a chance to run, along with anything that was on the event loop before the `gather`. As a result all of the coroutines in the `gather` make progress to completion at the same time, if this is possible. They are executed concurrently in the sense that you cannot be sure that `coroutine1` completes before `coroutine2` or `coroutine3` starts.

Canceling Tasks

In a single-threaded environment canceling a `Task` cannot mean canceling the thread because it has other work to do. If you use the `task.cancel` method then the `Task` is marked to receive a `CancelledError` exception the next time it runs on the event loop. If you don't handle the exception the `Task` simply dies silently. If you have any resources to close then you have to handle the exception to perform the cleanup. You can even opt to ignore the `CancelledError` exception altogether.

For example:

```
import uasyncio
async def test1(msg):
    try:
        await uasyncio.sleep(0)
    except:
        pass
    print(msg)
    return msg

async def main():
    t1 = uasyncio.create_task(test1("one"))
    await uasyncio.sleep(0)
    t1.cancel()
    print("Hello Coroutine World")
    await uasyncio.sleep(0)

uasyncio.run(main())
```

In this case the try suppresses the exception and everything works as if cancel had not been called. If you remove the try/except then you don't see one displayed as test1 is canceled.

Dealing with Exceptions

The fact that a Task is modeled on a Future should immediately tell you how to handle exceptions in asynchronous programs. The Task either returns a result or an exception object and by default the Exception object is used to raise the exception in the calling coroutine. For example:

```
import uasyncio

async def test(msg):
    print(msg)
    raise Exception("Test exception")

async def main():
    t1 = uasyncio.create_task(test("one"))
    try:
        await t1
    except:
        print("an exception has occurred")
    print("Hello Coroutine World")
    await uasyncio.sleep(0)

uasyncio.run(main())
```

In this case test raises an exception as soon as it is called. This is returned to the calling coroutine and raised again by the await operation.

303

If you want to access the exception object and handle it manually you will have to use one of the gather methods as await always consumes the Task and hence raises the exception whereas gather can return all results including exceptions. For example:

```
import uasyncio

async def test(msg):
    print(msg)
    raise Exception("Test exception")


async def main():
    t1=uasyncio.create_task(test("one"))
    result=None
    try:
        result = await uasyncio.gather(t1,return_exceptions=True)
    except:
        print("an exception has occurred")
    print("Hello Coroutine World")
    print(result)
    await uasyncio.sleep(0)

uasyncio.run(main())
```

displays:

```
one
Hello Coroutine World
[Exception('Test exception',)]
```

You can see that now you have the Exception object and you can choose to do what you like with it or raise it when you are ready.

Finally if you don't await a Task then any exceptions are ignored, just as any results are ignored. The Task fails silently, just as it succeeds silently if it is not awaited.

Shared Variables and Locks

Coroutines share global variables and have their own local variables as is the case for functions. If you are not used to asynchronous programming this can have some surprising consequences. The problem is that access to global resources by more than one task carries the risk of a race condition. For example, if two tasks attempt to update a resource and one is part way through an update when the other starts and begins its own update then the final outcome depends on which task gets to complete its update last. This is a "race condition". Given that uasyncio implements a form of asynchronous programming that only starts another Task if the currently running Task gives up the thread, i.e. it voluntarily allows another Task to start, this is far less of a problem. You can avoid it altogether by always making sure that any `Task` only gives up the thread when any use of a shared resource is complete. However, as hardware-oriented programs of the sort you run on the ESP32 tend to use shared hardware resources, this is more of a problem than in other situations. The solution is to use a lock of one sort or another so as to restrict access to the shared resource to one task at a time.

The `uasyncio` module contains asynchronous equivalents for most of the standard threading locks:

- ◆ Lock
  The `Lock` object has three methods that control the way that tasks interact with it:

  `lock.locked()` Returns `True` if locked

  `lock.acquire()` Waits for lock to be unlocked and then locks it

  `lock.release()` Unlocks the lock

The basic idea is that all of the tasks that want to access a shared resource follow the protocol that they first have to acquire the `Lock` object that is protecting it by using `acquire()`. If another task has already acquired the lock then subsequent attempts to acquire it suspend the task until the lock is released. When the lock is released one of the tasks waiting to acquire it is allowed to run. This means that only one task accesses the shared resource at a time and other tasks queue up to use it.

- ◆ Event

  The `Event` object has four methods:

  `is_set()` True if the event is set and `False` otherwise

  `set()` Sets the event, any waiting tasks can now run

  `clear()` Clears the event

  `wait()` Waits for the event to be set

The `Event` object is intended to be used to synchronize tasks. Any number of tasks can wait on an event and then any other task can set the event and allow the waiting tasks to be scheduled to run when the thread is free. For example, a set of tasks might process a file that is downloaded by another task. The downloading task can set the event to signal to the processing tasks that the data is ready to process.

- ◆ ThreadSafeFlag

  The `ThreadSafeFlag` has three methods:

  `set()` Sets the flag

  `clear` Clears the flag

  `wait` Waits for the flag to be set.

305

ThreadSafeFlag works like the Event object, but it can be used by functions that are not coroutines such as interrupt handlers.

The whole subject of locks and how to use them is complex and if you want to know more see ***Programmer's Python: Async***, ISBN:9781871962765. However, you need to be aware of the two big problems in using locks. The first is that they slow things down. Locks are slow to use and restrict access often unnecessarily. The second is the potential for deadlock – where one task is waiting on a lock that another holds while it is waiting for a lock that the first task is holding.

Consider the following example based on a simple counter updating a global variable, myCounter:

```
import uasyncio

async def count():
    global myCounter
    for i in range(1000):
        temp = myCounter+1
        await uasyncio.sleep(0)
        myCounter = temp

async def main():
    await uasyncio.gather(count(),count())
    print(myCounter)

myCounter=0
uasyncio.run(main())
```

Each task updates myCounter a thousand times and so the total should be 2000, but if you run the program you will find that it is 1000. Where have the other thousand updates gone?

Both t1 and t2 release the main thread in the middle of the update of the global variable. As a result each task updates myCounter at exactly the same time and as a result there is a perfect race condition on every update and the program displays 1000.

The simplest solution to this problem is not to release the main thread in the middle of an operation. As long as the task doesn't release the main thread it is an atomic operation. This is usually one of the benefits of using single-threaded multi-tasking.

If this approach cannot be used then there is no alternative but to add a lock. The uasyncio module provides its own locks. Rather than having to explicitly call acquire and release we can use "async with". This acquires the lock on entry to the block and automatically releases it on exit. This can only be used in a coroutine and can be suspended during the enter and exit phase:

```
import uasyncio

async def count():
    global myCounter
    global myLock
    for i in range(1000):
        async with myLock:
            temp=myCounter+1
            await uasyncio.sleep(0)
            myCounter=temp

async def main():
    await uasyncio.gather(count(),count())
    print(myCounter)

myCounter=0
myLock=uasyncio.Lock()
uasyncio.run(main())
```

Now t2 has to wait until t1 releases the lock before it can continue. Notice the use of "async with" rather than just "with". The program now displays 2000. In this case the problem has been caused deliberately, but when you are using coroutines there are occasions that you cannot modify in which locking is the only option.

Using uasyncio

When you first meet uasyncio, or its full Python equivalent asyncio, it is all too easy to see it as a total solution. The idea that you can structure a program as a collection of tasks which get to run when they are needed seems to be a simplification. However, the MicroPython implementation of uasyncio provides only two coroutines that free the thread – uasyncio.sleep() and uasyncio.sleep_ms(). There are also some network classes and methods which make uasyncio much more useful, but it is still worth looking at its more basic use.

The only sort of task you can write that actually gives up the thread, and hence take advantage of asynchronous implementation, are of the form:

```
async task1():
    while True:
        do something
        await uasyncio.sleep(t)
        do something
```

The call to sleep releases the thread and allows other tasks to run for at least t seconds. What this means is that all of the tasks you create have to be able to be suspended for a given amount of time to allow other tasks to run. Notice that there is no indication of how often any of the tasks will run. For example, if one of the tasks is designed to read a sensor every few seconds then there is no way that you can use an asynchronous approach to guarantee that this is the case unless you handcraft all of the other tasks to ensure that the sensor task gets its turn at the right time. This is just as difficult, if not more so, than writing a simple polling loop that calls the tasks in a fixed order.

Consider the following program modeled on the example in the documentation:

```
import uasyncio
from machine import Pin

async def blink(led, period_ms):
    while True:
        led.on()
        await uasyncio.sleep_ms(5)
        led.off()
        await uasyncio.sleep_ms(period_ms)

async def main(led1, led2):
    uasyncio.create_task(blink(led1, 700))
    uasyncio.create_task(blink(led2, 400))
    await uasyncio.sleep_ms(10_000)

uasyncio.run(main(Pin(2,Pin.OUT), Pin(4,Pin.OUT)))
```

This flashes two LEDs connected to GPIO2 and GPIO4. The blink coroutine turns the LED on and then sleeps for 5ms, giving other tasks a chance to run. It then switches the LED off and sleeps for a specified period. If you try this out you will find that you do get 5ms pulses spaced at 700ms and 400ms. However, none of the periods are guaranteed. All it takes is another task, or a set of tasks, that take longer to process than 5ms to disrupt the intended timing.

For example, we can introduce a task that simply wastes some time:

```
import uasyncio
from machine import Pin
from time import sleep_ms
async def blink(led, period_ms):
    while True:
        led.on()
        await uasyncio.sleep_ms(5)
        led.off()
        await uasyncio.sleep_ms(period_ms)

async def timewaste():
    while True:
        sleep_ms(10)
        await uasyncio.sleep_ms(0)


async def main(led1, led2):
    uasyncio.create_task(blink(led1, 700))
    uasyncio.create_task(blink(led2, 400))
    uasyncio.create_task(timewaste())
    await uasyncio.sleep_ms(10_000)

uasyncio.run(main(Pin(2,Pin.OUT), Pin(4,Pin.OUT)))
```

Now if you run the program you will discover that the pulses are now 10ms in size. The `timewaste` coroutine now hogs the only thread of execution, only giving it up every 10ms, which means that the `blink` coroutine only gets the thread back after at least 10ms whenever it gives it up.

Even if you find this difficult to understand, an additional negative point for the approach is that the timing of blink depends on the timing of the other tasks it finds itself running with.

Asynchronous approaches generally only work well when each task keeps the thread for a time that is much shorter than the time that each task needs to run – and this implies that the thread has to be idle for most of the time.

You can convert any polling interaction into an `uasyncio` task by using the `sleep_ms` method. All you have to do is write a small infinite pooling loop:

```
async def checkReady():
    while True:
        if read hardware state:
            process hardware
        await uasyncio.sleep_ms(10)
```

This can be run along with similar tasks and as long as none of them take longer to process the hardware than the sleep time they should all work together.

Async Networking

The Python `asyncio` module is primarily designed to work with asynchronous network connections. It doesn't provide high-level networking facilities. There is no asynchronous download of an HTML page, for example. However, it provides a class that caters for high-level clients and another for server objects which make working with general TCP connections very easy.

Communication with both client and server object is via streams which are modeled on files. Both client and server objects return streams to allow the TCP connection to be used. `uasyncio,` the MicroPython implementation of the module uses a single `Stream` object as a reader and a writer.

The supported `read` methods are:

- ◆ `read(n = -1)` Reads up to n bytes as a `bytes` object
  The default, `n = -1`, is to read until the end of the file signal (EOF) is received and return all read bytes
- ◆ `readline()` Reads a sequence of bytes ending with \n
  If EOF is received and \n was not found, the method returns partially read data. If EOF is received and the internal buffer is empty, returns an empty bytes object
- ◆ `readexactly(n)` Reads exactly n bytes and raises an EOF error if EOF is reached before n can be read
- ◆ `readinto(buf)` Reads up to `len(buf)` bytes into `buf`

Notice that all of the reading methods are coroutines as there may not be enough data ready to satisfy the call. In this case the coroutine is suspended and the main thread is freed. That is, calls to functions that read data are asynchronous coroutines. Also notice that while there are references to using EOF to signal the end of a transaction, in general EOF isn't particularly useful when dealing with sockets. Sockets tend to be left open until they are no longer required and data is usually sent in some sort of format that lets you work out when you have read a useful chunk of data that can be processed. Generally, if you wait for an EOF you will wait a long time until the server times out and closes the socket.

The only `write` method is:

- ◆ `write(buf)` Attempts to write the `buf` to the stream
  The data is only written following a call to the `drain()` method

It is not a coroutine and always returns immediately. However, the `drain()` coroutine, which waits until it is appropriate to resume writing to the stream, should be called after each `write` operation, for example:

```
stream.write(data)
await stream.drain()
```

The close() method closes both the stream and the underlying socket used in the TCP connection and should be used along with the wait_closed() coroutine:

```
stream.close()
await stream.wait_closed()
```

The logic is that there is no point in carrying on until the stream has been closed and so you might as well free the main thread. You can also use is_closing() to test whether the stream is closed or is in the process of closing.

Downloading A Web Page

We have already used the urequest module to download a web page and we have used sockets to do the same job asynchronously with non-blocking sockets. An alternative approach is to use uasyncio to do the job as part of an overall asynchronous system.

The coroutine:

```
uasyncio.open_connection(host,port)
```

uses sockets to open a connection to the host, specified as an IP address or a URL and a port. If successful this returns a (*reader, writer*) tuple which can be used to communicate with the server. The *reader* and *writer* are actually the same stream object, but for clarity we will make use of each one appropriately. For example, to connect to www.example.com as we did in the previous chapter you would use:

```
import uasyncio
from time import sleep_ms
from machine import Pin, Timer
import network
def setup(country, ssid, key):
        .   .   .
async def main():
    reader,writer= await uasyncio.open_connection(
                                "www.example.com",80)
    request = b"GET /index.html HTTP/1.1\r\n
                            Host:example.org\r\n\r\n"
    writer.write(request)
    await writer.drain()
    print(await reader.read(512))
    reader.close()
wifi=setup(country, ssid, key)
print("Connected")
print(wifi.ifconfig())
uasyncio.run(main())
```

What is the advantage of this approach? The simple answer is that it makes it easier to overlap downloads.

311

For example, if you convert the download actions into a function:

```
async def getPage(url):
    reader,writer= await uasyncio.open_connection(url,80)
    request = b"GET /index.html HTTP/1.1\r\n
                            Host:example.org\r\n\r\n"
    writer.write(request)
    await writer.drain()
    page=await reader.read(512)
    reader.close()
    return page
```

you can now call it sequentially or concurrently.

If you call it sequentially:

```
    results=await getPage('www.example.com')
    results=await getPage('www.example.com')
```

it takes 800ms to download the page twice.

However, if you call it concurrently:

```
results = await uasyncio.gather( getPage('www.example.com'),
                            getPage('www.example.com'))
```

it takes only 400ms, which is only a little more than the 350ms it takes to download the page once. The improvement is due to the fact that while the getPage coroutine is waiting for the download it releases the thread and the other coroutine can execute.

Server

As well as making a stream connection to a server, uasyncio also allows you to create a server that will accept incoming connections as streams:

```
asyncio.start_server(callback, host, port, backlog=5)
```

This starts a socket server, with a callback for each client connected. The return value is a Server object. When a client connects, the callback is passed two parameters, a reader and a writer, to communicate with the client. As in the case of the TCP client, these refer to the same Stream object. Each client connection is independent and can be continued until the transaction is complete. The callback can be a standard function, but this would block the event loop so it is usual to make it a coroutine.

The Server object has the following methods:

- ◆ close() Stops serving, closes listening sockets and sets the sockets attribute to None. The sockets that represent existing incoming client connections are left open and can continue to be used until they are closed.
- ◆ wait_closed() Waits until the stream has closed.

The Server object also supports use as an asynchronous context manager. When the with block is exited the server.close method is called.

312

A Web Server

Implementing a simple web server using the `Server` object is very easy.

First create the server:

```
async def main():
    await uasyncio.start_server(serve_client,
                          '192.168.253.58', 80,backlog=5)
    while True:
        print("heartbeat")
        await uasyncio.sleep(1)
```

The server will respond to requests on the network connections on port 80. After creating the server the `main` coroutine simply loops, printing a message and then going to sleep, so freeing the thread.

The `Server` object now monitors incoming TCP packets on the specified address and port. When a client sends a packet, the `Server` object calls the callback, `serve_client` in this case. Each client gets its own copy of `serve_client` which run asynchronously on the event loop. This means that you could have many requests handled using just a single thread. Our `serve_client` is going to be simple, it will return the HTML page giving the current temperature as done by the server at the end of the previous chapter.

The callback has a `reader writer` stream object passed to it which enables two-way communication with the client:

```
async def serve_client(reader,writer):
    print("client")
    print(await reader.read(512))
    DS.convert_temp()
    temp = DS.read_temp(roms[0])
    html = template.replace("<!--#temp-->",str(temp))
    headers = ("HTTP/1.1 200 OK\r\n"
            "Content-Type: text/html; charset=UTF-8\r\n"
            "Server:ESP32\r\n"
            f"Content-Length:{len(html)}\r\n\r\n"
            )
    buf = headers.encode("utf-8")+html.encode("utf-8")

    writer.write(buf)
    await writer.drain()
    writer.close()
    await writer.wait_closed()
```

The callback reads the request that the client has sent and, irrespective of what it is, obtains a temperature reading and sends this as part of the HTML page back to the client.

As before, the program ignores the request sent by the client, but in this case it is easy to correct. You can also add additional processing as part of the main coroutine or you can add tasks to the task queue.

After the setup function the rest of the program is, assuming DS18X20 is on GPIO4:

```
import uasyncio
import network
from machine import Pin, Timer
from time import sleep_ms
import onewire
import ds18x20

def setup(country, ssid, key):
    .   .   .

wifi=setup(country, ssid, key)
print("Connected")
print(wifi.ifconfig())

ow = onewire.OneWire(Pin(4))
presence = ow.reset()
if presence:
    print("Device present")
else:
    print("No device")

DS = ds18x20.DS18X20(ow)
roms = DS.scan()

template = """<!DOCTYPE html>
<html>
<head> <title>Temperature</title> </head>
<body> <h1>Current Temperature</h1>
Hello ESP32 Server World <br/>
The Temperature is: <!--#temp--><br/>
</body>
</html>
"""
async def serve_client(reader,writer):
    print("client")
    print(await reader.read(512))
    DS.convert_temp()
    temp = DS.read_temp(roms[0])
    html=template.replace("<!--#temp-->",str(temp))
    headers = ("HTTP/1.1 200 OK\r\n"
            "Content-Type: text/html; charset=UTF-8\r\n"
            "Server:ESP32\r\n"
            f"Content-Length:{len(html)}\r\n\r\n"
            )
```

```
    buf = headers.encode("utf-8")+html.encode("utf-8")
    writer.write(buf)
    await writer.drain()
    writer.close()
    await writer.wait_closed()

async def main():
    await uasyncio.start_server(serve_client, '192.168.253.24',
                                              80,backlog=5)
    while True:
        print("heartbeat")
        await uasyncio.sleep(1)

uasyncio.run(main())
```

Best Practice

How best to implement a server?

Although the uasyncio approach is attractive from a theoretical point of view, it is built using non-blocking sockets. If you really need to serve multiple clients at the same time then directly using non-blocking sockets is probably the best way to do the job from the point of not having additional overhead and having more control over timing in a polling loop.

Notice that uasyncio doesn't include any support for events and this is true of the full asyncio module. If the task loop could be modified to include event handlers then it might be more useful in an IoT context. The ESP32 has the hardware to work with events and it should be easy to add this to uasyncio by adding an event handling Task when an event occurs.

There is also a lot to be said for using a client to deliver data to a server via a PUT or POST request. This would save a lot of effort in implementing an asynchronous system and makes timing easier to deal with.

Summary

- The uasyncio module provides single-threaded multi-tasking.

- A coroutine is a function that can be suspended and resumed by the use of the await instruction.

- A coroutine has to be run in conjunction with an event loop. uasyncio.run creates an event loop and runs a coroutine as a task using it.

- A Task is a coroutine with some additional methods and it is what is added to the event loop's queue using uasyncio.create_task. The Task is run when the thread becomes free.

- When you await a coroutine it starts running to completion.

- When you await a Task, i.e. a coroutine already on the task loop, it only starts running if it isn't already completed.

- The await always returns the result of the Task, including any exceptions that might have occurred.

- You can use wait_for as a version of await with a timeout.

- Task coroutines can be executed in sequential order by awaiting each one in turn. They can be run concurrently by adding them to the queue or by using the gather coroutine.

- A task can be canceled but is up to you to handle the exception.

- A Task returns any exceptions to the awaiting coroutine – these can be raised or processed.

- Locks are less useful for coroutines because unless the thread is released they are atomic. If a race condition can occur there are asynchronous equivalents of some of the standard synchronization objects.

- The uasyncio module makes network connections easy and asynchronous.

- Implementing a web client is easy, but there is no high-level function which downloads an HTML page. You have to work with the HTTP protocol.

- Creating a web server is only slightly more difficult in that you have to support multiple potential clients.

Chapter 18

Direct To The Hardware

MicroPython provides classes and methods to let you access most of the major hardware features of the ESP32. They are very simple wrappers around the basic mechanism of working with the hardware – memory-mapped registers. Unfortunately at the time of writing there are many hardware features which are simply not exposed via MicroPython. In most cases it is possible to extend what you access using lower-level interactions with the hardware. This way you can stay in MicroPython while writing and reading the low-level, register-based hardware.

The obvious reason for knowing how to use memory-mapped registers is that if MicroPython doesn't provide a function that does just what you want, you simply create it! Perhaps a better reason is just to know how things work. In this chapter we take a look at how the ESP32 presents its hardware for you to use and how to access it via basic software.

Registers

Some processors have special ways of connecting devices, but the ESP32's processor uses the more common memory-mapping approach. In this, each external device is represented by a set of memory locations or "registers" that control it. Each bit in the register controls some aspect of the way the device behaves. Groups of bits also can be interpreted as short integers which set operating values or modes.

How do you access a register? MicroPython provides a number of ways of doing this but the simplest is to make use of the mem functions in the machine module:

machine.mem32[address]   Returns or sets a 32-bit value at the address

machine.mem16[address]   Returns or sets a 16-bit value at the address

machine.mem8[address]   Returns or sets an 8-bit value at the address

The only difficult part is in working out the address you need to use and the value that sets or resets the bits you need to modify. For example, if you look in the documentation for the ESP32 you will find that the GPIO registers start at address 0x3FF44000. However, if you look up the starting address for the ESP32 S3, you will find that they start at 0x60004000. You cannot assume that all versions of the ESP32 have the same memory map, but you can assume that the registers mostly work in the same way. The registers are defined by the offset from their starting address or an absolute address.

For the ESP32 S3, the start of the table of GPIO registers is:

Name	Description	Address	Access
GPIO_OUT_REG	GPIO 0-31 output register	0x60004004	R/W
GPIO_OUT_W1TS_REG	GPIO 0-31 output register_W1TS	0x60004008	WO
GPIO_OUT_W1TC_REG	GPIO 0-31 output register_W1TC	0x6000400C	WO

This gives an offset of 0x4, 0x8 and 0xC for each register. This is also true for the ESP32, but the offsets are relative to 0x3FF44000 giving addresses of 0x3FF44004 , 0x3FF44008 and 0x3FF4400C respectively.

This describes three registers which control the GPIOs in output mode. How the GPIO line gets into output mode is a matter of using other registers described later in the table. But if we assume that the GPIO line is fully configured in output mode then these three registers control the state of GPIO0 to GPIO31. There are three similar registers for GPIO32 to GPIO39.

The big problem in making use of this information is that the "Description" part of the table is cryptic and often incomplete. You almost have to know what sorts of things the register is used for before it makes any sense. The first register is simple – if you write a 1 to bit n then GPIOn will be set active, usually high voltage, and if you write a 0 to bit n then the line is deactivated, usually low voltage. The other two registers are slightly more difficult to understand due to the use of W1TS and W1TC – which stand for Write One To Set and Write One To Clear. Once you know this it is obvious that the first register is a bit-set register and the second a bit-clear register. That is, if you write a 1 to bit n using the W1TS register then GPIOn will be set active, but if you write it using the W1TC register, GPIOn will be deactivated.

You might wonder why we need three registers to control the GPIO lines? It is true that you don't need anything beyond the first, but the other two make things easier. By writing a bit pattern to GPIO_OUT_REG you set or reset all of the GPIO lines depending on whether there is a 1 or a 0 at bit n. If you only want to change a subset of lines then you have to read the current state of the lines, notice whether GPIO_OUT_REG has read or write access, and then modify just the bits corresponding to the lines you want to change.

This isn't difficult, but you can avoid having to do this by using GPIO_OUT_W1TS_REG with a bit pattern that sets just the lines that correspond to a 1 or GPIO_OUT_W1TC_REG which resets the same lines.

This becomes easier to understand after an example.

Blinky Revisited

Now we can re-write Blinky yet again, but this time using direct access to the GPIO registers.

```
from machine import mem32,Pin
from time import sleep_ms
led = Pin(2,mode=Pin.OUT)
GPIOSet = 0x60004008  #Change to 0x3FF44008 for the ESP32
GPIOClear = 0x6000400C #Change to 0x3FF4400C for the ESP32
mask = 1<<2
while True:
    mem32[GPIOSet] = mask
    sleep_ms(500)
    mem32[GPIOClear] = mask
    sleep_ms(500)
```

This program uses the standard MicroPython class to set the GPIO line to output. If you think that this is cheating, it is an exercise in setting the line correctly using the GPIO control register, but if you do this you risk getting out of sync with MicroPython's internal state. That is, if you set a GPIO line to output don't expect MicroPython to know anything about it.

To toggle GPIO2 we make use of the set and clear registers and a mask that has bit 2 set to 1. Notice that 1<<n is a bit pattern with bit n set to 1. Alternatively you could use:

```
mask = 0x02
```

Once we have the mask, the loop simply stores it in the set and clear register alternately. Notice that as only bit 2 is a 1 this only changes the state of GPIO2.

This raises the question of how fast is this direct manipulation of the GPIO line's state? Using the same optimizations we used in Chapter 4 gives:

```
from machine import mem32,Pin
from time import sleep_ms
@micropython.native
def blink():
    GPIOSet = 0x60004008  #Change to 0x3FF44008 for the ESP32
    GPIOClear = 0x6000400C #Change to 0x3FF4400C for the ESP32
    mask = 1<<2
    while True:
        mem32[GPIOSet] = mask
        mem32[GPIOClear] = mask
led = Pin(2,mode=Pin.OUT)
blink()
```

If you try this out you will find that the pulses are slightly faster at $1.8\mu s$ compared to $2.7\mu s$.

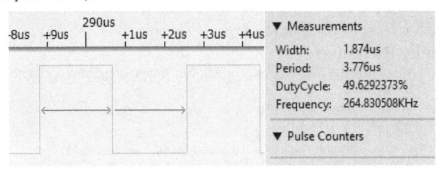

This example is a demonstration rather than being useful, but there are some very useful functions we can write using our knowledge of how the GPIO lines are controlled. For example, MicroPython is limited to controlling a single GPIO line at a time, but the hardware can change or read multiple GPIO lines in a single register operation. This was introduced in Chapter 4 but without explanation.

For example:

```
def gpio_get():
    return mem32[0x60004004]#Change to 0x3FF44004 for the ESP32
```

Here the get function simply reads the GPIO_OUT register which has a single bit for the output state of each GPIO line. Notice that GPIO lines that are set to output reflect their last written-to state – this is not a way of reading the line's current state.

A set function simply writes the mask to the GPIO_OUT_W1TS_REG register:

```
def gpio_set(mask):
    mem32[0x60004008] = mask #Change to 0x3FF44004 for the ESP32
```

A clear function is just as easy and writes to the GPIO_OUT_W1TC_REG register:

```
def gpio_clear(mask):
    mem32[0x6000400C] = mask #Change to 0x3FF4400C for the ESP32
```

As before, only the set bits in the mask are affected.

Example 1 - Simultaneous Setting of GPIO Lines

You use these two functions to set or clear any GPIO lines, but you often want to select a set of bits and set or clear them in one operation. For example, if you want to change two or more GPIO lines in phase, i.e. all high or all low, then you can use clear and set.

For example;

```
gpio_set(0x3)
gpio_clear(0x3)
```

sets the bottom 2 bits and so it toggles the GPIO0 and GPIO1. Both turn on and off at exactly the same time.

Now consider how you do the same thing but setting GPIO0 high when GPIO1 is low?

The best you can do is:

```
gpio_set(0x1)
gpio_clear(0x2)
gpio_set(0x2)
gpio_clear(0x1)
```

and, while this does set the GPIO lines correctly, the changes don't happen at the same time.

What we need is a function that will set any group of GPIO lines to 0 or 1 at the same time:

```
def gpio_setgroup(value, mask):
```

The mask gives the GPIO lines that need to be changed, i.e. it determines the group and the value gives the state they are to be set to. For example, if mask is 0111 and value is 0100 and the low four bits of the register are 1010 then reg & ~mask is 1000, value & mask is 0100 and finally reg | value is 1100. You can see that bits 0 to 3 have been set to 100 and bit 4 has been unchanged.

The trick to working out how to do this is to construct one mask to set the bits that need to be set and another to unset the bits that need to be unset. If a bit is to be set, it needs a 1 in the mask and a 1 in the data and the mask to set bits is:

```
setmask = mask & data
```

If a bit is to be unset it needs a 1 in the mask and 0 in the data, so the mask to reset bits is:

```
resetmask = mask & ~data
```

Applying both to the value gives the required result:

```
(value | setmask) & ~(resetmask) =
                    (value | (mask & data)) & ~(mask & ~ data)
```
which, after simplification, is:

```
value & ~mask | mask & data
```
Using this it is easy to create a function to do the job.

```
def gpio_setgroup(value, mask):
    reg = machine.mem32[0x60004004]
 #Change to 0x3FF44004 for the ESP32
    reg =  reg & ~mask
    value = value & mask
    reg = reg | value
    machine.mem32[0x60004004] = reg
 #Change to 0x3FF44004 for the ESP32
```

This function can be written more concisely by combining operations.
As demonstrated in Chapter 4, the value, mask function can be used to set GPIO lines simultaneously:

```
from machine import Pin
import machine
def gpio_setgroup(value, mask):
    machine.mem32[0x60004004] =
            machine.mem32[0x60004004] & ~mask | value & mask
  #Change to 0x3FF44004 for the ESP32
pin = Pin(2, Pin.OUT)
pin = Pin(4, Pin.OUT)
value1 = 1 << 2 | 0 << 4
value2 = 0 << 2 | 1 << 4
mask = 1 << 2 | 1 << 4
while True:
    gpio_setgroup(value1, mask)
    gpio_setgroup(value2, mask)`
```

As we are changing the same pins each time, we only need a single mask.
The value, however, changes each time. If you run this program, on an S3, you will see an almost perfect pair of out-of-phase $14\mu s$ pulses:

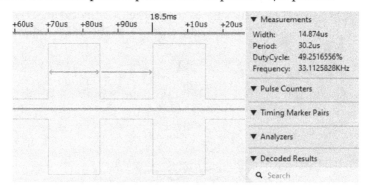

322

Example II – Sine Wave Generator

MicroPython doesn't provide access to the sine wave generator included in the ESP32's DAC. It is, however, fairly easy to configure and enable it by directly working with its registers. There is only one sine wave generator for both DACs, but each one can set its own scale, offset and phase. Notice that the ESP32 S3 doesn't have a DAC so this only works on an ESP32.

If you look at the manual you will find the analog register summary and listed are two registers for the DAC system:

DAC control registers			
Name	**Description**	**Address**	**Access**
SENS_SAR_DAC_CTRL1_REG	DAC control	0x3FF48898	R/W
SENS_SAR_DAC_CTRL2_REG	DAC output control	0x3FF4889C	R/W

Looking further at the details of the registers reveals:

Register 29.22. SENS_SAR_DAC_CTRL1_REG (0x0098)

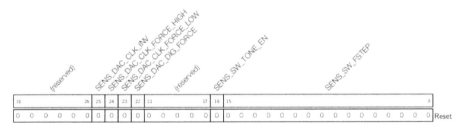

SENS_DAC_CLK_INV 1: inverts PDAC_CLK, 0: no inversion. (R/W)

SENS_DAC_CLK_FORCE_HIGH forces PDAC_CLK to be 1. (R/W)

SENS_DAC_CLK_FORCE_LOW forces PDAC_CLK to be 0. (R/W)

SENS_DAC_DIG_FORCE 1: DAC1 & DAC2 use DMA, 0: DAC1 & DAC2 do not use DMA. (R/W)

SENS_SW_TONE_EN 1: enable CW generator, 0: disable CW generator. (R/W)

SENS_SW_FSTEP Frequency step for CW generator; can be used to adjust the frequency. (R/W)

You can see that the first register has a single bit that enables the sine wave generator – bit 16, SENS_SW_TONE_EN and a 16-bit field, SENS_SW_FSTEP, that sets the frequency. Looking back at the description of the sine wave generator, we find the expression:

```
freq = dig_clk_rtc_freq · SENS_SAR_SW_FSTEP/65536
```

and that the clock is 8MHz. This gives:

```
step = int(f*65536/8000000) & 0xFFFF
```

Looking at the details of the second register:

SENS_DAC_CW_EN2 1: selects CW generator as source for PDAC2_DAC[7:0], 0: selects register reg_pdac2_dac[7:0] as source for PDAC2_DAC[7:0]. (R/W)

SENS_DAC_CW_EN1 1: selects CW generator as source for PDAC1_DAC[7:0], 0: selects register reg_pdac1_dac[7:0] as source for PDAC1_DAC[7:0]. (R/W)

SENS_DAC_INV2 DAC2, 00: does not invert any bits, 01: inverts all bits, 10: inverts MSB, 11: inverts all bits except for MSB. (R/W)

SENS_DAC_INV1 DAC1, 00: does not invert any bits, 01: inverts all bits, 10: inverts MSB, 11: inverts all bits except for MSB. (R/W)

SENS_DAC_SCALE2 DAC2, 00: no scale; 01: scale to 1/2; 10: scale to 1/4; 11: scale to 1/8. (R/W)

SENS_DAC_SCALE1 DAC1, 00: no scale; 01: scale to 1/2; 10: scale to 1/4; 11: scale to 1/8. (R/W)

SENS_DAC_DC2 DC offset for DAC2 CW generator. (R/W)

SENS_DAC_DC1 DC offset for DAC1 CW generator. (R/W)

You can see that there are two bits, SENS_DAC_CW_EN1 and SENS_DAC_CW_EN2, which select the input source for each DAC, 1 or 2 respectively. Setting either bit to 1 connects the DAC to the sine wave generator and setting it to 0 connects the DAC to the usual register that sets the output level.

The two 2-bit fields SENS_DAC_INV1 and SENS_DAC_INV2 are a mystery and don't seem to do what they were intended to. Setting the field to 00 or 10 produces a very strange waveform. Setting the field to 01 or 11 produces a pair of sine waves that differ by 180 degrees. The two settings 00 and 10 were intended to produce 90° and 270° phase shifts, but these don't seem to work.

The two 2-bit fields SENS_DAC_SCALE1 and SENS_DAC_SCALE2 scale the output by 00 = no scaling, 01 = 1/2, 10 = 1/4 and 11 = 1/8.

Finally the two 8-bit fields SENS_DAC_DC1 and SENS_DAC_DC2 set the offset.

We need a set of functions that set the appropriate bits in the control registers. The easiest three to set are phase, scale and offset. To set phase to p, a two-bit value, we need to change bits 20 and 21 for DAC 1 and 22 and 23 for DAC 2. This can be done using a single function:

```
def setPhase(chan,p):
    _reg_set(0x3FF4889c, p << (20 + 2 * (chan − 1)),
                               0x03 << (20 + 2 * (chan - 1)))
```

The mask is computed using the chan parameter which is 1 or 2. If it is 1 then the mask works out to:

```
0x03 << 20
```

which sets the mask to only allow modification of bits 20 and 21. If chan is 2 then mask works out to:

```
0x03 << 22
```

which allows modification of bits 22 and 23. The value is worked out in the same way so as to store the two-bit value in the same bits as the mask.

Once you have seen how to set a bit field with a specified size and location it is easy to generalize and setScale and setOff are:

```
def setScale(chan,s):
    _reg_set(0x3FF4889c, s << (16 + 2 * (chan - 1)),
                               0x03 << (16 + 2 * (chan - 1)))
def setOff(chan,off):
    _reg_set(0x3FF4889c, off << (8 * (chan - 1)),
                               0xFF << (8 * (chan - 1)))
```

A setFreq function is only slightly more difficult in that we have to calculate the step value from the specified frequency:

```
def setFreq(chan,f):
    if chan<1 or chan>2:
        return
    step = int(f*65536/8000000) & 0xFFFF
    _reg_set(0x3FF48898, step, 0x000FF)
```

Finally we need to enable the sine generator. It is assumed that the DAC is already set up correctly using MicroPython and all we have to do is set the additional bits to turn the sine wave generator on and connect it to the appropriate DAC,

A function to do this is now relatively easy:

```
def enableSin(chan,f):
    if chan<1 or chan>2:
        return
    setFreq(chan, f)
    setPhase(chan,0x2)
    #enable tone
    _reg_set(0x3FF48898, 0x10000, 0x10000)
    #select channel
    if chan==1:
        _reg_set(0x3FF4889c, 1<<24,0x1<<24)
    else:
        _reg_set(0x3FF4889c, 1<<25, 0x1 <<25)
```

Putting all this together gives us a complete set of functions to control the sine wave generator:

```
from machine import Pin, DAC, mem32
from time import sleep

def _reg_get(adr):
    return mem32[adr]

def _reg_set( adr,value, mask):
    mem32[adr] = mem32[adr] & ~mask | value & mask

def enableSin(chan,f):
    if chan<1 or chan>2:
        return
    setFreq(chan, f)
    setPhase(chan,0x2)
    #enable tone
    _reg_set(0x3FF48898, 0x10000, 0x10000)
    #select channel
    if chan==1:
        _reg_set(0x3FF4889c, 1<<24,0x1<<24)
    else:
        _reg_set(0x3FF4889c, 1<<25, 0x1 <<25)


def setFreq(chan,f):
    if chan<1 or chan>2:
        return
    step = int(f*65536/8000000) & 0xFFFF
    _reg_set(0x3FF48898, step, 0x000FF)

def setPhase(chan,p):
    _reg_set(0x3FF4889c, p << (20 + 2 * (chan − 1)),
                              0x03 << (20 + 2 * (chan - 1)))
```

326

```
def setScale(chan,s):
    _reg_set(0x3FF4889c, s << (16 + 2 * (chan - 1)),
                              0x03 << (16 + 2 * (chan - 1)))

def setOff(chan,off):
    _reg_set(0x3FF4889c, off << (8 * (chan - 1)),
                             0xFF << (8 * (chan - 1)))
```

The scale factor s is restricted to two bits and the scaling is given by 2^s. The offset is seven bits and if the scale factor isn't used clipping will occur. Phase is two bits and only 2 and 3 can be used, corresponding to phase shifts of 0 degrees and 180 degrees. Notice that the phase shift also shifts the offset, which is generally undesirable.

Once we have these functions we can make use of the sine wave generator:

```
dac1 = DAC(Pin(26))
```

```
enableSin(2,30000)
setScale(2,0x0)
setOff(2,0x0)
while(True):
    sleep(0.001)
    setPhase(2,0x3)
    sleep(.001)
    setPhase(2, 0x2)
```

The standard MicroPython DAC object is used to enable the DAC hardware. After this we can use the functions to modify the control registers. The example sets a frequency of 30KHz and then modulates its phase between 0 and 180 degrees.

RTC

The ESP32 has a built-in RTC (Real Time Clock) which, while not having a battery backup, can be kept accurate using the ntptime module to retrieve the time from the Internet.

You can set the system time using the ntptime module. This allows you to look up the time from an NTP (Network Time Protocol) server and to use it to set the RTC. The ntptime object has two properties and one method:

```
ntptime.host= ntpserver
ntptime.timeout= timeinmilliseconds
ntptime.settime()
```

The host that you set should be one of the many NTP pool servers. A pool server has a list of time servers that it issues in response to a DNS request so as to spread the load. For example, if you query pool.ntp.org or time.nist.gov then a different SNTP server is returned each time on a round robin basis so that the load is spread between the servers in the pool. The `settime` method sets the RTC to the current time in UTC. Currently time zones are not supported.

For example, to set the RTC you can use:

```
import ntptime
from machine import RTC
import network
from machine import Pin, Timer
from time import sleep_ms

def setup(country, ssid, key):
        .   .   .
wifi=setup(country, ssid, key)
print("Connected")
print(wifi.ifconfig())

ntptime.host="pool.ntp.org"
ntptime.timeout=1000
try:
    ntptime.settime()
except Exception:
    print("NTP server not available")
    pass
rtc = RTC()
print(rtc.datetime())
```

The `RTC` constructor also allows you to set the date and time:

```
RTC((year, month, day, weekday, hours, minutes,
                        seconds, microseconds))¶
```

The *weekday* value is Monday to Sunday corresponding to 0 to 6 and the *seconds* value has a fractional part accurate to the millisecond.

The `RTC` object has two methods:

- ◆ `RTC.datetime(datetimetuple)`¶

  Gets or sets the date and time of the RTC where *datetimetuple* is the same as for the constructor. With no arguments it returns a date, time tuple.

- ◆ `RTC.init(datetimetuple)`¶

  Initializes the RTC.

There is also a low-power memory associated with the RTC which can be used to store data while the processor is in deep sleep mode – see the next section.

Sleep

An important feature of the ESP32 is that it has a low-power sleep mode which make it suitable for battery operation. This is a big subject and can become very complicated but no look at the ESP32 would be complete without an insight into its power-saving modes.

The ESP32 has a complete low-power system based on the RTC. When the machine is put into sleep mode the processors and all of the power-hungry peripherals are off and only the RTC is running. That is, the RTC is the core of the reduced power system of the ESP32 and many of its features are prefixed with "RTC".

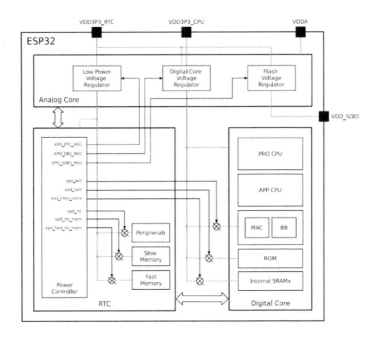

There are two standard functions which put the ESP32 to sleep:

- machine.lightsleep(*wakeuptime*)
- machine.deepsleep(*wakeuptime*)

The *wakeuptime* is the maximum number of milliseconds the machine will sleep for. That is, if it isn't woken up by some other event, it will wake up after *wakeuptime* milliseconds. The difference between the two is that in deepsleep the contents of main memory is lost and this has a big effect on the way MicroPython behaves.

In lightsleep the radio is switched off but the CPU is in standby. Power consumption in lightsleep is around 800µA and it takes around 1ms to wake up.

In deepsleep the CPU is powered down and all state information is lost. Power consumption can be anywhere between 10-150µA depending on what other peripherals are in use and wake up time is around 1ms. These figures should be compared to the 250mA to 800mA that the devices uses while active and using its radio.

The ESP32 supports several other power modes but MicroPython only makes lightsleep and deepsleep available. There are also more ad-hoc ways of saving power by reducing the CPU clock rate using the machine.freq function and the wifi.connect function with the listen_interval parameter. These can reduce power but they also reduce performance and need to be carefully tuned.

You can use the light-sleep mode to pause a program. The state of MicroPython is preserved as the memory is preserved during light sleep. This means that you can use lightsleep to pause polling loops etc. deepsleep on the other hand does not preserve main memory which means that when it ends the machine essentially reboots. This means that when MicroPython starts up and runs main.py the program that caused the deepsleep isn't automatically restarted. Two examples will make the difference clear.

First lightsleep can be used to pause a polling loop:

```
from machine import lightsleep
from time import sleep
for i in range(10):
    print("starting sleep",i)
    lightsleep(1000)
    print ("back from sleep",i)
```

If you run this program you will see the for loop pause while the machine is in light-sleep mode for one second. The for loop continues after the sleep without loss of data. In this sense lightsleep works in the same way as the much used sleep function but it switches off the radio hardware during the sleep period.

deepsleep doesn't restart your MicroPython program like lightsleep. Instead it causes the MicroPython system to be reloaded and main.py to be run just as if the machine had been just turned on. What this means is that if you want a program to persist across a deep sleep it has to be saved as main.py.

For example:

```
from machine import deepsleep
from time import sleep
for i in range(10):
    print("starting sleep",i)
sleep(2)
print('I am going to sleep')
deepsleep(1000)
```

If you save this as `main.py` and run it you will see the `for` loop print 0 to 9 and then `I am going to sleep`. After one second the ESP32 restarts and you will see a message from the ROM giving status information and then the program will start over. There is no easy way to suppress the status message from the ROM. Notice that there is a danger that you lose control of the ESP32 – the `sleep(2)` is to give you time to interrupt the program while it is not sleeping. If this happens, reflash the MicroPython system to reset the ESP32.

If all of the data is lost after a deep sleep, how can this be useful? In most cases you need to keep some state data when the program restarts. The RTC has a 2KB memory which is maintained during deep sleep. The RTC method:

```
rtc.memory(data)
```

stores the byte data in the memory and

```
data = rtc.memory()
```

stores the contents of the memory in the byte object data.

To keep the state between deep sleeps you have to save it in the RTC memory before calling `deepsleep` and you have to restore it when the program starts.

For a very simple example, we can create a `for` loop that counts on 10 more values each time the program wakes up:

```
from machine import deepsleep, RTC
from time import sleep
sleep(3)
rtc = RTC()
if len(rtc.memory())==0:
    start=0
else:
    start = int.from_bytes(rtc.memory(),"big")
for i in range(start,start+10):
    print(i)
print("starting sleep")
rtc.memory((i+1).to_bytes(4,"big"))
deepsleep(1000)
```

If you run this you will see that the loop moves on by 10 each time it is restarted. The key to the program is that, if there is nothing in the memory, the byte object it returns is zero length, which allows us to distinguish the first time the program runs. The only practical complication with the program is the way you have to pack the state data into a `bytes` object and then recover it. If you want to know more about working with data in this way see **_Programmer's Python: Everything is Data_**, ISBN: 978-1871962595.

A bigger problem is maintaining any objects you may be using. Of course these are destroyed when you enter a deepsleep and you have to recreate them. This is generally easy for simple objects - save their properties in the RTC memory and restore them on wake up. Hardware-connected objects are more difficult. In general, you have to assume that hardware objects – SPI, DAC, ADC, etc are associated with initialized hardware and you have to recreate them. Also there is the problem of what to do about WiFi. You need to use code something like:

```
wifi = network.WLAN(network.STA_IF)
if not wifi.isconnected():
    setup(country, ssid, key)
```

to keep the WiFi connected on restart. Of course, you can store any WiFi parameters in the RTC memory.

In the case of `lightsleep` things are very much simpler as the WiFi connection is maintained as MicroPython isn't restarted. Even so, you should check that the network is still connected:

```
from machine import lightsleep,Pin, Timer
from machine import
import network

def setup(country, ssid, key):
    . . .


wifi = network.WLAN(network.STA_IF)

for i in range(10):
    print(wifi.isconnected())
    if not wifi.isconnected():
        setup(country, ssid, key)
    print("starting sleep",i)
    lightsleep(1000)
    print ("back from sleep",i)
```

Wake Using ULP

We have already seen that the ESP32 can wake after a set time, but there are also other events that can wake it up before this time is up. You can set the touch inputs to wake the device or some of the GPIO lines and a third way of waking up the ESP32 is to use the ULP (Ultra Low Power) processor. This is a very simple processor that uses very little power and can be programmed to use peripherals such as the I2C, SPI or any GPIO line while the main processor is sleeping. It can also wake the processor when a condition is satisfied. The ULP processor provides a way to monitor and collect data while the main processor is sleeping and this is very useful. Deep-sleep consumes 10μA without the ULP processor. Adding the ULP adds typically 100μA. Unfortunately it has to be programmed using a simple assembler rather than either MicroPython or Python and its use is beyond the scope of this book.

Wake Using EXT0 and EXT1

There are two external wake-up signals, EXT0 and EXT1. The only difference between them is that EXT0 will wake the device based on the state of a single GPIO line whereas EXT1 can monitor multiple GPIO lines:

```
esp32.wake_on_ext0(pin, level)
esp32.wake_on_ext1(pins, level)
```

The parameter *pin* is a Pin object and *pins* is a tuple or List of Pin objects. The *level* parameter determines what state wakes the system:

```
esp32.WAKEUP_ALL_LOW
esp32.WAKEUP_ANY_HIGH
```

You can see that the first provides an AND-like condition and the second provides an OR-like one. This works with deepsleep or lightsleep. For example:

```
from machine import lightsleep,Pin
import esp32

wakePin = Pin(2,Pin.IN,pull=None)
esp32.wake_on_ext0(wakePin,esp32.WAKEUP_ANY_HIGH)
for i in range(10):
    print("starting sleep",i)
    lightsleep()
    print ("back from sleep",i)
```

This pauses the for loop in a lightsleep state until GPIO2 goes high.

This is simple enough, but there are some subtle points. The GPIO lines that wake up the device from sleep are part of the RTC low power domain. These

RTC GPIO lines are separate from the standard GPIO lines and are used to conserve power while in sleep mode. Not all of the standard GPIO lines have RTC GPIO equivalents. What this means is that you can only use GPIO lines 0, 2, 4, 12-15, 25-27, 32-39 as these are the only ones duplicated as RTC GPIO hardware and hence the only ones connected to the RTC.

When entering a deepsleep state any pullup/down resistors are maintained. This can result in wasted power so setting `pull` to `None` just before entering sleep is a good idea. In general RTC GPIO capable pins retain their state. However, non-RTC GPIO lines are disconnected and to keep their state you need to turn PAD hold on using the hold `parameter` in the `Pin` constructor. However, notice that setting `hold` to `True` also stops any change in configuration being applied until `hold` is set to `False`. You can also set all of the non-RTC GPIO lines to `hold` using:

```
esp32.gpio_deep_sleep_hold(True)
```

Wake Using TouchPads

You can also use any of the TouchPads to wake the ESP32:

```
esp32.wake_on_touch(True)
```

If any of the touch inputs exceed the set threshold they are considered "touched" and the device wakes up.

You can find out what woke the system using:

```
machine.reset_cause()
```

it returns one of:

- ◆ `machine.WLAN_WAKE`
- ◆ `machine.PIN_WAKE`
- ◆ `machine.RTC_WAKE`

While the WiFi can wake the ESP32, MicroPython doesn't currently support this.

Watchdog

One piece of hardware that we haven't yet considered is the watchdog timer. This is a very simple idea and once you have encountered it there are few problems in using it. A standard problem for any IoT device is how to cope with a system crash – caused by software or hardware. Clearly you need to protect your system from crashes as much as possible, but despite precautions bad things still happen. What should your system do if it crashes? The usual, but not universal, answer is that it should restart and try to pick up where it left off. This is what a watchdog timer is all about. It has to be a very reliable piece of hardware, preferably implemented separately from the main system and, if possible, powered separately. In practice, most processors have a watchdog timer built in, which makes them easy to implement, but not as robust as you might like. The watchdog timer simply counts down at a steady rate and when it reaches zero it applies a hardware reset signal to the main processor. The application software sets the countdown time and before this interval is up it resets the timer. Resetting the timer is an "I'm alive and well" signal that stops the system from being restarted. If the application has crashed then the timer will not be reset and the system will restart.

You start the watchdog timer using:

```
from machine import WDT
wdt = WDT(timeout=2000)
```

where `timeout` sets the countdown in milliseconds with a minimum of one second. Once set you cannot stop or modify the watchdog timer but you can feed it:

```
wdt.feed()
```

which restarts the countdown.

If the watchdog does timeout it restarts the ESP32 and this restarts the MicroPython interpreter. It doesn't automatically restart the program that started the watchdog timer. So how do you keep an application running? The answer is that if your MicroPython program is called main.py then it will be automatically loaded and run when the system is powered on or reset by the watchdog timer. This is exactly the same as the situation in which you restart following a deep sleep and you can use the same techniques to maintain state, including the RTC memory.

You also need to make sure that you include a pause while developing the program to ensure that you can interrupt the program:

```
from machine import WDT
from time import sleep
sleep(4)
print("starting")
wdt = WDT(timeout=4000)
wdt.feed()
while True:
    sleep(0.1)
    print("still running")
    pass
```

If you name it main.py it will start running every time the ESP32 starts. The watchdog timer will restart the MicroPython interpreter every four seconds and this in turn will load and run main.py. The sleep at the start of the program gives you four seconds to stop the interpreter. Without it you would need to reflash MicroPython to stop the program.

Flash Memory

There are a number of different objects and methods that allow you to work with the ESP32's built-in flash memory. You can also easily add external removable flash memory in the form of an SD card reader.

First there are some very low-level methods provided by the `Partition` class. Flash memory is divided up into partitions for different uses. There are two general types of partition:

```
Partition.TYPE_APP
Partition.TYPE_DATA
```

These roughly correspond to programs and data. You can find out what partitions are present in your ESP32 using:

```
from esp32 import Partition
print(Partition.find(Partition.TYPE_APP, subtype=0xFF, label=None))
print(Partition.find(Partition.TYPE_DATA, subtype=0xFF,
                                                   label=None))
```

where `subtype=0xFF` and `label=None` match anything.

Typically you will see:

```
[<Partition type=0, subtype=0, address=65536, size=2031616,
                              label=factory, encrypted=0>]

[<Partition type=1, subtype=2, address=36864, size=24576,
                                    label=nvs, encrypted=0>,
 <Partition type=1, subtype=1, address=61440, size=4096,
                               label=phy_init, encrypted=0>,
 <Partition type=1, subtype=129, address=2097152, size=2097152,
                                    label=vfs, encrypted=0>]
```

The first partition, `factory`, holds the MicroPython interpreter. The second, `nvs`, hosts the Non Volatile Storage system and the third, `vfs` or `ffat`, is the filing system used to store MicroPython programs. You can use both `nvs` and `vfs` in your own programs without having to worry about managing storage blocks.

To work with a partition you create an instance of Partition using:

```
part = esp32.Partition(id, block_size=4096)
```

where id is the label of the block or one of:

```
Partition.BOOT¶
Partition.RUNNING
```

which gives you the boot partition or the partition that the running program came from. For example, to work with the `nvs` partition you could use:

```
part = Partition("nvs")
```

Once you have an instance you can use:

```
part.info()
```

which returns a 6-tuple (`type`, `subtype`, `addr`, `size`, `label`, `encrypted`) or any of the following methods:

- ◆ `part.readblocks(block_num, buf, offset)`
- ◆ `part.writeblocks(block_num, buf, offset)`
- ◆ `part.ioctl(cmd, arg)`

These methods implement the simple and extended block protocol defined by `os.AbstractBlockDev`.

There are three methods that can be used to implement OTA (Over The Air) updates of the MicroPython system:

- ◆ `part.set_boot()`

sets the partition as the boot partition

- ◆ `Partition.get_next_update()`¶

gets the next update partition after this one, and returns a new `Partition` object.

```
classmethodPartition.mark_app_valid_cancel_rollback()
```

If you want to use these you need to compile or find a version of MicroPython that has OTA enabled. This creates a Flash layout that has two partitions `ota_0` and `ota_1` which can be used to store a complete MicroPython interpreter. The OTA update works by downloading the new version of MicroPython to the free OTA partition. Exactly how to implement this is beyond the scope of this book but you need to use the OTA ready version of MicroPython.

You can use the read/write blocks methods to load and store data, but you would have to keep track of which blocks were in use. This is usually the task of a file system and MicroPython provides two file systems on the ESP32 and they are built on top of the block methods listed above.

The File System

The ESP32 supports two general file systems, a traditional FAT system and MicroPython's own littlefs v2. You can create either type of file system on an available partition – which is usually named `vfs`. The ESP32 provides a global variable `bdev` which points to the partition to be used for the file system. This is most often the `vfs` partition.

When you first install MicroPython it creates a FAT file system for you to use and you can simply make use of a subset of the standard Python file handling functions in the os module:

os.chdir(path)	Changes current directory
os.getcwd()	Gets the current directory
os.ilistdir(dir)	Iterates through directories returns (name, type, inode[, size])
os.listdir(dir)	Lists the given directory
os.mkdir(path)	Creates a new directory
os.remove(path)	Removes a file
os.rmdir(path)	Removes a directory
os.rename(old_path, new_path)	Renames a file
os.stat(path)	Gets the status of a file or directory
os.sync()	Syncs all file systems

There is also os.statvfs(path) which gets the status of a file system and returns a tuple with the file system information in the following order:

f_bsizefile	system block size
f_frsize	fragment size
f_blocks	size of fs in f_frsize units
f_bfree	number of free blocks
f_bavail	number of free blocks for unprivileged users
f_files	number of inodes
f_ffree	number of free inodes
f_favail	number of free inodes for unprivileged users
f_flag	mount flags
f_namemax	maximum filename length

You can also open a file and work with it using the standard stream functions, read(), write(), readinto(), seek(), flush() and close().

For example:

```
f = open("Hello.txt","wt")
f.write("Hello World")
f.close
f = open("Hello.txt","rt")
s = f.read()
f.close
print(s)
```

If you try this out you will discover that there is a new file called Hello.txt and you should see its contents displayed.

As this is non-volatile storage you can use it to save state when the system goes to sleep, but notice that it is slower than using the RTC's memory.

Non-Volatile Storage

To make it even easier to use flash storage for saving state, the ESP32 implements Non-Volatile Storage, NVS. This isn't anything new in the sense you could just write a file with the same data, but NVS is easier to use as it provides key/value storage. The NVS storage is usually provided by the partition called nvs.

Keys are strings and values are either 32-bit signed integers or binary blobs, i.e. bytes, bytearrays or strings.

To use it you simply create an instance of NVS:

```
nvs = esp32.NVS(namespace)
```

You can think of *namespace* as a sort of file name and if it doesn't already exist it is created.

You save and load the key value-pairs using:

```
nvs.set_i32(key, value)
nvs.set_blob(key, value)
```

and you can retrieve values using:

```
nvs.get_i32(key)
nvs.get_blob(key, buffer)
```

The system always writes and reads a sequence of bytes irrespective of the type stored. It returns the actual length read and raises an OSError if the key does not exist, has a different type, or if the buffer is too small.

Finally:

```
nvs.erase_key(key)
```

erases a key-value pair.

It is important to notice that any setting of key-value pairs is postponed until you use:

```
nvs.commit()
```

For example, the deepsleep for loop given earlier can be implemented to save its current start value using NVS:

```
from machine import deepsleep
from time import sleep
from esp32 import NVS
sleep(3)
start = 0
nvsState = NVS("state")
try:
    start = nvsState.get_i32("start")
except OSError:
    pass
for i in range(start,start+10):
    print(i)
print("starting sleep")
nvsState.set_i32("start",i+1)
nvsState.commit()
deepsleep(1000)
```

Notice that the NVS namespace is called state and we can have other namespaces if we need to. The start value is stored and retrieved as a key value pair. Don't forget to save this as main.py if you want it to work.

Installing File Systems

If the preinstalled file system doesn't do what you want you can install your own. The ESP32 supports the FAT and the littlefs v2. The advantage of FAT is that it is a standard file system that can be read by other devices, but as we are using the internal flash memory this isn't relevant. FAT is more prone to errors than the alternative littlefs v2.

To work with a file system you first have to create it in a suitable partition, usually indicated by bdev:

```
os.VfsFat.mkfs(block_dev)
```

creates a FAT file system and:

```
os.VfsLfs2.mkfs(block_dev, readsize=32, progsize=32,
                                lookahead=32, mtime=True)
```

creates a littlefs v2 file system. Creating a file system on a partition is essentially formatting it and hence all existing data is lost.

Once you have created a file system it can be mounted either as the root file system or on any existing subdirectory.

```
os.mount(fsobj, mount_point, *, readonly)
```

To make modifications to the file system you have to unmount it:

```
os.umount(mount_point)
```

For example, to replace the default FAT file system with a littlefs v2 file system you would use:

```
os.umount('/')
os.VfsLfs2.mkfs(bdev)
os.mount(bdev, '/')
```

Notice that this erases all of the files and folders in the `vfs` partition.

External SD

Although the ESP32 generally doesn't have an SD card reader, it is fairly easy to add one. Add-on SD card readers are available to order at very reasonable prices, see the Resources section of the book's webpage for stockists.

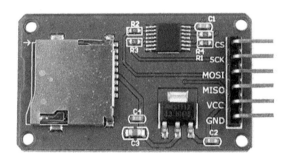

The only problem is that most have zero documentation or specification and they lack a card-detect and a write-protect pin. Connection to the ESP32 is fairly easy via one of the two SPI buses. The only complication is that most of the devices need a 5V supply. They work at 3.3V logic levels and so can be directly connected to the ESP32 and have an onboard voltage regulator to reduce the supply to 3.3V. Most claim to work if powered from 3.3V, but this depends on the regulator used and some fail or become unreliable. The ESP32 has a suitable 5V supply pin and in most cases this is the VCC connection to use, The ESP32 S3 often cannot supply enough 5V current to operate a card reader.

As we have already discussed there are four SPI interfaces, but two are dedicated to SD use and it is easier to use one of the remaining two, i.e. SPI2 HSPI or SPI3 VSPI. The SDCard object can be configured to work with any of the SD interfaces, but most of the add-on hardware will only work with the SPI interfaces.

Selecting pin assignments that work with the ESP32 or the ESP32 S3 – any other reasonable selection should also:

	ESP32/S3	Nano ESP32
sck	GPIO18	GPIO18 D9
cs	GPIO5	GPIO5 D2
miso	GPIO4	GPIO4 A3
mosi	GPIO14	GPIO14 A7

You can use any GPIO line for any of the SPI signals. The connections are as shown below:

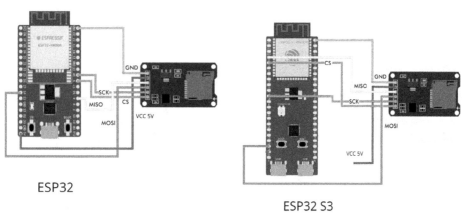

ESP32

ESP32 S3

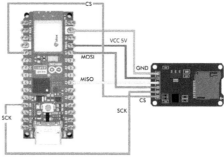

Nano ESP32

The ESP32 has has enough power to supply 5V to most card adapters but the ESP32 S3 generally hasn't and you need to provide a separate 5V supply unless the adapter works at 3.3V. If the software reports a time out and the SD card is good and the wiring correct then the most likely reason is an inadequate power supply. If the software reports a CRC error then the connecting cables are too long and you need to reduce the clock speed.

Once you have this wired up you need an SD card freshly formatted using FAT and a single partition – which is what you get if you use a new just out of the packet formatted SD card. If the card isn't new then partition and format it in another machine. You can partition and format cards using the ESP32 but getting started is easier with a pre-formatted card. Make sure the card is correctly inserted before moving on to the software.

To use the SD card you have to create an instance of the SDCard class:

```
machine.SDCard(slot=1, width=1, cd=None, wp=None,
        sck=None, miso=None, mosi=None, cs=None, freq=20000000)
```

All standard SPI interfaces use width=1, i.e. one data line. Most add-on SD readers don't support card detect (cd) and write protect (wp). If they are supported they can set the GPIO pins that they are connected to. You can also set a Pin object to sck, miso, mosi and cs if you want to use something other than the default. The freq parameter is sometimes needed to slow things down if you are experiencing read errors.

In most cases the defaults are what you want and this means you can create an SDCard object using:

```
sd =machine.SDCard(slot=2, sck=18, miso=4, mosi=14, cs=5, freq=400)
```

Starting with a frequency of 400kHz is good because this the frequency of the initial probe irrespective of what frequency you set for the rest of the transaction. If the card reader doesn't work at this frequency it is unlikely to work at all. Once you have the setup working you can adjust the frequency up to see how high the reader will go. The frequency depends on the length and quality of the wiring.

Once you have an sd instance you can treat it as a partition and mount it:

```
os.mount(sd, "/sd")
```

and from here you can treat it like an other partition in the file system:

```
f = open('/sd/Hello.txt', 'w')
f.write('Hello World')
f.close()
print(os.listdir('/sd'))
f = open('/sd/Hello.txt', 'r')
s=f.read()
f.close()
print(s)
```

The complete program is:

```
import machine
import os
sd =machine.SDCard(slot=2, sck=18, miso=4, mosi=15, cs=5, freq=400)
print(sd)

os.mount(sd, "/sd")
f = open('/sd/Hello.txt', 'w')
f.write('Hello World')
f.close()

print(os.listdir('/sd'))

f = open('/sd/Hello.txt', 'r')
s=f.read()
f.close()
print(s)
```

You can also use the other partition function with an SDCard object. For example, to format an SD card to a FAT file system use:

```
import machine
import os
sd =machine.SDCard(slot=2, sck=18, miso=4, mosi=14, cs=5, freq=400)
os.VfsFat.mkfs(sd)
os.mount(sd, "/sd")
```

After this you will find that the SD mounted has nothing stored on it.

Digging Deeper

There is much more to explore about the ESP32 hardware, but you now should have the confidence to read the datasheet to find out how the registers control things and to implement MicroPython functions to extend what you can do.

The biggest difficulty is finding the register that contains the bits that reflect the status or that control whatever it is you are interested in. Once you have found this out, the only remaining problem is in working out how to set or clear the bits you need to work with without changing other bits. It also has to be said that hardware documentation at this level is often incomplete due to assumptions the writer makes about what you should already know. In such a circumstance your best approach is the experimental method. Work out the simplest program you can think of to verify that you understand what the hardware does – and if you are wrong always check the addresses and bits you are changing before concluding that things work differently from the documentation.

Summary

- All of the ESP32's peripherals, including the GPIO lines, are controlled by registers – special memory locations that you write and read to configure and use the hardware.

- Exactly where the registers are positioned in the address space is given in the documentation as a base address used for all of the similar registers and an offset that has to be added to the base to get the address of a particular register.

- With knowledge of how things work, you can add functions that are missing from MicroPython, changing GPIO lines at the same time.

- You can also use features of peripherals that MicroPython doesn't support like the sine wave generator connected to the DACs.

- There is a Real Time Clock, RTC, that you can set using the ntptime object.

- If you want to use the ESP32 with a battery source then you need to work with power saving modes.

- Low-power modes are implemented as part of the RTC. Some GPIO lines have low-power counterparts RTC GPIO.

- Light sleep is easy to work with because it saves the current state of the system and you can restart your program from where it entered light sleep.

- Deep sleep saves more power, but the CPU is switched off and the system loses track of its state. The entire MicroPython system is restarted when it wakes up and your program has to restore its state.

- The system can be woken up either by a set time, a change in RTC GPIO lines or a Touch input.

- The watchdog timer can be used to make your program reliable.

- You can work with the ESP32's internal flash memory as partitions and you can install file systems onto partitions and then work with files.

- The NVS object allows you to save key value pairs to the internal flash memory.

- If you add an external SD card reader you can work with an SD card using the same techniques as used for the internal flash memory.

Index

356

Programming The ESP32 In C Using The Espressif IDF
ISBN: 978-1871962918

C is the ideal choice of language to program the ESP32, ensuring that your programs are fast and efficient, and here it is used with the Espressif IoT Development Framework, ESP-IDF and VS Code, a combination which makes it simple to get started and provides a wealth of functions not found elsewhere.

The purpose of this book is to reveal what you can do with the ESP32's GPIO lines together with widely used sensors, servos and motors and ADCs. After covering the GPIO, outputs and inputs, events and interrupts, it gives you hands-on experience of PWM (Pulse Width Modulation), PWM for Motor control, the SPI bus, the I2C bus and the 1-Wire bus, the UARTs and of course WiFi. To round out, it covers direct access to the hardware, adding an SD Card reader, sleep states to save power, the RTC, RMT and touch sensors. It also devotes a chapter to FreeRTOS which takes us into the realm of asynchronous processing.

Programming the ESP32
In C Using the Arduino Library
ISBN: 978-1871962925

C is the ideal choice of language to program the ESP32, ensuring that your programs are fast and efficient, and here it is used with the customized ESP version of the Arduino library and its associated IDE which makes the device as easy to use as possible. The Arduino library runs on top of the official Espressif ESP32 IoT Development Framework as a simplifying layer and you can always drop down a level and make use of its additional features when required.

The purpose of this book is to reveal what you can do with the ESP32's GPIO lines together with widely used sensors, servos and motors and ADCs. After covering the GPIO, outputs and inputs, events and interrupts, it gives you hands-on experience of PWM (Pulse Width Modulation), the SPI bus, the I2C bus and the 1-Wire bus, the UARTs and, of course, WiFi. To round out, it covers direct access to the hardware, adding an SD Card reader, sleep states to save power, the RTC, RMT and touch sensors. It also devotes a chapter to FreeRTOS which takes us into the realm of asynchronous processing.

Programmer's Python: Everything is an Object, Second Edition
ISBN: 978-1871962741

This is the first in the Something Completely Different series of book that look at what makes Python special and sets it apart from other programming languages. It explains the deeper logic in the approach that Python 3 takes to classes and objects. The subject is roughly speaking everything to do with the way Python implements objects - metaclass; class; object; attribute; and all of the other facilities such as functions, methods and the many "magic methods" that Python uses to make it all work.

Programmer's Python: Everything is Data
ISBN: 978-1871962595

Following the same philosophy, this book shows how Python treats data in a distinctly Pythonic way. Python's data objects are both very usable and very extensible. From the unlimited precision integers, referred to as bignums, through the choice of a list to play the role of the array, to the availability of the dictionary as a built-in data type, This book is what you need to help you make the most of these special features.

Programmer's Python: Async
ISBN: 978-1871962595

An application that doesn't make use of async code is wasting a huge amount of the machine's potential. Subtitled "Threads, processes, asyncio & more, this volume is about asynchronous programming, something that is is hard to get right, but well worth the trouble and reveals how Python tackles the problems in its own unique way.

Programming The Raspberry Pi Pico/W In C, 2nd Edition
ISBN: 978-1871962796

This book explains the many reasons for wanting to use C with the Pico, not least of which is the fact that it is much faster. This makes it ideal for serious experimentation and delving into parts of the hardware that are otherwise inaccessible. Using C is the way to get the maximum from the Pico and to really understand how it works.

Master the Raspberry Pi Pico
ISBN: 978-1871962819

There is far too much to the Pico to cover in a single book and this follow-on volume takes your Pico C programming to the next level. Chapters are devoted to more advanced PIO programming, using the second core and many of the more advanced hardware features such as DMA, watchdog timer and saving power. For the Pico W it covers TLS/HTTPS connections, access point mode, other protocols and using FreeRTOS.

Programming the Raspberry Pi Pico/W in MicroPython, Second Edition
ISBN: 978-1871962802

MicroPython is a good choice of language to program the Pico. It isn't the fastest way, but in most cases it is fast enough to interface with the Pico's hardware and its big advantage is that it is easy to use.

The purpose of the book is to reveal what you can do with the Pico's GPIO lines together with widely used sensors, servos and motors and ADCs. One of the key advantages of the Pico is its PIO (Programmable I/O) and while this is an advanced feature, it is introduced in this book. After finding out how the PIO works, we apply it to writing a PIO program for the DHT22 and the 1-Wire bus.

Raspberry Pi IoT In C, 3rd Edition
ISBN: 978-1871962840

This book takes a practical approach to understanding electronic circuits and datasheets and translating this to code, specifically using the C programming language. The main reason for choosing C is speed, a crucial factor when you are writing programs to communicate with the outside world. If you are familiar with another programming language, C shouldn't be hard to pick up. This third edition has been brought up-to-date and focuses mainly on the Pi 4, Pi5 and the Pi Zero.

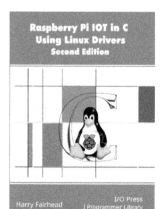

Raspberry Pi IoT in C With Linux Drivers, 2nd Edition
ISBN: 978-1871962857

This second edition has been updated and expanded to cover the Raspberry Pi 5 and the Raspberry Pi Zero W/2W. There are Linux drivers for many off-the-shelf IoT devices and they provide a very easy-to-use, high-level way of working. The big problem is that there is very little documentation to help you get started. This book explains the principles so that you can tackle new devices.

Micro:bit IoT In C, 2nd Edition
ISBN: 978-1871962673

The second edition of this book covers V2, the revised version of the micro:bit. The other important change is that it now uses the highly popular VS Code for offline development and let's you get started the easy way by providing downloadable templates for both V1 and V2 of the micro:bit.

The micro:bit lacks WiFi connectivity but using a low-cost device we enable a connection to the Internet via its serial port which allows it to become a server. The book rounds out with a new chapter on the micro:bit's radio and the V2's sound capabilities

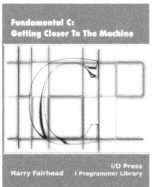

Fundamental C: Getting Closer To The Machine
ISBN: 978-1871962604

For beginners, the book covers installing an IDE and GCC before writing a Hello World program and then presents the fundamental building blocks of any program - variables, assignment and expressions, flow of control using conditionals and loops.

When programming in C you need to think about the way data is represented, and this book emphasizes the idea of modifying how a bit pattern is treated using type punning and unions and tackles the topic of undefined behavior, which is ignored in many books on C.

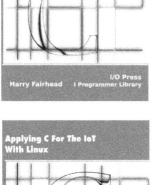

Applying C For The IoT With Linux
ISBN: 978-1871962611

If you are using C to write low-level code using small Single Board Computers (SBCs) that run Linux, or if you do any coding in C that interacts with the hardware, this book brings together low-level, hardware-oriented and often hardware-specific information.

It starts by looking at how programs work with user-mode Linux. When working with hardware, arithmetic cannot be ignored, so separate chapters are devoted to integer, fixed-point and floating-point arithmetic. It goes on to the pseudo file system, memory-mapped files and sockets as a general-purpose way of communicating over networks and similar infrastructure. It continues by looking at multitasking, locking, using mutex and condition variables, and scheduling. It rounds out with a short look at how to mix assembler with C.

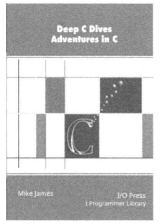

Deep C Dives: Adventures in C
ISBN: 978-1871962888

This book provides in-depth exploration of the essence of C, identifying the strengths of its distinctive traits. This reveals that C has a very special place among the programming languages of today as a powerful and versatile option for low-level programming, something that is often overlooked in books written by programmers who would really rather be using a higher-level language. To emphasize the way in which chapters of this book focus on specific topics, they are referred to as "dives", something that also implies a deep examination of the subject.